China's Students

China's Students

The struggle for democracy

Ruth Cherrington

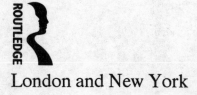

London and New York

First published 1991
by Routledge
11 New Fetter Lane, London EC4P 4EE

Simultaneously published in the USA and Canada
by Routledge
a division of Routledge, Chapman and Hall, Inc.
29 West 35th Street, New York, NY 10001

Typeset by NWL Editorial Services, Langport, Somerset
Printed and bound in Great Britain by
Biddles Ltd, Guildford and King's Lynn

British Library Cataloguing in Publication Data
Cherrington, Ruth 1955–
    China's students: the struggle for democracy.
    1 China. Students. Protest movements, history
    I Title
    322.40951

    ISBN 0–415–05291–2

Library of Congress Cataloguing-in-Publication Data
Cherrington, Ruth, 1955–
    China's students: the struggle for democracy/Ruth
    Cherrington.
        p. cm.
    Includes bibliographical references and index.
    ISBN 0–415–05291–2
    1 Students – China – Political activity – History.
    2 Student movements – China – History.
    3 China – History – Tiananmen Square incident, 1989.
    I. Title.
    LA1133.7.C515 1991   90–45301
    378. 1'981 – dc20   CIP

*To all the Chinese students who have helped me in
so many ways over the years*

Contents

Acknowledgements

I have received the assistance and advice of many people, both before and during the preparation of this work. I would like to offer sincere thanks to the following people for all their varied help and support: Gary, Kiao Wei, Sandra, Stella, Margaret, Brie, Kate, Robyn, Xiao Ping, my colleagues at Harrow College of Higher Education and my family. Also, thanks to my friends, who have been very supportive, David Kelly at the Australian National University, James Miles of the BBC World Service, and Xandra Hardie drew my attention to some useful materials.

A note on Chinese words and phrases used in the text

The standard modern form of romanisation of Chinese characters, 'Pinyin', will generally be used in this work, as it is now commonly employed in most western texts. Only where quotes or references to older works are cited will the more traditional form be used. Given below are some of the more frequently occurring forms in both Pinyin and the older form of English representation.

Pinyin	Traditional
Beijing	Peking
Changjiang	Yangtse River
Deng Xiaoping	Teng Hsiao-Ping
Guangzhou	Canton
Guomindang (GMD)	Kuomintang (KMT)
Hua Guofeng	Hua Kuofeng
Liu Shaoqi	Liu Shao-ch'i
Mao Zedong	Mao Tse'tung
Nanjing	Nanking
Qingnian (youth)	Ch'ing-nien
Sichuan	Szechwan
Tianjin	Tientsin
Yanan	Yenan
Xinjiang	Sinkiang
Zhongguo (China)	Chung-kuo
Zhou Enlai	Chou En'lai

Common abbreviations

BR	*Beijing Review*
CASS	Chinese Academy of Social Sciences
CCP	Chinese Communist Party
CCTV	Central Chinese Television
CPPCC	Chinese People's Political Consultative Conference
CR	*China Reconstructs*
CYL	Communist Youth League
ECMM	Extracts from *China Mainland* magazines
FBIS	Foreign Broadcast Information Service
FEER	*Far Eastern Economic Review*
GMD	Guomindang
GMRB	*Guangming Ribao (Enlightenment Daily)*
NPC	National People's Congress
PLA	People's Liberation Army
PRC	People's Republic of China
RMRB	*Renmin Ribao (People's Daily)*
SCMM	Selections from *China Mainland* magazines
SCMP	Survey of *China Mainland* Press
SEC	State Education Commission
ZGQN	*Zhongguo Qingnian (Chinese Youth)* magazine

Introduction

During the night of 3 June 1989, an unknown number of students were fatally wounded by armed troops in and around Tiananmen Square at the heart of the Chinese capital, Beijing. Also killed and injured at this time and on subsequent days were scores of other people, from young children to elderly Beijing residents. The death toll has been estimated to run into thousands, although the official count by the Chinese authorities has generally been much lower at around several hundred dead with 'thousands' injured. There is also dispute about whether anyone actually died in Tiananmen Square itself. The authorities and some western observers claim that no deaths occurred there.[1]

What we do have is a clear record of the sudden anger, fear and violence which swept through the streets which, moments earlier, had been the scene of massive peaceful demonstrations calling for more democracy and freedom in Chinese society. This weekend was the tragic climax to nearly two months of a popular campaign for social and political change, spearheaded by students from many of the capital's campuses. Similar massive displays of 'people power' took place in Eastern Europe a few months after what became known as the 'Tiananmen Massacre'. These resulted largely in peaceful victories for those calling for democratic reforms, with the exception of Romania, where violence and bloodshed occurred before the final overthrow of the Ceaucescu regime.

In China, perhaps a source of inspiration for the eastern bloc, the initial result was not victory for the people but punishment, repression and fear. The act of defiance against their ageing communist leaders began as a public display of mourning for a former party chief, Hu Yaobang, who had fallen from grace two years earlier. The students felt that comrade Hu had been wronged in his later years; that they themselves were being unfairly treated by the government; that the Chinese nation was itself in jeopardy because of the economic and political ills the leaders seemed too incompetent or reluctant to remedy. The students had decided to point out and protest against the shortcomings of the ruling elite, acting out the traditional role of advisers to the state in the modern setting of the Deng Xiaoping's reform decade.[2]

The result was catastrophic, not just for individual members of this generation of intellectuals, but for the country as a whole which sorely needs the talents of those with higher education. 'Young intellectuals should play a leading role in modernisation', more than one university student told me during my time in China. 'We should be the main force in developing our country', was a belief shared by many frustrated young people wishing to apply their knowledge and skills in China's development programme, both before and during the pro-democracy campaign.

Their aspirations were abruptly ended by the Chinese leadership, as the young intelligentsia became the target of a military crackdown. Deng Xiaoping, previously heralded as a political pragmatist and reformer, donned the mantle of a 'hardline conservative' as the government strove to regain both physical and ideological control of a capital overtaken by 'democracy fever'.

In the aftermath of the June massacre, when the symbolic centre of the nation became associated with tragedy and the main thoroughfare of Beijing was renamed by local residents 'blood road', numerous questions were raised about the nature of politics in modern China. The students had called into question the legitimacy of the ageing communists and demanded political reforms. The leadership's reply was not just dismissive but showed repression at its most extreme. The optimism and progress of a decade of economic development and change was harshly betrayed. The scale of the massacre and subsequent repression may never be known but there is a need to make some sense of the events which culminated in the scenes witnessed during that historic weekend. This book is an attempt to explain the extraordinary developments in China during spring 1989, but it cannot account for the scale of the violence used by those in power to suppress the student-led 'patriotic democracy movement'.[3]

A strong case can be made for the view that this social and political movement was almost inevitable given the far-reaching and rapid changes of the previous ten years and certain historical factors such as the traditional role of Chinese intellectuals as the 'conscience' of the state. The tensions between those who live by mental rather than manual labour and the Communist Party also added potentially explosive features to the political scene in contemporary China.

Students in 1989 had inherited elements from the tradition of scholarly protest and added their own particular characteristics which reflected contemporary political and social experiences. Their ambiguous and highly unstable position as both the most vociferous supporters and sharpest critics of the reform programme initiated by Deng Xiaoping will be analysed in this book.

As a brief introduction, it will be seen that the students were following the tradition of outspokenness laid down by their Beijing University predecessors during the 'May Fourth' movement of 1919. By publicly expressing their opposition to the unfavourable terms of the Versailles Peace Treaty in their march on Tiananmen, the students inspired the nation and instigated widespread debate about social and political problems in post-imperial China. Others joined in as nearly every aspect of Chinese social and cultural life was called into question.

Even before 1919, however, scholars had an obligation to point out to the ruler any poor judgements or corruption, even at the risk of incurring punishment as a reward. In his admirable work *Chinese Democracy*, A. J. Nathan describes this role as 'remonstrance',[4] offering evidence for the existence of a tradition of intellectual self-sacrifice which dates back to the last century. The students who occupied Tiananmen Square in spring 1989, were probably well aware of these earlier examples of remonstrance, having conscientiously studied Chinese history, their 'revolutionary' predecessors and intellectual antecedents. They may well have been seeking to revive some of the debates silenced first by the republican government, then by the Guomindang[5] and finally by the communist rulers.

During the post-1919 republican era, students often acted as the social conscience of the nation governed by the nationalists under Chiang Kaishek. They sometimes paid with their lives for demonstrating or even just speaking out against the government. The intellectual search for a suitable form of democracy in China was suspended as the struggle for national survival predominated. Both nationalists and the outlawed communists vied for the support of the students during this turbulent period and the rallying point was often the banner of patriotism, especially at the time of Japanese invasion in the thirties.

Under the communist rule established in 1949 by the victorious Chairman Mao, the situation for intellectuals remained difficult. Fear and suspicion pervaded academic institutions with regular 'purges' instigated by the regime in the name of achieving genuine socialism. That intellectuals could not be trusted but were to be used when and where necessary, was the clear message coming from the leadership. They were to be restrained from independent research and thought, operating only under the control of the party. Mao Zedong likened them to rubber balls in a bucket of water: if you don't press hard enough on them, they keep coming back up. Consequently whenever they dared to offer any criticism of the system, even when urged to do so during the so-called 'One Hundred Flowers' movement in 1956–7, they were strictly suppressed.

Hence this generation of intellectuals became 'tame', according to a graduate of the 1980s. They learned the hard way not to go beyond the official boundary of dissent and into the unacceptable realms of 'bourgeois liberalism' – an umbrella-term used to describe unhealthy thoughts and actions. It was interesting to see members of this generation, now middle-aged, motivated to speak out again during the 1989 campaign. Their memories were mixed, with ideas of free speech and democracy coloured by the harsh punishments many received thirty years before.

Those who had been 'educated youth' during the 1960s also had their own bitter memories. The 'Great Proletarian Cultural Revolution' instigated by Chairman Mao in 1966 mobilised millions of young people to be the 'shock troops' of a new revolutionary movement. They were to attack the 'four olds' left over from the past, i.e. old customs, habits, thoughts and culture, and those who harboured them, as well as rooting out any members of the Communist Party at all levels who were taking the 'capitalist road' and thus threatening the success of the communist revolution.

Many undertook this historical task with great fervour and dedication, but some interpreted their role too freely, their actions uncomfortably radical for the Chairman, whose very control over the movement was doubtful. Different Red Guard factions acted independently of any authorities in their efforts to establish true 'proletarian democracy' at the local level. Mao had to resort to using the People's Liberation Army (PLA) to quell the overzealous Red Guards and thousands were severely punished for going beyond his decrees. Unknown numbers died either through summary execution, in labour camps or in harsh border regions where many were sent to work. The use of the military in 1989 was not, unfortunately, without precedent in contemporary Chinese history. Banishment to the extreme provinces has an even longer tradition in China.

By the end of the Cultural Revolution, several millions of young people, the educated elite of the nation, languished in the countryside. Many felt disappointed, disillusioned and betrayed. Their efforts to dedicate themselves to rebuilding the 'socialist motherland' seemed to have achieved little but personal loss and national disaster. The memories of this period lingered on well into the 1980s, as did the persistent doubt that the Party could not reform the political system. The sort of changes first articulated clearly during the 'May Fourth' movement, under the broad term of 'democracy' remained as goals for some members of the intelligentsia but seemed a long way off, even unmentionable in public.

There was some optimism as Deng Xiaoping consolidated his power through a series of important meetings in 1978, but this was hedged by the doubts which usually accompany any hope for change held by Chinese intellectuals. Even as Deng rose to the position of paramount leader, he crushed a burgeoning pro-democracy movement centred on Xidan Wall in Beijing. Ten years before the brutal onslaught on the students in Tiananmen Square, young activists of the 'Democracy Wall' movement were being arrested and imprisoned for demanding democracy in China, what was called the 'fifth modernisation'. This was a direct reference to Deng's reform programme which emphasised the realisation by the year 2000 of the 'four modernisations' of industry, agriculture, defence and science/technology. The Chinese government often use slogans containing numbers in their political campaigns: the 'four olds' have already been mentioned. 'Democracy Wall' activists of late 1978 and early 1979 discussed the need for the 'fifth modernisation' of democracy without which they believed the others could not be realised.

Wei Jingsheng, a leading 'Democracy Wall' activist, articulated this demand in several unofficial publications and posters during the short life of this movement. He questioned the sincerity of Deng's plans and launched a scathing attack on China's emergent leader. His unorthodox views and outspokenness led to his arrest, a well-publicised trial and fifteen years of imprisonment. It took another ten years for others to be convinced by his warnings that without political reform China would remain a backward nation.

The rising generation of students in the 1980s were aware of these major events, both past and more contemporary, and also conscious of their own position in Chinese society. Initially encouraged by the 'open door' and reform policies of the leadership, they attempted to assimilate the rapid changes and concentrate their own energies in developing knowledge and skills in many fields. Early optimism was quickly overwhelmed, however, by disappointment as the situation for intellectuals actually deteriorated in material terms, leaving them behind in the economic 'rat-race'. Worsening conditions in education, fewer opportunities than expected for advanced study and good jobs along with rising inflation were some of the factors deepening the frustration throughout China's institutions of higher learning during the 1980s. The queues of students and teachers waiting to register for TOEFL[6] examinations in an effort to go abroad, reflected considerable disillusionment with Deng's reform programme.

Students increasingly perceived themselves as the victims rather than beneficiaries of reform and there were notable clashes between them and the authorities over the lack of democratisation. Nurtured on reform ideology and propaganda, the cream of China's educated youth really wanted to 'emancipate the mind', to bring their talents 'into full play' and work hard for the much-publicised 'four modernisations'.[7] But there seemed to be no way to realise their own potential whilst political and administrative structures remained ossified reminders of the 'old style' state communism, which itself seemed out of place in the new era of economic liberalisation. The lack of any substantial change in the authoritarian political system was inevitably an issue of contention between the government and young intellectuals. Although there were promises and debate about modernising the edifices of the Stalinist-type structures, few real changes had occurred. Young people in the universities felt acutely underprivileged in comparison to their western counterparts, about whom they had increasing knowledge and more actual contact. 'We want to do what we want to do, not what the Party tells us to do. We simply do not have enough freedom', I was told on numerous occasions by students and young teachers.

Issues such as corruption within the Party ranks and excessive bureaucracy also intensified debate and led to mounting discontent. Examining these factors in greater depth through the use of selected documentary sources, personal experiences in China since 1984 and numerous students' and young intellectuals' own accounts of their hopes and expectations, this book will seek to explain the origins, contents and characteristics of the 1989 student-led, pro-democracy movement. In making demands for reforms which were not acceptable to the Chinese leadership, the young people ventured beyond the limits imposed by Deng and the Party faithful. The students revived some of the debates begun during the 'May Fourth' period and conducted them on the sites of the government headquarters; in Tiananmen and outside Zhongnanhai on Changan Avenue in Beijing. Like some of the Red Guards during the 1960s, they 'went too far'. Acting in an autocratic manner, Deng Xiaoping put an end to their movement and discussions. There was to be no divergence from the orthodox Party line, no independent thought or freedom of expression. The crackdown inevitably wiped out a great deal of support for the decade of reform and Deng's popularity plummeted even further both inside and outside of China. Dissent, however, could only be temporarily silenced.

The outcome could have been different for the 'patriotic democracy movement'. Ironically the East German leadership, one of China's first allies to congratulate the government on its suppression of the 'counter-revolutionary rebellion', as it was labelled, was soon to give in to 'people power'. Other communist regimes were reluctant to use the 'Chinese solution' to suppress pro-democracy movements. The different elements of the situation in China at that particular time along with chance occurrences and personalities, however, all had their part to play in bringing about the final outcome during the weekend of 3–4 June.

Many of the events of spring 1989 caught Chinese leaders off guard and took many of the nation's citizens (as well as foreign observers) by surprise. Some of the developments were simply remarkable by any account and they merit consideration in an analysis of the students' 'patriotic democracy movement'.

I had left China at the beginning of 1989 aware of the mood of the students and believing that 'something' would happen. The year 1988 had seemed to be a watershed, when the problems and deficiencies of the reform programme were becoming increasingly apparent. No-one could foresee the sudden death in early April of Hu Yaobang, a well-liked leader in his day, which triggered off a chain reaction, resulting ultimately in more death. Nor could anyone have gauged the degree of contempt engendered amongst the students by the *People's Daily* editorial of 26 April. This represented the official judgement of student demonstrations initiated after Hu's death. Its harsh tone warned of severe repercussions if they did not return to their classrooms and cease their demands for political change. Instead of frightening students into submission, however, it caused further anger. The pro-democracy campaign snowballed, overtaking the planned celebrations for the seventieth anniversary of 'May Fourth' and President Gorbachev's historic visit from the Soviet Union. Students 'seized the moment' and put their own mark onto these important events, capturing the attention of the world's media and antagonising the old communist diehards. Taking a famous quote from Mao at face value, they acted. 'The world is yours and ours but in the final analysis, it is yours', he had said to a group of young people in 1957.[8]

For several weeks in May 1989 Beijing at least appeared to belong to its youth. Virtually seizing control of the capital in a peaceful manner, students inspired people from all walks of life to join in their campaign against the weaknesses of government and the political system. They tapped an underlying current of discontent, bringing people to their side in an unprecedented manner with calls for democratic reforms and a firm line against corruption. It seemed a truly 'popular' movement with a level of support almost inconceivable even a few months before.

Even the student 'leaders' who emerged at that time appeared to be taken aback by the appeal of the movement they helped to orchestrate. Young people like Chai Ling, Wang Dan and Wu'Er Kaixi[9] were suddenly thrust into important positions, seen as leaders, spokespersons, even 'heroes' of the pro-democracy campaign. They were not prepared for their sudden international fame but developed their own abilities as best they could as the movement grew almost beyond their control. They were well aware, right from the start, of the risks they took in speaking openly for different student bodies and challenging the communist authorities. This book is not about the personalities of the movement, rather the role played by these young people will be considered as part of an attempt to explain what took place in Beijing during those spring months.

Media coverage was wide and in-depth, providing a good source of information. I also saw the situation for myself, spending time with students in Tiananmen Square and at other Beijing locations during the final week of the movement. 'Please tell out story', I was implored in the days before the tanks and troops moved into the city and eventually the square, where I saw people shot and wounded. I had promised to tell the story of China's educated youth long before this student movement had begun, in response to requests of those 'victims of reform' who expressed their overwhelming disappointment, frustration and sadness. 'We have already been let down, many times. Tell people what it is like for us here', one student had asked me, just before leaving China at the start of 1989.

I shall begin their story in history, outlining major features and events in China's past which can shed light on the present situation. No aspect of Chinese society can be adequately described without some reference to its long, complex and often troubled past. The students and their association with ideas of democracy are no exception. The struggle began a long time before April 1989. Following history through to the communist regime, the importance of the students' so-called 'revolutionary tradition' will become apparent but it is a tradition not always linked to clear goals and ends. Some of the confusion and disagreements between participants of the 1989 pro-democracy campaign were not unlike those of preceding movements. The difficulties and contradictions facing young intellectuals in the Mao and post-Mao periods will also be introduced as part of the general background and I shall attempt to highlight the problems facing students today who wish to formulate political objectives outside of the Party's control. Calls for 'democracy', therefore, can be viewed largely as criticisms of the dominant political system and the desire for more freedoms and choice rather than a concrete programme of action. This is not to dismiss the students as naive idealists nor to deny that new policies for reform could not have evolved if the pro-democracy movement was not ended so abruptly.

At various points during the reform decade, students have criticised the quality, quantity and direction of the Party's reforms. The results have usually followed a pattern, with official claims of 'bourgeois liberalism' and a stress on 'ideological work', or propaganda. But the problems never went away and demands for democracy, human rights, more personal freedom and less corruption were to return.

Clearing Tiananmen Square with tanks and guns was a drastic measure by an unstable leadership, but it will probably fail to eliminate the desires shared not only by many students but by other sections of Chinese society. The students were not the only 'victims of reform'. This book is about them because they were the most vocal in airing their grievances.

1 Tracing the heritage of the 'Patriotic Democratic Movement'

OVERVIEW

'How can they be prepared to starve to death for the ideal of democracy yet remain dedicated to socialism?', one baffled foreign observer asked about the student hunger strikers occupying the now famous Tiananmen Square in May 1989. In China, I will argue, this is understandable given complex cultural and traditional features dating back to ancient times. Intellectuals have always played a special social role, handed down through the generations in various forms. Even in 1989, students carried with them the 'survivals of the past' (Goldman *et al*. 1987: 2), and these ideas affected their beliefs and behaviour, driving many of them to sacrifice their liberty and lives for the greater good of the 'motherland'. An analysis of the intellectual's role in Chinese history will unravel some of the strands of thoughts predominant during the 1989 'patriotic democratic movement'. It will also help to explain the events which took place at the heart of the Chinese capital during that time.

THE LEGACY OF THE PAST

The Communist Party's brutal suppression of the students' pro-democracy movement in 1989 recalled the intolerance and terror of earlier periods when intellectuals often trod a precarious path through life. Qin Shi Huang, the first ruler to unify the state of China, which was known as 'Zhongguo' (the Middle Kingdom) in 221 BC, was very suspicious of intellectuals. This was mainly because he wanted to apply a legalist framework to the government of the newly unified state rather than the traditional Confucian ethics and virtues upheld by the intellectuals.

Qin's achievements include his impressive underground tomb located near Xian in north-west China, which is 'guarded' by hundreds of life-like terracotta warriors and has been visited by over one million foreign tourists during the last decade. It is a spectacular monument to a ruler who had grand plans for the Chinese state and his own place in history. He was also responsible for linking the defences along the Great Wall, establishing a massive bureaucracy, standardising weights, measures and script across the vast territory of the 'Middle Kingdom'. He viewed scholars as a threat, according to Cleverley (1985) because they praised the ancient rulers with their codes of virtue and would not accept the new military state as the great achievement perceived by Emperor Qin. He allegedly ordered 460 Confucian scholars to be buried alive because of their dissent and burned Confucian ethical and political writings. Qin demanded complete obedience from all his subjects.

Contemporary intellectuals have traced the source of their troubles back to Qin's rule. There could be no independent thought because all intellectual activity had to serve the state. Whilst Qin's attempts to unify and strengthen the nation are often viewed with approval, his cruel, despotic manner is seen in more negative terms. The patriotic desire for a strong and powerful China, capable of warding off foreign aggressors, is a continuing phenomenon. This was an aim repeated throughout the centuries and was one of many on the lips of students in Tiananmen Square during the heady days of the patriotic democracy movement.

After Qin, other rulers adopted a similar autocratic approach to governing China. Fortunately they did not all bury scholars, but the social position of those whose livelihood depended on learning and books was often uncertain. Intellectuals were seen as necessary adjuncts to the imperial system and over time tradition decreed that they should fulfil two main functions: (1) serving the state in its day-to-day administrative and bureaucratic procedures and (2) acting as 'moral critics' of the ruler (Goldman *et al*. 1987: 3). These roles did not always coalesce and in the upshot scholars had limited scope for individual freedom of thought or autonomous intellectual activity. Scholars could be accepted and firmly integrated into the imperial establishment as bureaucrats or 'literati' but only if they did not go beyond the official limits of thought and deed. They were expected, however, to speak out if the ruler was governing unwisely, in line with the tradition of 'remonstrance' (Nathan 1986: 24).

In ancient times, intellectuals may have gained important insights about the nation through their studies and knowledge just as in recent times. By speaking out, giving warning or merely pointing to the error of the emperor's ways, they were seen to be remonstrating. Whether or not the ruler acted on their information was another matter. There was always the risk of being punished for daring to remonstrate, even though it was a form of patriotism rather than rebellion. Some emperors could accept criticism less well than others, just as with Communist Party leaders in modern times. Banishment to the harsh border regions, torture, imprisonment, even execution were not uncommon for outspoken 'literati' who lost their status even if they kept their lives. They became common criminals and here there is a parallel with more recent events. When discussing the so-called 'counter-revolutionary rebellion' of spring 1989, Premier Li Peng said that students who took any part in the uprising were no more than criminals.[1] Their actions had deprived them of their scholarly status and any privileges this may have brought.

The students in 1989 were latter-day remonstrators. In raising their voices in protest against corruption and questioning the regime's political, social and economic policies, they were not rebelling but expressing their patriotism, which literally translates from the Chinese as 'love of the country'. Nathan describes how, 'tradition insists that the remonstrators were always unselfish', risking their own livelihood and safety to 'awaken the ruler to his own interests and those of the state' (Nathan 1986: 24). There probably were elements of self-interest, both in the past and during the movement of 1989, but the survival of another legacy from the past is interesting. It is also part of the inherited dilemma of modern-day intellectuals regarding their social position and role. Students find themselves a 'privileged' group in society, a position with associated duties and difficulties.

It must be asked why some intellectuals were driven by their social conscience to point out the wrongdoing of their ruler. John Cleverley refers to the so-called 'mandate of heaven', seen as legitimising the emperor's right to rule, as similar to the idea of 'divine right'. Emperors were expected to rule in a sound and ethical manner in return for the loyalty and obedience of their subjects. If the head of state did not set a good example, then others might behave badly and the delicate balance in the social hierarchy would be upset. With people doing as they pleased rather than showing passive loyalty, then 'great chaos' or *da luan* would result, a condition feared by the Chinese from ancient times.

Chaos, things falling apart at the centre if the ruler neglects his duties, was viewed as the major threat to the survival of the Chinese state. Dr Sun Yatsen (Zhongshan), the intellectual usually portrayed as the founder of modern China, referred to the country as a pile of loose, shifting sand, which needed to be kept together by sound leadership. Internal turmoil could also attract the unwanted attention of predatory states. Therefore, unity and order had to be maintained at all costs. Members of the intelligentsia, usually patriots, probably shared this fear of *da luan* and may have been prompted into remonstrance to help the nation avoid adverse conditions. Such actions, however, often gave rise to conflict with the authorities, leading to ambivalence about speaking out and taking risks.

Earlier generations of scholars were mostly the sons of the wealthier 'gentry' families, schooled in the classics and prepared for office in the imperial civil service. Girls would only receive limited education in the more enlightened families. The gentry family, is, as M. J. Levy reminds us, often viewed as the 'typical' family of traditional China, but of course only represents one section of the population (Levy 1968: 43). The majority of people had different domestic arrangements. Only a small but important social class received education. The family portrayed in the classical Chinese novel, *The Dream of the Red Mansion*[2] is perhaps a good illustration here with the much cosseted son, Pao Yu, a typical example of the scholars being referred to.

The education of such young men had the all-important imperial examinations as the ultimate goal, just as in more recent times Chinese schools geared the curriculum increasingly to the national university entrance exams. Although thousands of years separated the two academic qualifications, both resulted in similar limitations of educational experience, content and pedagogy. In traditional education the boys were schooled strictly and often without mercy until they knew by heart the classical texts required. Besides reading and writing, the Confucian code of morality was also of great importance because the social order was largely based upon this philosophical footing. Ideals such as 'san gang wu chang',[3] the three cardinal principles and five constant virtues were invoked here as the basis for respect and obedience. The former states that the ruler 'guides' his subjects, the father 'guides' his son and the husband 'guides' the wife. This sacred order had to be maintained otherwise chaos would ensue. The five constant virtues – benevolence, righteousness, propriety, wisdom and fidelity – were also specified in the feudal ethical code of behaviour. These were to foster a sense of 'filial piety' - reverence and obedience to parents and ancestors. The overall result would be continued social stability, maintenance of the status quo and the avoidance of *da luan*.

Obviously this type of education minimised individual development. As Levy points out, the son was seen 'primarily as the property of the ancestors' (Levy 1968: 75). By the end of the initial period of schooling, a submissive pattern had already been established, often literally beaten into the boy through severe corporal punishment. In the classical novel already cited, Pao Yu is nearly beaten to death for misbehaving[4] and this fictional example is not inaccurate. As Levy describes it, there were no limits to punishments meted out by fathers to their sons, for they were the property of the family, not the state. Cases of severe beatings were frequent, and there have even been cases of sons beaten to death by the fathers. (Levy 1968: 76). Levy remarks that if any rebelliousness remained after this time, it was probably there for good and the young man would become one of the few non-conforming outsiders. (Pao Yu, incidentally, became a monk, one of the few ways out for those who could not conform.)

Under all this pressure, however, most sons accepted their position in the hierarchy and this had important repercussions for the status quo. To cite Levy once more, he writes that a proper family, imbued with filial piety, could not in the nature of things 'produce a member who would act contrary to the interests of the state' (Levy 1968: 164) Loyalty to the social unit of the family would be extended to the state. Consequently, after success in the imperial examinations the young educated elite would step into important bureaucratic roles and be suitably rewarded. They themselves would then go on to help reproduce the system in their work and domestic lives. It was always made abundantly clear that they owed their livelihood to the emperor and gratitude should be expressed regularly. Independent intellectual activity was usually out of the question: everything had to be granted the imperial seal of approval. Goldman *et al.* remind us that the scholars sacrificed their auto- nomy for guaranteed work and status but were expected to sacrifice their security if remonstrance was necessary. Their position was, therefore, always volatile, dependent on the character and personality of the ruler.

The system did not always run smoothly, as already indicated. Some young scholars did 'drop out' or failed the examinations and so could not assume their designated place in society. The examinations were open to cheating, bribery and nepotism as influential fathers sought to 'assist' their sons. Although in theory available to everyone, large sections of society were excluded and this was a deep source of frustration. The students' claims in 1989 of nepotism and corruption, limited access to higher education and narrowness in the curriculum were not unlike the criticisms levelled at the imperial system by their scholarly predecessors.

Nevertheless, the old ways persisted with the Chinese dynasties managing to contain the negative aspects of the system. China was virtually closed to the outside world for so long that there was little external impetus for change. The imperial examination system, with its associated educational doctrines and Confucian morality, which had been codified at the end of 900 AD, but had its origins even earlier, remained more or less intact.

The social order, as a result, hardly changed, with most young intellectuals being assimilated into the bureaucratic hierarchy in return for their loyalty and passive obedience. They were a privileged but passive group.

By the nineteenth century, a time of serious foreign incursions into the Chinese mainland, the strains and deficiencies in the system were becoming less manageable. Young intellectuals were finding the situation increasingly intolerable. There were demands for educational reforms from those who saw the classics as outdated and irrelevant. Imperial decline, corruption, mass poverty and the encroachment of foreign powers were pressing problems. China was in a period of transition, caught between traditional and modern society but the ultimate direction of change was far from clear.

At the forefront of the growing movement for change were young intellectuals. Although schooled largely in the old ways, many had visions of a China free from restrictive traditions and customs. This period was a turning point for the country as well as for the young people who spearheaded what has been referred to as China's 'youth movement' (Wang 1928). Every area of social life would be examined and found wanting but the students were not to free themselves totally from the shackles of the past. Traditions were transformed rather than eliminated as what began to some extent as a cultural movement was overtaken by political struggle.

REFORMS, THE REPUBLIC AND 'MAY FOURTH'

The modern era brought further conflicts for intellectuals. The incursions of the 'imperialist' powers of Britain, Japan, Russia and Germany from the early decades of the nineteenth century onwards, were largely unwelcome. They caused national humiliation as China lost territory to the foreign invaders, for example the forced 'leasing' of Hong Kong to Britain in 1848. But there was the unanticipated offshoot of interest in new ideas which the foreigners brought with them. The young intellectuals were both interested in and receptive to currents of scientific, political and social thought, but they remained intensely patriotic, determined to save China from the 'Waiguoren' or foreigners, as well as from its own internal decline.

There was an ambivalent stance towards the 'foreign devils': their ideas were welcomed and considered useful to the struggling nation, but China was fearful of being swamped by westernisation. The old feudalistic and 'backward' ways were severely criticised by the rising generation of intellectuals as the nineteenth century drew to a close, but most of them believed in building a strong nation capable of repelling the invaders. The somewhat contradictory attitude towards foreigners which resulted would also be apparent in the 1980s, when the Chinese people were called on to use all things foreign in national reconstruction but reject the negative western traits, usually labelled as 'bourgeois liberalism'.[5]

At the turn of the century, though, educated people had begun to learn foreign languages and to read the philosophical and political writings which entered China during the nineteenth century. There was a lively interest in science, viewed as the epitome of modernity and necessary to ensure national progress. Political works on democracy, liberalism and social evolution were read, also the works of Rousseau, Hobbes, Darwin and other European thinkers. There was at this time, as pointed out by Schwartz[6] no direct input of socialist writings. Marxism as a possible ideology and foundation for a new political system arrived several decades later.

Groups of intellectuals started to go abroad for study purposes. The first known Chinese overseas student, Yung Wing, left for the USA in 1847, but few joined him at first (Wang 1928: 44). He had difficulty persuading the Chinese government to send more young people overseas to study, but by the turn of the century the trickle had become a tide. Heading for Japan, Europe and the USA, educated youth became further dissatisfied with conditions in China and many wanted to act on their return to improve their 'motherland'.

According to Nathan, an important protest by imperial examination candidates in 1895, 'set China on the path to democracy' (Nathan 1986: 45), one which would be strayed from and rediscovered several times before 1989. This early example of student demonstration in China was led by Kang Youwei, who as a candidate for examination and not an official, had no right to criticise the government, let alone take action. Such audacity was unheard of, but he succeeded in organising over 1,000 other candidates in Beijing to sign a petition calling for the rejection of the disastrous peace treaty with Japan[7] and demanding 'fundamental government reforms' (Nathan 1986: 45). They were concerned about the crisis facing their nation and wanted immediate action to remedy some of the ills. Nathan describes how on 2 May they marched to the Censorate offices, located on the site later to become Tiananmen Square, and offered their petition in a manner befitting their gentlemanly status. Just as with the students in 1989 who presented a list of their demands to the leaders, kneeling deferentially on the steps of the Great Hall of the People, with the document held high in a submissive, respectful gesture, their 'remonstrance' met with disapproval.

The rejections on both occasions served only to deepen the sense of dissatisfaction with the encumbent leadership and strengthened the calls for reform. 'Democracy' was a central theme in both of these protests spanning nearly one hundred years. Kang Youwei, the organiser in 1895, had read widely in an intellectual search for a suitable political system for modern China. He considered constitutional monarchy a possibility. The old imperial regime would have to be radically reformed but there was still room for a symbolic head of state. Other thinkers were convinced that a republic was the only way because there was no tradition of democracy in China and the rulers had a historical preference to autocracy. Debate continued in intellectual circles as the reform movement grew.

The important point to stress is that the students were spurred on not just by high-sounding ideals of equality and social justice but also by their intense sense of national pride. They wanted China to face adversaries like Japan and Britain from a position of strength, not the weakness which had resulted in a succession of humiliating peace treaties throughout the nineteenth century. It was commonly assumed that a well-run, powerful state would automatically benefit all the constituent parts of Chinese society. 'Democracy', therefore, was for the well-being of the state as a whole rather than its individual members, who, following the logic of this political view, could only benefit if the national interests were placed first. Traditional repression of individuals and suppression of dissent was given a more modern setting and legitimacy.

A clear precedent was consequently laid down for the type of democracy later propounded by the communists, i.e. 'dictatorship of the proletariat'. With the centralised party representing the best interests of the masses, it could legitimately govern without resorting to the 'façade' of bourgeois democracy. The scholars demanding reform at the end of the nineteenth century paved the way in their brief, incomplete explorations of democratic ideas for another form of autocratic government.

One hundred years ago it could be said that new ideas were 'flooding' into China but there was still only limited access to foreign works and an obvious lack of experience of alternative political processes and structures in action. Only those who had studied abroad had such experience. China was still ruled by an emperor and struggled along in a backward state of 'semi-feudalism'. Young people continued to be taught largely in the traditional ways, supplementing their education where possible with science and other western-style subjects. The intellectuals' proposals were slowly beginning to have an impact as the necessity for social and political change became more urgent.

1898 saw '100 days of reform', launched by the emperor himself after accepting the advice of scholars, which lasted from 11 June to 21

September. Nathan writes that many of the reforms Kang Youwei and other leading intellectuals previously proposed were implemented. Education was to be modernised as a way of halting China's decline and moves were made to establish a free press. These measures were viewed favourably by many of the 'modernisers', but those with vested interests in the traditional ways saw them in a more menacing light. The '100 days' ended tragically with the powerful and ruthless empress dowager Cixi deposing the weak Guangxu emperor and executing the leading reformers. Kang and his close follower Liang Qichao were among those who managed to escape to Japan. From there, they saw the reforms overturned and many of the despised old ways reinstated. With the old empress firmly in control, there seemed little hope for change. Yet the seeds of reform had been planted. The violent ending of this movement could not halt the trend towards modernisation. Liang Qichao, exiled in Japan, turned to writing and became the ersatz leader of the reform movement, influencing many young people with his explorations of western thought. His work was smuggled into China and he became an underground hero, looked to for ideological guidance.

Another important exile at this time was Dr Sun Yatsen who followed the republican line. These two intellectuals along with other 'dangerous' exiles, watched China teeter on the brink of collapse as they travelled the world, often revising and perfecting their ideas. They were eventually able to return home as the ancient imperial dynastic rule finally came to an end. Dr Sun was invited to return to China to lead the 1911 revolution, the eleventh attempt to overthrow the imperial system.[8] It was not, however, the exiles which brought down the empire, 'but the new imperial army headed by Yuan Shikai' (Wang 1985: 6). Sun Yatsen agreed to step in as provisional president only when the Republic was established in 1912.

It was something of an anticlimax. The child emperor, Aisin Guoro Pu Yi, put on the throne by the Dowager Empress Cixi before her death, abdicated. His lifestory, turned into a film and a television series in China, shows the country caught midway between the old and the new. The 'warlords' who exercised political power through their military might were cowed by the republican army. China appeared to be entering a new era free of its feudalistic past. But thousands of years of history could not be dismissed overnight and change was not immediately noticeable.

The early hopes of young intellectuals were soon disappointed as the new leaders 'sold the old medicine', behind 'the false signboard of "Chinese Republic" (Schwartz 1966: 13). The general leader Yuan Shikai quickly styled himself a new 'emperor', and after his death in 1916 the warlords resumed their military activity. The future security of the new republic was not at all certain as internal struggles threatened to pull the nation apart and foreign nations continued to view China's vast territories in terms of potential imperialistic expansion. Students looked on with anger and anxiety.

By this point they were more recognisable as students in a modern sense. The establishment of a number of higher education institutions during the latter part of the nineteenth century had a significant effect on the composition as well as the general situation of the student population. From naval academies to engineering and teaching colleges, more young people from increasingly diverse backgrounds, including women, were pursuing courses of education and training. The curriculum was no longer dominated by the imperial examinations, abolished in 1905, and more western-style teaching methods were being tried out in the new colleges. Teaching itself was becoming a profession rather than a job only taken up by exam failures, and a few important colleges were founded, such as Beijing Normal (Teaching) University in 1902. The majority of young people still received little or no education, but there was a growing, recognisable student body in China.

These fortunate young people also experienced a degree of freedom not only in their studies but in their everyday life. Taking lessons outside of the home, in a campus environment was a truly 'liberating' experience in itself, as was the more relaxed atmosphere and social association feasible under these changed study conditions. Away from the strict confines of the traditional Chinese family, young men and women were coming together more freely than ever before, exchanging ideas and experiences and breaking down social barriers. Discussion groups and societies were formed addressing all the major facets of Chinese life and society, from philosophy and culture to economics and politics. It seemed that nothing was to be ruled out of bounds for the students, who increasingly perceived themselves as a social group rather than a collection of individuals. T. C. Wang, in his study of students in the early decades of this century, refers to these developments as the growth of a 'youth movement' in China, similar to those in other countries. The changing circumstances bringing young people together for study purposes had profound social consequences. Whilst developing a 'group identity' they were simultaneously becoming aware of their individuality, no longer belonging to family or emperor but to themselves. Intellectual explorations into concepts of the 'individual' were a significant break with tradition, but the Chinese students were not about to adopt western versions uncritically. At this time, the state remained the source of rights and duties, without which an individual could not exist autonomously. The relationship was still one of dependency.

Thus, the centrality of the state predominated in the thought of China's 'new youth',[9] an important point already referred to which will re-emerge as part of the 'legacy' handed down from the past. The duty of remonstrance, formerly a matter of individual conscience, was being transferred to the growing student body. It would be the students, as the youth movement of China, who would offer their services as saviours of the nation. They were certainly becoming an increasingly articulate group whose intellectual explorations were preparing them to take a pioneering role in political and social affairs. Like their successors seventy years later, they were developing skills as opinion leaders. The Chinese government seemed to stumble along the road to political oblivion, unable to control the warlord factions and foreign intruders. China appeared to be breaking up, like the 'loose sand' already referred to. Who would do something about it? Levy points out that it was the Chinese students and intellectuals who were 'the most articulate performers' in expressing personal dissatisfactions and political frustrations (Levy 1968: 346). They were not alone in harbouring grievances.

These suppressed grievances were to erupt during the historic 'May Fourth' movement of 1919 which began at the prestigious Beijing University. At one time called the National University, 'Beida', as it is usually referred to, was established in 1898 and quickly became the centre of intellectual activity and radicalism. There was a society for the study of Marxism set up in 1918, one of the first attempts by Chinese scholars to come to grips with socialist theory.[10] The 'Renaissance Society' was also organised there in the same year and its publication, 'attempted to give an active portrayal of the new student life' (Wang 1928: 111). Beida was developing a 'corporate identity' as China's leading educational establishment and the 'chaos and confusion of Peking society ... heightened the sense of solidarity prevailing in the university'. It was like a magnet for young intellectuals and student numbers rose from 818 in 1912 to 2,228 in 1919 (Wang 1928: 110).

This tradition was visible from 'May Fourth' onwards, handed down lovingly to successive generations. 'To know and understand Beida students is to know and understand the hearts of all China's students', I was advised in 1988. Going back to 1919 provides an important link in the legacy of student protest and demands for democracy with their impact upon wider society.

The students went onto the streets of the capital on 4 May 1919 as a last resort. They had already held mass meetings on the issues of 'militarism' and 'world peace', usually joined by hundreds of colleagues from other Beijing campuses. When the news broke of the Versailles Peace Treaty, demonstrations were the inevitable result of simmering student unrest. The Chinese leaders had accepted without protest the handing over of parts of China from one imperialist power to another. Japan was to acquire large parts of Shandong province from the defeated Germans, incensing the students who insisted these territories should be returned. At a meeting on 3 May, the loss of land was attributed to official corruption and injustice. One student, according to the account of a participant, cut his finger deliberately and wrote with his blood, 'Return our Tsingtao'[11](Wang 1928: 164). Nationalistic fervour was rising as well as anger at the government's lack of political will.

On the morning of 4 May, representatives from different Beijing colleges met and planned the march for the afternoon. They were warned not to go, 'but we refused to listen', wrote one protester (Wang 1928: 164). About 10,000 students marched peacefully to the heart of the city, Tiananmen.

Some had posters bearing slogans about the treaty and the government, while others bore the characters for democracy and science, believed to be the pillars of the modernisation process so badly needed in China. 'May Fourth' was largely but not solely about an injured sense of national pride; it was also about solutions for the nation's problems.

The demonstration started a movement which rapidly spread because it touched a nerve in the population, sensitive to the image of China as the 'sick man of Asia', exploited by foreigners. It raised calls for action on government corruption, political reforms, democratisation, free speech, and more and better education. 'May Fourth' also exhibited the ambivalence towards foreigners pointed out earlier. As Cleverley writes, it was 'anti-Western' in the political sphere but 'pro-Western' in its intellectual commitment (Cleverley 1985: 49). The treaty had been the spark, and soon all the pent-up grievances of the Republican era erupted. The population was enthused by the students' bold actions. Over thirty had been arrested but were later released after further protests. Support flooded into Beijing and demonstrations broke out in other cities. The authorities used brute force to restore order but could not suppress this burgeoning national movement. Intellectually, the spirit of 'May Fourth' was to continue because the 'sick man' of the East could no longer take the 'old medicine'. A new cure was needed and many felt that cure lay within the broad concept of democracy.

But what form exactly? The discussions inside and outside the universities were more or less theoretically based since experience of democracy in practice was limited. Schwartz describes the predominant version of democracy at this time as 'Manchester liberalism' (Schwartz 1966: 9), while J. Wang refers to it as 'Fabian socialism' (Wang 1985: 8). Basically, it was a pragmatic form of democracy in which the individual had to be free to compete without the fetters of tradition in order to revitalise society and bring about progress. It was not particularly egalitarian or idealistic, stressing instead what the individual could do for the nation, not vice versa, in a modern political environment. My own suspicion that many of the influential 'May Fourth' thinkers had not truly liberated themselves from the traditional Confucian background is shared by Schwartz. He suggests that the idea of the individual having to justify himself by serving the social order was still 'lurking in the background' (Schwartz 1966: 9). There was an understandable stress on nationalism as foreign powers attempted to divide China. This tendency towards a particular form of democracy and the predominance of nationalism led many young intellectuals into acceptance of western individualism by 'default' rather than desire. Increasing numbers were becoming aware of Marxism, especially in its Leninist 'export package' from Moscow, which seemed to be more suited to China' polity than pure Marxism. The anti-imperialist content was especially appealing to Chinese intellectuals.

The Bolshevik Revolution of 1917 had repercussions within the intellectual community in China and the fledgeling society for the study of Marxism at Beida attracted many eminent people. The young Mao Zedong, for example, was a member. He acted as assistant to the prominent intellectual Li Dazhao in the library at Beida. As other scholars became increasingly disillusioned with the western democracies because of their imperialist tendencies, they looked to the new socialist model of development being built in Russia.

A period of intense intellectual activity followed 'May Fourth'. The poet Wang Zhangqi remarked that 'all kinds of ideologies have reached China, they all compete' (Wang Zhangqi 1989).[12] These ideologies were certainly in competition during the early decades of this century as they were during the student movement of 1989. Intellectuals during 'May Fourth' were 'flirting with every conceivable variety of doctrine' (Schwartz 1966: 25), finding good and bad in all of them.

The Chinese Communist Party (CCP) was founded in 1921, two years after the student demonstrations. Some of the country's leading intellectuals decided to opt for the communist line of development. The Third Communist International (Comintern) set up in Russia by Lenin in order to export revolution offered guidance on Marxist-Leninist ideology and practical assistance in political organisation. The first leader of the CCP was Chen Duxiu of Beijing University, who had a few years before been more interested in the promise of democracy and science. Many students agreed with the strategy of taking Russian advice and followed their teachers across the line from 'bourgeois liberalism' into communism, seeing it as the only solution for China's problems.

Not all agreed, however, on the appropriateness of this approach. Ideological debate continued, but the worsening conditions in China forced their hand. They had to 'jump' one way or the other during this period of internal strife, civil war and increasing Japanese aggression.

STUDENTS AND THE BATTLES FOR IDEOLOGICAL AND POLITICAL SUPREMACY

Some intellectuals remained unconvinced by Communism and clung to more traditional views about how China should be governed, while others retained their allegiance to republicanism more or less in line with the nationalist doctrine of Sun Yatsen. Marxism in any guise was viewed as too extreme among some sections of the educated class, but it still had growing appeal for those totally disillusioned by the old ways. An extreme solution was considered necessary to meet the needs of the situation. Communism also had a 'youthful' image in the early days, in contrast to the 1980s and the communist 'gerontocracy'. The search for a political identity was an expression of the strains of this 'transitional' phase. Many aspects of Chinese society were changing rapidly and the incompetent leadership could not control the situation. The depredations of warlords and foreign aggression also exacerbated matters. Even the much revered leader Sun Yatsen at one point had to seek the protection of the southern warlord in Canton as his enemies gathered around him.

The newly formed CCP also feared for their safety in this uncertain political environment. The first congress to establish the party took place in Shanghai, July 1921 but was broken up by the police and the participants had to scatter.[13] Despite its shaky start, however, it began to take root. Intellectuals were advised by Moscow to preach Marxism to the masses and make links with the growing urban proletariat. Many workers suffering the degradations of long hours, low pay, and poor working conditions in the factories had already formed their own trade unions, facilitating political organisation. The situation seemed ripe for making the links, mobilising the masses swiftly and totally reforming Chinese society along communist lines. Chen Duxiu, the party leader, was optimistic about early success, but the Russians did not share his enthusiasm, envisaging a longer, more protracted struggle. There were internal wranglings within the party as to the exact strategy to follow and whether to accept wholeheartedly Moscow's lead. The advice given, especially after Stalin came to power, was not always unanimously received. Besides, it sometimes led to disastrous consequences, thus further alienating some Chinese communists from their Soviet allies. It was no longer a matter of theoretical debate but serious political decision-making as the communists' enemies gathered strength.

In 1922, Sun Yatsen was forced to flee Canton to Shanghai, where help was on offer from a Comintern agent. Under his guidance, Sun reorganised the Nationalist Party (Guomindang-GMD) in 1923 along Leninist lines, aiming for it to be the Chinese equivalent of the Soviet Communist Party. The Russian analysis of the situation led them to believe that the nationalist ticket was most likely to succeed rather than the straightforward communist line, which still had many people to win over. As a result, from 1923, Chinese communists joined the GMD, as suggested by Moscow, to form an alliance. Many did so reluctantly, suspicious of this co-operation with the nationalists and well aware of the fundamental differences in ideology. They would have preferred to have built up the CCP as a separate entity. The untimely death of Sun in 1925 did little to allay their fears and further problems were caused when Chiang Kaishek, a military man, took his place as GMD leader. The rifts between the right and the left within the party became apparent.

Meanwhile, China was being increasingly threatened both in military and economic terms by Japan. Manchuria in the north-east was on the verge of annexation and the various warlords, themselves hopelessly divided, could do little to halt the Japanese advance. Students and workers demon- strated regularly, largely motivated by patriotic sentiments and feelings of social injustice. The year 1919 had set a pattern, as Israel writes in his work on student nationalism in China.[14] 'During the next three decades (1919–49) it became common to see thousands of high school and college youths surging through the streets demanding resistance to imperialist insults or an end to unpopular policies of their own government' (Israel 1966: 3). In this sense, Russian support for the Nationalists may have been well founded, as the Chinese grew increasingly concerned about foreign imperialism. Vociferous students, often joined by other intellectuals and workers, followed their scholarly ancestors by pointing out the errors of the government and remonstrating with a sense of urgency.

On 30 May 1925, for example, students in Shanghai protested about the murder of a Chinese worker by a Japanese foreman in a textile mill. The British-led police fired at the demonstrators, killing thirteen and injuring many more. The Chinese government did little to redress these deaths. Also in Shanghai, in June of the same year, more people died when English and French troops machine-gunned students and workers in another anti-imperialism demonstration. On 18 March 1926, forty-seven young people were killed during a demonstration against the Japanese which had gathered in Tiananmen Square. A famous and very moving essay was composed by the renowned intellectual Lu Xun, 'In Memory of Miss Liu Hezhen',[15] dedicated to one of his young students, relating how she and her friend were shot and beaten to death by the warlord's troops and labelled as 'rioters and hooligans'. Such brutal actions only further incited the students and their teachers, turning them further away from the existing regime and its complicity with the foreigners. More moved into the communist camp, which provided answers, at least in theory, for imperialist aggression.

Chiang Kaishek was worried by the lure of communism, for his own position as leader of the GMD would be threatened by an independent uprising. He decided to act quickly against the Marxist threat. During the so-called 'Northern Expedition' of the combined nationalist-communist forces to defeat the warlord factions and unite China, Chiang turned on the communists. On 12 April 1927 a wholesale massacre took place in Shanghai, which was under the control of the workers, on the orders of the 'generalissimo'. The town was to be taken by force. Some of the communist leaders managed to escape, but thousands of communists and their sympathisers were subsequently rounded up and the Soviet advisers expelled. This eventuality had been suspected and feared by the communists. Further attacks on the communists left many more dead and imprisoned in July and August 1927. This action by the GMD would leave an indelible mark on the young communists who survived and later were to become China's leaders, e.g. Deng Xiaoping.

The alliance suggested by Moscow had not only failed but led to thousands of deaths, imprisonment and repression. The CCP was virtually wiped out and Chiang was able to assume supreme power. No mercy was shown for communist sympathisers. Those who escaped fled to the hills, while the victorious head of the GMD set up his nationalist government in the southern capital of Nanjing.

The 'May Fourth' period was over, although many of its conceptual elements were to recur throughout the following decades. Some of the ideas were in fact translated into concrete programmes after the People's Republic was established, according to J. Wang and other commentators.[16] The impact and influence of 'May Fourth' probably went further than the students in 1919 could have anticipated. But after Chiang came to power academic debates and explorations were secondary to the struggle for survival. Conditions had been deteriorating since the turn of the century for scholars, no longer assured employment since the abolition of the imperial examinations and with few opportunities taking the place of traditional posts. (A parallel situation can be seen with the proposed reform of the graduate assignment system in 1988. Although despised by the students, as were the imperial exams, it did at least mean a job on graduation. Without it, the prospect of unemployment loomed large.) Israel writes that compared to the 'scholarly gentry of earlier times', students in the 1920s were 'psychologically and socially, displaced persons' (Israel 1966: 1). They were also often very poor. Both the nationalists and communists offered them ideological 'homes' and the promise of a better life.

Chiang combined repression with the occasional concessions, as when he attempted to improve conditions in education and win over the intellectuals, but these were largely superficial. The government could not hide the massive poverty and injustice in China, the corruption within the GMD's ranks and their brutal treatment of communists and other political opponents. Chiang's regime also seemed to be ineffectual in checking the Japanese moves to overrun China. Students and their teachers were often at the forefront of oppositional activity, although the nationalists tried to bring them into line. There were frequent purges of intellectuals who were suspected of communist sympathies. The overall effect of Chiang's repression served only to further alienate the educated elite, even those who were not Marxists. To the outside world. the 'generalissimo' appeared to be bringing China into the twentieth century with new industry and large-scale building projects, but political and social discontent increased with his attempts to wipe out all opposition to his regime. The students, still extremely patriotic, could not be politically neutral and had to choose between the nationalists and communists.

The expected annexation of Manchuria by Japan in 1931 heightened the political complexities. Chiang still saw the communists as his main enemies and did little to halt the invaders. Mao Zedong, by this time the leader of the small Chinese Soviet Republic in Jiangxi province, declared war on the Japanese and called on all Chinese people to resist the aggressors. Over the succeeding years students repeatedly urged the nationalist government to fight the Japanese, but Chiang resisted this pressure. It was not until 1937 that a united communist-nationalist front was formed to drive out the invaders, who by now were well established in China. Naturally there was suspicion and hatred on both sides. The communists still had bitter memories of 1927, but the future of the nation itself was at stake so old rivalries were temporarily put aside.

Chiang only reluctantly agreed to the alliance after being 'kidnapped' by communists near Xian.[17] Over the next few years, millions of Chinese from all walks of life and political persuasions lost their lives in the anti-Japanese struggle as the uneasy alliance held firm.

The communists' numbers had been further depleted during the tortuous 'Long March' from their base in Jiangxi to Yanan in 1936–7, as Chiang's forces tried to annihilate them. Only an approximate 20,000 had survived the march, making it to the north-western territory and the communist base.[18] Cleverley talks of Yanan being an, 'extraordinary place for young people who flocked there to fight the Japanese and for other reasons' (Cleverley 1985: 104). It became known as 'student city', with many political movements having their origins there. This greatly annoyed Chiang, who could do little to redress his apparent unpopularity among educated youth while involved in the anti-Japanese alliance. The nationalists had their youth movements too, but they were often ill-conceived and did not attract students into the GMD camp. Many young people had died because of GMD policies, a factor which was not forgotten. Yanan, with its youthful vitality and patriotic appeal, its novelty and 'fresh start' image, was the more attractive.

Sometimes, however, the idealism of the young people went beyond the party's plans and stretched the patience of some of the older comrades. The so-called 'youth transformation groups' had to be disbanded in what was a forerunner of the Red Guard brigades and their attacks on everything 'old'. This would not be the last time the party was to run into conflict with its younger members, who wished to take matters further than they proposed. Also during the Yanan period the party's ambiguous attitude towards intellectuals became apparent. Some of the leading CCP members were themselves intellectuals but as Cleverley points out, they were suspicious of intellectuals as such because of their predominantly 'bourgeois' background. Mao's feelings towards intellectuals were mixed, at times antagonist, at others supportive, a characteristic which had disastrous consequences for scholars in the years after the communist victory. Few intellectuals were given full party membership and if things went wrong, they were often made the scapegoats. Students, therefore, were welcome at Yanan but were also kept at a distance even when they made sacrifices and undertook hard work in the struggle against the Japanese.

The students had by now established a tradition of patriotic protest which was in many ways an autonomous movement, involving action outside the Party's control. This was another worrying feature for Party leaders. 'December Ninth', for example, had become another 'legend' in the students' history of protests to add to 'May Fourth'. Before the 'combined front' against the Japanese had been formed, large-scale demonstrations against the Japanese had been held in Beijing on December 9th, 1935. The students had defied official warnings not to go out onto the streets and they began their march to Tiananmen. The events leading to this protest can be found in the years before, when Chiang had tried to strangle student opposition. But growing resentment in Beijing academic circles could hardly be restrained as Japan looked set to annex other parts of China. The Beijing Student Union had been revived in November 1935 and actively spread from there. Edgar Snow, a well-known and respected friend of communism in China, had supported the idea of mass demonstrations with his Beijing University colleagues. According to Israel, he said 'Time is running out'. If students were to have any impact on public opinion, they would have to 'move rapidly' (Israel 1966: 119).

Accounts of the demonstration foreshadow the speeches and emotions of the 'patriotic democracy movement' of 1989.[19] The students wanted to avoid conflict, but would risk injury and death to bring to people's notice the terrible situation and danger facing China. The Japanese had to be repelled. News of the events in Beijing quickly spread to the rest of the country, causing further protests and strikes. Mao sent a message that the Communist Youth Corps 'lauded the new movement but warned students to seek support from workers, peasants, and merchants' (Israel 1966: 129) if they wished to avoid defeat. The Beijing students had started a movement that roused many from apathy and refuted the regnant idea that 'nothing can be done' to save China. By the end of December, approximately 65 demonstrations had occurred in 32 different areas, with numerous student strikes and other forms of oppositional activity. Students even went out into the countryside, in 'rural crusades' to win over the peasantry to their cause.

Such was the legacy which educated youth brought with them to Yanan. It is no wonder that Mao and other party leaders had some doubts about the students, who had such an impressive record of protest and mass mobilisation. Mao probably made a mental note that this patriotic zeal should be contained and transformed into action for the 'revolution', fully inside of party control. This would not always be possible. Meanwhile, the main problems related to defeating the Japanese and preparing for the ultimate showdown with Chiang's nationalist forces. It was obvious that once the invaders had been driven out, the old hostilities between the nationalists and communists would resume. And they did.

Chiang was backed by western money and arms, with his forces superior to the 'ragtag' communists, but his GMD government was seen as ideologically and politically bankrupt. He had little support from the people. Many more intellectuals had joined the communist cause because of its 'moral superiority', and they worked together with workers and peasants to defeat the enemies. Marxism-Leninism, as preached by the CCP under the charismatic leadership of Chairman Mao Zedong, had great appeal, not just as a doctrine but as a way of life to the hard-pressed population. Years of civil war and fighting the Japanese had made them hungry for a strong, united China. The communists offered this along with food to eat and clothes to wear. They had the support of the people and in the end were victorious in the struggle, pushing Chiang and the remnants of his army off the mainland to Taiwan at the end of 1949. A few intellectuals went with him but many stayed, believing that communism offered the best hope for China.

The unresolved questions raised by 'May Fourth', however, would have to be addressed. What was the best form of government for a modern Chinese state? What should be the relationship between the government and its intellectuals? These and many issues continued to cause problems for the new government, as shall be discussed in the following chapter. Many intellectuals had willingly exchanged their academic and political autonomy for the promises offered by the communists. Would they be disappointed?

The legacy of the past had given students a sense of duty to their 'motherland' and the idea that they should play a leading role in national reconstruction. They had their own historical traditions going back to before 'May Fourth', but their movements during the twentieth century had defined their role as critics of the state. They were prepared to support the CCP to assist in China's development, but they still had ambitions remaining from the earlier periods of protests: free speech, free channels of communication, educational opportunities and independent academic lives, as well as the various ideas associated with the term 'democracy'. Although most students were willing communists, their enthusiasm was due to the promises it held not just for China but for the individuals within the state. Democracy had not been scrapped as an ideal and the students had their own legacy of protest and dissent to fall back on if the communist way did not eventually work out.

2 Shaping the revolutionary successors
Students under Mao

OVERVIEW

In 1949, a war-torn China was faced with the urgent tasks of material reconstruction and national reconciliation, to be carried out according to socialist principles. Students had already contributed greatly to the Communist Party's cause both in the countryside and the cities, forsaking their studies to organise, campaign and fight where necessary. After 1949, they were to be schooled in Mao Zedong thought in order to further the revolution and subjected to massive political indoctrination. Campaigns like the 'anti-rightist' movement of 1957 actively involved them in the criticism of teachers and other intellectuals, but the results were not always as expected. Mao attempted to define the limits with which the young people could operate and the socialist rather than the 'bourgeois' version of democracy was held up as the model. But a number of unresolved problems and dilemmas continued to lie underneath the surface. Some of the major reasons why attempts to create genuine 'revolutionary successors' through political socialisation, ideological education and coercion instead produced a 'lost generation' will be suggested and discussed in this chapter. Although the search for democracy appeared to have reached a 'cul-de-sac', there remained outbursts of pro-democratic sentiment, in opposition to the party's official line, coming from students and other young intellectuals. These can be understood when examined within the context of Mao's plans for his youthful successors.

SHOULDERING THE HISTORICAL TASK OF CARRYING THE REVOLUTION FORWARD

The leading role played by Chinese students in political campaigns and social reform programmes during the first half of the century has already been pointed out. James Townsend writes that after the founding of the People's Republic, 'youth ... assumed an even more prominent role' (Townsend 1980: 9). The major difference, it can be argued, is that there was less opportunity for spontaneity and autonomy in their actions with the party as the all-powerful political authority. The numerous street demonstrations seen during the anti-Japanese period were now in the past, not only because the enemy had been defeated but because the party leaders would not permit such autonomous campaigning. The students were no longer organising themselves but were mobilised by the authorities, who faced a task common to all post-revolutionary governments: that of ensuring the continuation of their success and preventing a return to previous political and social arrangement. The new regime needed not just the support of youth but total commitment to the socialist cause, viewed as a 'political imperative' (Townsend 1980: 10).

Young people had to be thoroughly 'red', i.e. possessing true socialist values, attitudes and beliefs, otherwise the continuation of the revolution could not be assured. But educated youth were also required to be 'expert', possessing skills in various fields in order to help rebuild China. Knowledge, however, could lead to dissent from the party line, and when 'class struggle' was emphasized, Mao indicated his mistrust of intellectuals and their potential power. This was the 'red and expert' dilemma which the party has never properly resolved.[1] Intellectuals had to be kept in line, especially the younger elements who shouldered the task of continuing the struggle for socialism while simultaneously being educated in a manner suitable for China's development. Great efforts went into the political socialisation of this group in order to instil the appropriate morality and ensure adherence to the so-called 'socialist road'.

As part of their large-scale plans, the communists re-established the Youth League in Beijing in April 1949.[2] It was renamed the New Democratic Youth League of China in line with Mao's stated policy of 'new democracy' of the socialist variety, but there was little scope for its members to set their own agenda. The League was not a grassroots movement but a 'top down' one, similar to other official organisations like the All China Students' Federation. The party aimed to use the League as a 'nucleus for mobilising China's youth, serving as both auxiliary and reserve strength of the Communist Party' (*People's China* 1950 7: 10). It was to contain model youth, not just students but young workers, who could all set good examples for their peers to follow. These could be publicised through the League's own journal *China's Youth* (*Zhongguo Qingnian*) and other channels of the mass media.

By the time of its second national congress in June 1953, its membership had risen to nine million of China's 15 to 25 year-olds who were eligible to join.[3]

The constitution of the League was revised slightly to fit the contemporary stress on industrialisation and 'transition to socialism'. Youth all over China were urged to study and work harder for the good of the country by the League's secretary, Hu Yaobang. This was the start of his long association with the young people of China. At the Third Congress in May 1957, the name was changed again to Communist Youth League (CYL) and there were now twenty-three million members (Townsend 1980: 14).

There was more enthusiasm and genuine interest during the early years after 'liberation' than later on when apathy set in. It was viewed increasingly in terms of what benefits it could bring to the individual, being an acknowledged route to full membership of the Communist Party itself. Like a form of political apprenticeship, any self-respecting socialist had to apply for membership of this elite group in order to further his/her own political career. Self-interest, therefore, soon became intertwined with the purely patriotic motives of rebuilding China and dedicating one's life to the national good. Students were supposed to be inspired by such slogans as, 'All for the Motherland!', 'All for socialist construction!', but social status and material gains could accrue from active league and party membership. This naturally set up an underlying tension which would later cause problems not just for the young people caught up in political campaigns but for the country as a whole.[4]

Young applicants had to prove their suitability by carrying out good deeds and passing overtly political criteria to gain membership. Urban youth probably had some advantage over their rural counterparts because of relatively easier access to schools and party officialdom. Students who went on to higher education were more likely than not to be league members unless their applications had been blocked because of 'bad class' background, e.g. children of former 'exploiting' classes such as industrialists. Schooled on party propaganda and slogans these young communists would be called on to show their dedication to the motherland in a number of ways, not only to prove their 'redness' but also that 'the greatest happiness of youth is to work for the happiness of the country and its people' (*People's China* 1955 14: 20).

The League was also intended to be a forum for discussing problems facing young people and pages of *Zhongguo Qingnian* aired both the problems and the official answers. 'Lost' revolutionary youth could rediscover the right direction they should be taking in life. There was

also ample advice about how to avoid the temptations of the bourgeoisie. Young people had to be constantly alert because these people
were ready to steal their loyalty and lead them astray. There was also a
strong element of religious fervour in the descriptions of ideological
salvation through the League. By accepting the true 'faith' of communism, young people could find peace of mind, but they would have to
accept the dictates of strict socialist morality. It was good for the 'soul'
as well as a source of companionship. Young people were encouraged
to look upon the League as, 'their own good friend' (*People's China* 1955
14: 20), rather than just a mouthpiece for the party, able to give advice
on all areas of life from career to choice of marriage partners.

Even early on, however, a sense of alienation existed amongst
Chinese youth as the NDYL was a poor substitute for a real and sound
relationship between youth and party officialdom. It was a go-between,
papering over an underlying problem which would later erupt on several
important occasions. Some claimed this problem was the result of the
absence of true democracy within the Party and its associated
institutions like the League. Such views were, of course, strongly
rejected because democracy had already been achieved according to the
logic of Mao's socialism. In spite of this intensive propaganda, the
underlying tension between youth and the party leaders was unresolved.

The tasks facing youth, especially those in higher education, were
defined clearly in terms of selfless dedication to the cause of national
reconstruction. When the newly established People's Republic entered
the Korean War in 1950, it took thousands of young students to the
battlefront. Most young people, it was claimed, were willing to
contribute their best efforts and go wherever the Party needed them, but
'a few' did have 'shortcomings' because they were raised during the 'dark
days' before communism and that left a regrettable impression on them.
The League, in a combined effort with socialist educators and
ideological workers, could help erase the 'backward influences' of the
old society, freeing youth from bourgeois impurity so they could
successfully further the revolutionary cause. Three decades later, the
opposite reason was given for young people's shortcomings, i.e. their
lack of experience of the old society, according to the authorities.[5] The
League was part of the attack on 'bad' influences.

The reorganisation of higher education was also part of the overall
plan for transforming China into a socialist nation and a good deal of
advice was forthcoming from their only major international ally, the
USSR. The first minister for higher education told his colleagues to 'put
aside lingering fancies of knowledge for its own sake' (Cleverley 1985:
129), since everything taught was to be for the benefit of the nation.

There was an inbuilt emphasis on technical subjects to match the growth of the industrial sector. Russian assistance and advice were welcomed. With a strict timetable of practical classes, political study and physical education, the students would be physically, mentally and ideologically healthy. There would be little time for idle chatter about foreign political systems, bourgeois democracy or individuality as in previous times. Chinese students had come a long way since 'May Fourth', it was proclaimed in the media, but now needed to go no further than their Soviet counterparts for inspiration and advice. They could not, in reality, go anywhere else because China had effectively cut itself off from the western world by entering the Korean War.

In spite of its narrow orientations, higher education was very popular, with thousands seeking the highly valued places, but not all the candidates were inspired by socialist idealism. As with membership of the League, joining this exclusive club could bring material and social benefits, especially in the early years of communist rule when conditions for academics improved.[6] Increasing numbers of senior middle-school graduates competed for entry. Selection was based not just on academic ability but political criteria and physical fitness. At times when party policy emphasised 'redness', the political criteria counted far more importantly than educational achievements, but when expertise was needed for the reconstruction effort, ability was rated highly. The ideal candidate would fulfil all the criteria, but there were few truly 'proletarian intellectuals', much to the dismay of Chairman Mao, who would ultimately throw the country into disarray in order to produce the real heirs to the revolution. With this aim apparently uppermost, Mao led the party into the 'anti-rightist' campaign.

THE ANTI-RIGHTIST CAMPAIGN OF 1957 AND ITS AFTERMATH

This campaign actively involved the students in order to 'steel' them into true socialist fighters. There had already been struggles against intellectuals throughout the 1950s and many had suffered because of their bad class background, associations with western imperialism and bourgeois ideology. The year 1957 was significant not just because of the large numbers of people who were adversely labelled and mistreated for years to come but because it marked the end of any real hope that the party could accept advice or tolerate criticism from intellectuals. The message put across very clearly was: if you are not totally for us, you are against us. The Party defined exactly what constituted patriotism: love of the motherland and 'redness'. The anti-rightist campaign would root out, punish and reform those who harboured the wrong ideology and thereby constituted a threat to the future of socialism in China. The leaders called upon students in colleges and schools to help in this important task. Educated youth were implored by the Party leaders to actively defend the socialist creed by seeking out those who harboured 'bourgeois' beliefs or acted contrary to the interests of the Party.

Coming one year after the euphemistically named 'One Hundred Flowers' movement initiated by Mao, the purges of so-called 'poisonous weeds', i.e. bourgeois intellectuals, seemed like a betrayal of trust. There has been the suggestion of a 'big plot', that encouraging intellectuals to speak out freely during 1956 was intended to sound out potential dissidence and opposition to the Communist Party. It is difficult to prove or disprove this theory of an official conspiracy against leading academics and other 'mental' workers.[7] The implications are vast in terms of who was aware of what was going to happen and how they acted together in a concerted effort to mislead the nation's intellectuals. Probably the only person who knew this was the Chairman himself and he took this knowledge with him to the grave.

What it did reflect, however, were underlying disagreements on the correct handling of intellectuals. At the beginning of 1956 a special conference had been called to deal with this issue and Zhou Enlai claimed that the majority of intellectuals were by this time working class, not bourgeoisie. They should be given better conditions and above all, trusted, even those who belonged to the 'democratic parties', small and ineffective groups represented in the National People's Congress but having no power. This was an umbrella term for remnants of groups which had their origin in the pre-liberation era.

Mao took Zhou's words even further with his 'let one hundred flowers bloom and one hundred schools of thought contend', speech of May 1956, inviting criticism from all quarters about party policies and socialist development. It was stressed that intellectuals' objective views would be welcome because they could help improve the workings of the socialist state. There would be no recriminations against those who were less than sympathetic to communism. 'Speak freely' was the call. Only those who were genuine bourgeois, perhaps around one per cent, would have anything to fear. But the attempts to downplay the suspicion held by many did not work at first and only a few spoke out, the rest fearing 'an early spring followed by a cold spell' which would damage the 'flowers'.

Eventually, more spoke out and the campaign really got underway during the spring of 1957 with many intellectuals and students freely coming forward to express their views. But these often read like a catalogue of complaints and disillusionment as intellectuals let off steam after nearly a decade of socialism. Some were personal complaints; others were more profound criticisms about the way in which the party ran China. There were calls for more free speech and a more open academic and intellectual environment. The fact that non-party personnel had no real power in the running of the country, with no real division between the Party and the government was noted with regret. Democracy was needed, not just the adoption of the western forms, but one suitable for the Chinese situation. As one important poster put up at Beijing University read, 'Genuine socialism should be very democratic, but ours is undemocratic. I venture to say that our society is a socialist one erected on feudal foundations; it is not typical socialism and we must struggle for genuine socialism' (Gittings 1989: 71). There was even a 'Democracy Square' at Beida where, as Gittings points out, the tradition of student protest was revived. Hun- dreds of *dazibao* (large character wall-posters) appeared on some days, mostly supporting socialism but taking to task the negative features of the Chinese version. Gittings also suggests that the tone of these posters anticipated the 'Democracy Wall' of two decades later.

The students, like their teachers and other intellectuals, often spoke out because of their concern for the nation and their desire to see healthy development. In this sense, they were following their 'May Fourth' predecessors and their outcries were partly along the lines of remonstrance rather than protest. The results of these outpourings, however, were catastrophic not only for their authors but for China as a whole. Mao turned quickly on those who dared to 'bloom and contend' and the category of 'rightists' was added to the list of enemies of the people. Thousands of intellectuals who spoke out were put into this category with enduring, damaging consequences. The 'one per cent' of rightists that Mao had alluded to grew to over five per cent. The 'big plot' theory, to lure the 'snakes out of their caves', has already been mentioned, but a conspiracy against certain intellectuals cannot be proved. Some institutions took the percentage literally and tried to find the appropriate number of 'rightists' in each department as if filling a quota. There were divisions within the party about the wisdom of this purge, but Mao's wishes seemed to prevail as the cry, 'Down with the rightists!', went out across China.

Intellectuals lost their jobs, their livelihoods and their liberty; an unknown number were killed. A whole generation of educated people, some of them life-long supporters of communism even if not Party members, was blighted by the 'rightist' label. Their position in society remained tenuous, their life still fraught with difficulties, this time because of Party dictates. If they did not totally support the Party then they were against it: there was no independent third road. 'Those who labour under the illusion are ultimately obliged to choose either one of two roads', read a *Zhongguo Qingnian* editorial summing up the campaign two years later (ECMM 170: 25). In order to serve the nation, the intellectuals had, according to Goldman and Cheek, already acquiesced in the Party's control over their professional activities and organisations. Now they were faced with further limitations on academic and professional autonomy.

A brief look at the examples of two intellectuals of the time illustrates the situation. Wu Ningkun returned to China in 1951, suspending his doctoral research in the USA to answer a call from Beijing University to teach English and American Literature. He had received 'glowing reports' about the People's Republic, established during his many years of absence from China. He returned with enthusiasm, willing to make a contribution to the new China and leaving his relatively comfortable American life behind. Arriving in the midst of the anti-US imperialism campaign, his welcome was lukewarm and he was soon subjected to criticism and discrimination because of his American associations. Teaching English at Beida was fraught with difficulties and once classified as a 'backward element', he was moved out of the capital to teach elsewhere. A brief period of 'rehabilitation' was followed by more personal calamity with the onset of the anti-rightist campaign. His label was changed to 'ultra-rightist' and he was sent to an 'education through labour' reform camp where he nearly died. Other inmates did not survive the harsh regime. All of them were locked up without trial or hearing, their crime as enemies of the people existing somewhere in their bourgeois pasts. Wu's wife managed to secure his release in 1960, but his derogatory class label was not immediately removed.[8] He would suffer again in later political campaigns against 'backward elements'.

Liu Pinyen, the other example, was a staff writer on *Zhongguo Qingnian* and a Youth League cadre (official). He had been a Party member for thirteen years, yet apparently declared. 'I never felt that the party was mine' (SCMP 1583: 11). It was full of 'yes men and flatterers', while the regional cadres behaved like 'local emperors'. Communism was cold according to Liu and the Youth League lacked human nature, actually oppressing the young rather than bringing out their revolutionary potential. His criticisms of the actual operation of socialism were wide-ranging and he advocated more activity by young people to help change the system and possibly set up some kind of alternative Party. Such ideas would be echoed more than thirty years later by students in Tiananmen Square, but in 1957 these remarks exposed him as an 'anti-party, anti-socialist bourgeois writer'. In the midst of the League itself there was a 'poisonous weed' who had to be struggled against and denounced by his fellow writers. 'Down with Liu Pinyen!' Yet Liu probably spoke for a number of his colleagues and the young people he was concerned with. He referred to their sense of alienation from the Party and socialism. They had to be given more rights to speak out. The 'dictatorship of proletariat' and 'socialist democracy' did not live up to the expectations of the early days of the People's Republic, but intellectuals had to accept the party line or suffer the consequences. It is hardly surprising that the survivors of the anti-rightist campaign became 'tame' as referred to previously.

The Party mobilised students as much as possible at the height of the campaign to seek out bad elements amongst the students and staff at educational institutions. The year 1957 was described as 'an unusual year ... the most important year to each youth in the history of our life' (SCMP 1584: 2). The anti-rightist struggle was of particular importance to the young people, especially educated youth, who were more susceptible to rightist ideas. By being vigilant they could observe the mistakes of their classmates and teachers and avoid bourgeois traps. Thus teachers and academics were denounced by their students in response to the Party's call. 'Are there rightists among university students?', was the question posed in 1957 with the official answer in the affirmative. Young communists were urged to play an active role in the struggle, even against other students. Participation in the campaign could prove a student's allegiance to socialism while non-participation could indicate their own rightist tendencies. There was probably little choice about involvement in this mass campaign, although some, no doubt, genuinely believed in the truth of what they were being asked to do and the ultimate correctness of their search to eradicate 'poisonous weeds'.

The fighting talk and stress on 'struggle' was typical of the language used by the Party. There were no real battles for the revolutionary successors to fight, so an ideological 'front' was envisaged where young people could earn their socialist medals. This strategy fulfilled several functions for the authorities: it fully occupied students outside of their classes and gave them a sense of social purpose; it provided the Party with assistance to root out any potential opposition, a form of secondary policing infiltrating all layers of society; it diverted attention from other pressing issues such as economic problems; and it bolstered up Mao's image as supreme ruler of China, ensuring the complicity and acquiescence of the next generation of intellectuals. Mobilising educated youth against their elders became an established diversionary tactic of the regime and provided a scapegoat for China's troubles – the rightist category. It would eventually misfire as students attempted to take the law into their own hands during the Cultural Revolution.

The authorities were also having practical problems with young people. The growing numbers of graduates from high schools were putting strains on the higher education system. The demand was too great and industry could not absorb the excess of school leavers who failed to find college places. Expectations had been raised in the optimism of the early 1950s, but disappointment was almost unavoidable as more educated youth entered the labour market, some-times over-qualified for any work available. One solution was to send them to the rural areas to take part in what was officially described as the 'agricultural front', another military analogy. A typical article of the time offered this advice for students who failed to gain admission to higher education: 'Become the first generation of educated peasants in the motherland!' (*People's Daily*, 22. 8. 1957: 17). It stated that although 250,000 young people took part in the national university entrance examination, only 107,000 new students could be enrolled. Many of those who could not fulfil their educational ambitions had apparently expressed the desire to go to the countryside, but some had 'more consideration for their personal tastes and interests than the needs of the nation', and needed to be convinced of the importance of agriculture for socialist construction. A great deal of propaganda was produced to help change their minds so they would go willingly to the villages, fields and distant border regions. Such action was consistent with the 'May Fourth' tradition, young people were reminded, when students took their messages to the rural areas and worked alongside the peasants.

But for many young people, it was certainly a raw deal. College or a good job in the city was more desirable than muckraking and hoeing down on the farm, yet with few options, thousands left their homes voluntarily for the countryside, putting their nation first. Some hoped, however, that after a year or so, they could return. Many never did, being refused permission to take up urban residence again. By 1957 approxim-ately eight million youths had 'gone down to the fields' according to Cleverley and the *xiafang* movement was set to continue until the 1970s.[9]

This stress on agricultural work also formed part of the 'Great Leap Forward', a mass campaign launched by Mao in 1958. Everyone was encouraged to work harder, produce more and be more efficient. Students were once again urged to go where the Party needed them. Study was geared towards practical subjects and military training, with less emphasis on the arts and humanities. University candidates from 'proletarian' backgrounds were given preference over those with academic abilities in an attempt to produce more 'working-class intellectuals'. Productive, manual work was incorporated into the curriculum across the board, with colleges opening factories on campuses and 'work study' programmes becoming part of the educational process. Producing second-rate steel from home-made blast furnaces was deemed more valuable than study and many students spent increasing amounts of time in employment. The attempt to break down the barrier between mental and manual labour had ideological and political motivations, but the economic and social consequences were inevitable.

The 'Great Leap Forward', however, was abandoned by 1960 amidst a series of crises, exacerbated by large-scale famines in the countryside. Many of the 'red and expert universities' closed down and numbers of students started to decline after several years of rapid growth. Some of the students who went to the countryside to make their national contribution started to drift back to the cities and school. Life on the farm was hard. After the initial excitement of a hero's send-off, the reality of rural conditions was too much for many youngsters to cope with. The peasants, from whom the students were supposed to learn, often could not help them to integrate into village life, and the extra mouths to feed were not always welcome. As a result, many of these 'rusticated' youth became dissatisfied, wanting to go home. But for many, this was simply not possible.

The question of what to do with the middle-school and college graduates remained a pressing social and economic problem. The leadership continued to use the countryside as a dump for the surplus of new young workers entering the labour market. *Zhongguo Qingnian*, for example, bombarded young people with appeals to dedicate themselves to the socialist motherland on the agricultural front. 'Young comrades, expand your chests, carry the heavy task of time on your shoulders and march to the rural areas with big strides' (ZGQN 1. 6. 1962). The Socialist Education Movement of 1962–4 was also an attempt to produce so-called 'peasant intellectuals'. Using educated urban youth as teachers in the countryside was one way of involving them more in rural life as well as a method of employing those who could not be placed in the cities. As China's industrial and economic development lagged behind the education 'boom' of the early 1950s, political ideals and economic imperatives were curiously intertwined in this period between the end of the 'Great Leap Forward' and beginning of the Cultural Revolution.

Party members did not all agree on where the stress in education should lie. Leading figures like Deng Xiaoping and Liu Shaoqi were seen as 'modernisers', or even 'developmentalists',[10] believing that skills not slogans were needed to repair the damage caused by excessive political campaigns. At certain junctures during these years, they had a degree of influence and power in the Party, for instance between 1959–63 (White 1981: 13). When they did, intellectuals were given more to do, for more recompense both in material and status terms. Their overall market situation improved. Some of those driven out of the universities during the periods of class struggle were restored to their posts, but few intellectuals could believe that drives to produce 'experts' in the fields of technology and science were permanent. They knew their position was insecure, largely dependent upon the patronage of Party leaders whose own fortunes which were liable to alter according to the way the political wind was blowing.

In the early 1960s, Mao was already preparing a campaign which would shake the nation with its strong gust of 'leftism' and return to class struggle. Educated youth were about to be put back at the centre stage of politics. The Chairman was not prepared, however, for the un-expected revival, even if on a small scale, of open discussions of the nature of democracy within socialist China nor for the students' acting independently and throwing off Party control. The launching of the 'Great Proletarian Cultural Revolution' politicised young people in unexpected ways and the consequences for China are still being assessed.

THE CULTURAL REVOLUTION PERIOD

Indications of this campaign can be traced back to Mao's thought and utterances in the early 1960s about the revolution being endangered by 'capitalist roaders' and 'revisionists', the latter category being frequently used to describe their former Soviet allies, with whom the Chinese now had little contact. The apparent rise of a privileged stratum of party bureaucrats in Russia described as the 'new class' was viewed as a danger facing Chinese socialism. According to Mao, there were many 'enemies of the people' who had infiltrated the ranks of the party. Their tendencies to 'revise' socialist ideology and policy to include elements of capitalism and feudalism would lead to the overturning of the revolution. The achievements of journalism would be usurped by the 'capitalist roaders', thus robbing the people of their rightful dues.

Other dangers lay in China's long past and the continuing influence of feudalism over cultural and social life. The old ways could not be eliminated overnight but the revival of former bad practices was to be stamped out. A mass movement was therefore needed to eradicate these dangers within Chinese society itself which would also restore Mao's supremacy.

The student population was the group to be mobilised *en masse* to help fulfil this 'great historic task', because they were the revolutionary successors'. Their eager participation would bring the country to the brink of civil war. Two decades later, students with no personal experience of the Cultural Revolution would be well aware of the terror, injustice and hardships caused in the name of 'class struggle'. This probably contributed to a certain tendency amongst them to be more wary of political campaigns. The 1980s generation wanted their own ideals rather than an idol to follow. It is necessary to remember, however, that youth in the 1960s did not all follow blindly. The concept of democracy may have been lost in the rhetoric of class struggle but was by no means non-existent. Ronald Montaperto reminds us not to accept, 'simplistic explanations of China's students as the unwitting dupes of cynical politicians, as self-seeking opportunists, as immature youngsters out for a lark or as idealist young warriors actively striving for a union between workers and peasants' (Montaperto in Scalapino 1972: 575). Their behaviour was a combination of all these factors plus others which a few foreign researchers have examined in detail, for example, Chan in *Children of Mao*, Montaperto, Susan Shirk among others.[11] Whilst largely following Mao's dictates, the students had their own ideas and this eventually led to clashes with the authorities as well as among themselves.

Mao probably intended the Cultural Revolution to run according to some grand plan. Early in 1966 he carefully orchestrated the outset of the campaign through political manoeuvring in various important meetings and by issuing a number of proclamations which would later serve as guidelines for its development. After several difficult years when his leadership had been eroded by the 'modernisers' and other 'opportunists', Mao was trying to regain power and influence. Yet the responsibility for the actual start of the mass movement was nearly taken out of his hands by one of his close confidants, Kang Sheng. He took the significant 'May 16th' document containing directives for criticising 'revisionism' in education to Beijing University ahead of schedule, while Mao was out of the capital. This document had Kang's signature on it as well as the Chairman's, a point noted in a Chinese account of this period called *Ten Years of Turmoil*.[12]

What took place next is a matter of history, well documented by China watchers. Given Beida's reputation as a centre of radicalism and the trendsetter for student movements, it may not be surprising that the Cultural Revolution started on its famous notice boards. A Party official and lecturer in the philosophy departments, Nie Yuanzi joined together with six other colleagues and put up a long *dazibao* on 25 May, criticising the Beida administration for their revisionist tendencies. That same day, more than 1,000 other *dazibao* had appeared, both supporting and opposing the original one, whose motives may not have been totally revolutionary. A poster fight got under way and Beida was the centre of attention once again. Many students and staff had complaints about the university administration, the 'faceless bureaucrats' as well as about the general state of education. Pent-up grievances which had previously found no channel for expression now emerged. It had been nearly ten years since the Beida 'spring' with its short-lived 'democracy corner'.

The party was worried about the unrest, however, and in Mao's absence sent a 'troubleshooting' team to Beida to defuse the situation. Zhou Enlai, so often cast in the role of moderator, was responsible for efforts to try and restore calm at the university. Kang Sheng and his colleagues did not wish to see a settlement and hastily sent a copy of the original poster to Mao, who on receiving it in Wuhan immediately proclaimed it to be the 'first Marxist-Leninist poster' in the country. It was to be broadcast at once and classes halted in order for its contents to be properly studied. The *People's Daily* carried it under the headline banner 'Poster Uncovers a Big Plot' (2. 6. 1966). This return to talk of conspiracies worried the modernisers in the party as well as the moderates, many of whom would be purged before long as 'capitalist roaders'.

A *Zhongguo Qingnian* editorial on 5 July declared that class struggle was the most important subject for young people to study but the 'bourgeois representatives in educational departments refused to allow them to take part'. Education was not for 'revisionism', it was claimed, but for 'training successors to the proletarian revolution' (SCMP 3731: 2). Schools were to be closed and the Central Party Committee (CPC) decided to postpone the enrolment of new students into higher education to enable young people to devote their time to furthering 'class struggle'. The most important task now facing the nation, according to Mao, was to rescue the revolution and ensure the continuation of socialism. The education of hundreds of thousands of young people was to be interrupted to further this end. The emphasis was on 'redress' rather than 'expertise' as the Cultural Revolution got underway.

Elements within student bodies at schools and colleges were enthusiastic about taking on this task. Education appeared to offer them little opportunity for worthwhile careers or the chance to show their potential as 'revolutionary successors'. All through childhood, this post-liberation generation had been subjected to overtly political socialisation and Mao had been at the centre of their lives, the 'sun in their hearts'.[13] The propaganda had convinced them of their uniqueness and their leading role in the transformation to full socialism. In the years before 1966, the agricultural 'front' was the main choice offered, but this fell far short of expectations in spite of official propaganda. So the Cultural Revolution presented a long-awaited opportunity to prove their 'redness' and ability to carry out the historic tasks assigned to them.

Pupils at Qinghua University's Middle School[14] decided to dedicate themselves to 'an education through struggle and to a politics course not given in the classroom' (Cleverley 1985: 164). Calling themselves 'Red Guards' (*hongweibing*), they were praised and encouraged by Mao.

With an apparent air of satisfaction, the Chairman reviewed one million Red Guards in Tiananmen Square in August 1966. The party had accepted the need for this political campaign and any members who harboured doubts about it were advised to keep silent. The young people who had swelled the ranks of the Red Guard believed they had an important mission to fulfil.

With something approaching religious fanaticism thousands travelled to the capital, hoping for a glimpse of the 'great helmsman' and his approval to seek out the bourgeois infiltrators who threatened to rob them of their socialist future. 'Down with the capitalist roaders! Smash the four olds!', were the cries echoing first around Tiananmen and then throughout China.

Older intellectuals still wearing their 'rightist' labels could guess what was coming. Wu Ningkun, mentioned in the earlier discussion of the anti-rightist campaign, said simply, 'So, I was in for it again' (*Cambridge Review* 1986: 105). He was dragged out of bed in the middle of the night by his students and pushed outside to a basketball court where many other lecturers were on their knees. Students screamed abuse at them, and beat and kicked their teachers into confessing their 'crimes'. Similar scenes were reported throughout China as Red Guard brigades were formed on most campuses. Their first and most accessible targets were their own teachers. Some intellectuals committed suicide before the 'mob' could get to them. Others died during the 'struggle' sessions. Torture, beatings, humiliation and death were witnessed on campuses, as in 1957, in the attempt to wipe out revisionism. 'Senior staff were paraded through the campuses wearing dunce's caps, and set to mop latrines and clean out pig sties. Things went harder for those who attempted to fight back.' (Cleverley 1985: 173). Those students who did not feel the revolutionary zeal of their comrades had little choice but to become involved and thus prove their loyalty to the cause. Many never questioned whether what they were doing was right or wrong; it was justified by the propaganda and was what they were expected to do.

Even so, the sudden change in the young people from apparent docility to open rebellion took many Chinese people, as P. Liu writes, completely by surprise. Explicable to some extent by their political socialisation, it was nevertheless hard to accept. The viciousness of some Red Guard groups was alarming and frightening. Chan argues that the 'authoritarian personality' became the dominant characteristic of these young people,[15] with devastating results for those on the receiving end of their criticism. Red Guards attacked not only intellectuals but all figures of authority. In what Liu describes as a 'revolt against excessive political regimentation' (Liu 1976: 114), they took matters into their own hands, acting with a degree of autonomy unanticipated by Mao.

Official organisations like the Youth League, with its millions of student members, were simply ignored. They set up their own groups which began to liaise with one another as the 'great link up' (*da chuan lian*)[16] got under way and Red Guards went touring the country both to exchange revolutionary experiences and learn more from the people. Free from schools, colleges and the control of parents, the young people set about making revolution in their own way, often creating chaos in doing so. Slogans like 'Revolution is not criminal: to rebel is reasonable',[17] and the backing of Mao justified their activities. They used posters and their own pamphlets to publicise the messages of the Cultural Revolution, as official state-run media were rejected as too 'bureaucratic' or 'instruments of the bourgeoisie'. But the messages were becoming increasingly complicated as the months went by and uncertainty about the future of China increased. Different groups had different perceptions of the contemporary situation and the disagreements were not confined to verbal clashes. Fighting on the streets was common between the young rebels, whose numbers were swollen by discontented rusticated youth who seized the opportunity to return to the cities and also by unemployed workers.

Attempts were made to commandeer elements of the party bureaucracy. In November 1966, Red Guards tried to take over *Liberation Daily*, (*Jiefang Ribao*) and there were clashes between radical students and workers. Other organisations were attacked as centres of bureaucracy, stealing power from the masses and therefore anti-socialist. Some Red Guard groups suggested that people should take control of Party organisations and establish 'real' socialist democracy. They made moves to 'seize power' from organs of state bureaucracy at various levels, which needless to say were worrying developments for the authorities. Gittings writes how they used the label of 'commune' to embody their principles (Gittings 1989: 76). This was a direct reference to the Paris Commune of 1871 described by Marx in his essay *The Civil War in France* (Mclellan, 1977: 539–558) a work not unfamiliar to many educated young people. The attempt by the Paris communists to establish a working democracy based on universal suffrage with leaders elected by the people and ultimately responsible to them, was viewed as a model to be emulated by some Red Guard groups. It would be referred to again in later political movements where the nature of democracy was called into question.

The Paris Commune version of democratic socialism was at variance with the CCP's preferred model, where the interests of the masses are seen to be best represented through the party which takes the leading role. This was also similar to the political system in the USSR, until President Gorbachev called this long-standing tenet into question in early 1990. In communist China, there is little scope for grassroots movements where people elect their own representatives and have power over them. The party had eliminated most forms of participatory democracy and proclaimed itself the true protector of the interests of the people. The power flows downwards to the masses, not the other way round.

During the Cultural Revolution, these arrangements began to come under attack. In Shanghai during the early part of 1967, a Red Guard faction set up the 'Shanghai Commune', intended as a 'completely new organisational form of political power suited to the socialist economic base' (Gittings 1989: 76). This set an example and there were soon other communes in major Chinese cities. These moves threatened the party's leading role, for if people began to govern themselves there would be no need for the party machinery and its bureaucrats. This was not seen as the correct road for socialism by the leaders, who appeared worried at the prospect of the masses taking control. The Shanghai Commune, however, was not founded on a real mass base, according to Gittings, but like other hastily established communes was the result of in-fighting between Red Guard factions struggling to establish power bases. They were for this reason doomed to failure, quite apart from their confrontational stance with party bureaucracy. The leadership was not about to support them and the ordinary people were also unsure of these new developments. The communes received heavy criticism.

The party was by now trying to contain this movement and rein in the disorderly young rebels who were instigating more 'trouble' than 'revolution'. The authorities had some success in re-establishing their control but fighting and ideological conflict continued to divide the country and its people throughout 1967. Where was China heading?

This important question formed the basis of a famous essay published by the 'Shengwulian' group in Hunan province, set up in October 1967.[18] Their discussion of communist ideology, the party, the nature of socialist development and other issues was bold in its attempt to make political statements outside of the CPP's authority. Their arguments in 'Whither China?'[19] were negative about party control and the version of socialist democracy on offer in China. They hinted that the people should seize power and run the country in the interests of the masses. It was, as Gittings sums up, 'a radical challenge from the grassroots', and while it was not the only one, it was the main challenge that foreign observers were aware of. 'Shengwulian stands in a classic line of revolutionary challenge which extends from Mao's own pronouncements through the Beida protests of the Hundred Flowers to the post-Mao democracy movement' (Gittings 1989: 81). In between the lines of its Marxist terminology was the call for people to be free to run their own lives and for a 'real' revolution to bring this about.

This was too radical for the party leadership, who continued to stress the central role of the party. Shengwulian was dismissed at first as irrelevant and then as 'counter-revolutionary'. The call for the 'smashing of bureaucracy' was not to be carried out as literally as envisaged by groups such as the one established in Hunan. 'The Marxist principle of smashing the old state machinery must be observed,' they had written. 'The old state machinery must be smashed utterly' ('Whither China?' SCMP 4190). The Shengwulian group had also called into question the role of the army in a state which had witnessed the rise of a new 'red capitalist' class. It was seen as inevitable that the PLA would serve the interests of this new exploiting class, in the words of the 'Whither China?' essay. The party authorities were angered by this view. The PLA was to be beyond reproach, seen as the 'Great Wall' protecting the people and the Cultural Revolution. The army was after all the 'People's Army.'

When Mao toured the country at various times during 1967 and saw for himself the civil disorder and near anarchy the Red Guards were causing, his earlier satisfaction turned into concern. Documents like that written by the Shengwulian group would only stir up further trouble. Civil war had become a real possibility. Throughout 1968 Mao called in units of PLA troops to help restore law and order. Students were sent back to school and college; workers to the factories. The army was accompanied by 'Mao Zedong Thought Propaganda teams', who were to carry out ideological work on wayward students.

They were sometimes met, however, with armed resistance. Qinghua University, for example, the 'home' of the Red Guards, 'was in a state of virtual anarchy at this time, Red Guard factions operating out of fortified buildings and fighting each other with an armoury of machine-guns, rifles, poison gas, mines, hand-grenades and homemade tanks' (Cleverley 1985: 174). The PLA and worker units sent in on 27 July 1968, eventually regained control and restored order. Then the ideological teams got to work. Similar events were witnessed elsewhere. By the end of 1968, a semblance of normality was restored but some schools and colleges remained closed. Education continued to be disrupted well into the 1970s because of changing policies on the part of the leadership and disagreements among local party officials about higher education.

Young people, especially former Red Guard activists, were once more sent to the countryside to learn from the peasants. From mid-1968, convoys of trucks began taking university and college staff as well as students to the rural areas where a hard and often hostile environment awaited them. This mass relocation of personnel effectively split up Red Guard brigades and factions, thus defusing the growing opposition to the bureaucratic structures of the party. Some Red Guard leaders were jailed or executed for their actions during the Cultural Revolution. Others fled to Hong Kong, fearing punishment and tired of failed political campaigns. Anita Chan's informants in her in-depth study of the Red Guard generation were former activists who became disillusioned with Mao's politics and decided to take their chances in Hong Kong instead.

The Ninth Party Congress in April 1969 is a convenient marker for the end of the Cultural Revolution proper because party rule was reimposed on the country. But the disruption and chaos did not really end until the death of Mao in September 1976 and in some commentaries this later date is given as the termination of 'ten years of chaos'. A sense of betrayal was common amongst the students of the 1960s, now referred to as the 'lost generation'. They had caused suffering and many had subsequently suffered themselves. Not all were Red Guard activists bent on class struggle. There were extremists, but others found the period to be instructive, their travels around the country giving them direct experience of China's social problems. Wei Jingsheng, for example, who would later become a leading 'Democracy Wall' activist, was a former Red Guard who travelled extensively during the 'Great Link-up'. He was shocked by the poverty and backwardness in many regions and his questioning of the socialist system grew out of these observations.

The reputation of the 'great helmsman', however, remained largely intact, such was his popularity and ideological hold over those who had memorised his 'little red book'. 'I cried when I heard of his death, even though he had caused me so much misery', one woman in her early thirties told me. 'My youth was wasted in the countryside and I nearly died of starvation but Mao's death seemed like a great loss', she continued. Her ambivalent attitude towards the leader of revolutionary China epitomises that of a whole generation of educated youth. His death was the end of an era for them and for China.

A NOTE ON THE 'GANG OF FOUR' AND THE 'TIANANMEN INCIDENT'

No account of this period would be complete without reference to the so-called 'Gang of Four', who were later to be blamed for many of China's ills and the events in Tiananmen Square in early April 1976. The four 'radicals' led by Mao's wife Jiang Qing had exerted increasing influence over party policy-making during Mao's final years as his health deteriorated. They attempted to orchestrate a number of campaigns during the 1970s to reassert the ultra-leftist line over the more pragmatic one proposed by Zhou Enlai and Deng Xiaoping. (Liu Shaoqi was already dead, probably as a result of treatment received for being labelled a 'capitalist roader'.) In the gang's view, the Cultural Revolution had been correct in its stress on class struggle and some of those subsequently punished for their actions were not guilty of any crime. They were concerned that the 'revisionist' policies of their political rival Deng would reappear. They had little support amongst the populace, however, who were tired of political movements. There was a distinct lack of enthusiasm for the gang's politicking.

In January 1976, Premier Zhou Enlai, the target of many of their attacks, died of cancer. He was well-loved by the people and had frequently intervened to spare many people from the excesses of the ultra-leftist policies. During the Qing Ming festival in April, a traditional period for Chinese to remember their dead, what seemed a spontaneous display of mourning took place in Tiananmen Square as thousands turned out to lay wreaths and dedicate poems to the former leader. The Gang of Four were opposed to this show of support for their former rival. Their criticisms only served to incense the people even more. Thirteen years later in the same place, a similar spontaneous act of mass grief would trigger another student movement. In 1976 it signalled the demise of Jiang Qing and her three associates.

They had the square cleared during the night of 4 April and Deng was blamed for provoking the incident to further his own political ambitions. It is not clear how many were killed or injured at this time, but hundreds were arrested in the crackdown. The people's anger was clear in what became known as the 'April Fifth' movement. They had to wait for Mao's death to see the 'gang' punished for their actions. The four ultra-leftists were arrested in October 1976, one month after Mao had died, thus marking the final episode of the Great Proletarian Cultural Revolution.

Relief was mixed with uncertainty about the future direction of the nation, but there was widespread hope that class struggle was finally over. Students were keen to return to their classrooms, although millions were still working in the countryside and over the normal age for study. The search for a form of democracy suitable for conditions in China had taken different forms during these years, but it had not been abandoned. This generation of students had been politicised to the extreme and now had the potential to become staunch critics of the future government. There were still unsettled issues from previous years to be addressed, ready to resurface once China had resumed a more normal pattern of social life. The desire for a political system which would prevent a recurrence of another Cultural Revolution was stronger than ever, as the new party leaders would soon discover.

3 New Beginnings
Students in the era of reform

OVERVIEW

The death of Chairman Mao led to a brief power vacuum because this one man had dominated Chinese politics for over three decades. There were no clear constitutional or democratic procedures for political succession. The arrest of the 'Gang of Four' in October 1976 eliminated them from the power struggle. Deng Xiaoping, the moderniser, had survived several purges and was now able to rise to power and take centre stage. Following on from the former Premier Zhou Enlai, Deng began an ambitious programme of economic reforms. These inspired the Chinese people and within a few years, there had been major efforts to move away from the centralised, planned economic system which was typical of communist regimes. Allowing small farmers in the countryside to be responsible for their own plots of land and to sell any surplus above the state quota on the free market and the encouragement of small-scale private enterprises in urban areas brought about great changes in Chinese society. It appeared that China had 'changed face'. Students, swept along on a wave of optimism, were not alone in their desires for political changes to match those taking place in the economic sphere. They placed their hopes on the 'little man from Sichuan'. Deng, however, showed very early on that he remained loyal to Marxist-Leninist-Maoist thought and the centrality of the party. The so-called 'fifth modernisation', democratisation, appeared to be on the agenda, but groups of student activists soon discovered that this was fraught with difficulty and contradiction.

THE RISE OF DENG XIAOPING, THE PROMISE OF REFORM AND THE DENIAL OF DEMOCRACY

Mao Zedong had apparently selected his successor, Hua Guofeng, from the favoured few still eligible for political power. Much was made of a note addressed to Hua stating, 'with you in charge, I'm at ease', in an effort to legitimise his succession.[1] It was Hua who gave the order for Jiang Qing and her associates to be arrested along with many of their supporters. Mao's widow had been eager to assume the leadership of the CCP, a prospect not welcomed among the party faithful and the general population. But even with this threat eliminated, Hua's reign was to be short-lived.

Deng Xiaoping had been out of circulation since being accused of provoking the Tiananmen Incident.[2] This was only a temporary setback to the Long March veteran who had survived a number of purges over previous decades when 'redness' was valued more than 'expertise'. Deng's developmentalist stance had not always endeared him to Mao, but had aligned him to some extent with Premier Zhou, who also saw overly radical, leftist policies as a threat to China's economic and social development. Zhou had shielded Deng from the extremists when 'class struggle' was predominant rather than economic development. Other valuable people were beyond saving, however, as the party was purged of the so-called 'capitalist roaders' during the Cultural Revolution. Liu Shaoqi, for example, had been more of a moderniser like Deng, suggesting that too much emphasis on leftist policies harmed China's future. He had died as a result of being labelled a 'capitalist roader' and 'revisionist', although he was later posthumously rehabilitated and praised by the Party. Deng Xiaoping managed to stay alive and did not wish to wait for his own death before being given any credit. He wanted to contribute actively to governing the country once more and have influence in policy making. By biding his time in the immediate aftermath of Mao's death, he could prepare for a rise to power in the CCP.

Hua Guofeng's unswerving loyalty to Mao became a liability as the 'great helmsman's' career was reassessed in a more objective and critical light. The blame for the excesses of the Cultural Revolution could all be placed onto the 'Gang of Four'. Hua's policy of the 'two whatevers', i.e. to (1) resolutely uphold whatever decisions Mao had made and (2) carry out whatever the Chairman had instructed, were to cause him some difficulties in a changing political environment. During the two years from the end of 1976 to the end of 1978, Deng became an increasingly popular candidate for Party leadership as support for Hua Guofeng evaporated. Hua's reluctance to admit that Mao had made mistakes contrasted with Deng's hints regarding the fallibility of the former supreme leader.

Drawing on support from leading Party members, such as Zhao Ziyang and Hu Yaobang and his popular appeal among the people, Deng was eventually formally restored to his government posts in July

1977. He was able to address the Eleventh Party Congress in August that year and emphasised the need for 'less empty talk and more hard work' (quoted in Benewick and Wingrove 1988: 14). The programme of 'Four Modernisations', originally proposed by Deng's former ally Premier Zhou Enlai in 1975, was revived and adopted as a priority in the new Party Constitution in 1977. This bolstered Deng's own position and as Gardner writes, 'Deng lost little time in directing his efforts to the pursuit of modernisation' (Benewick and Wingrove: 14). Training scientific and technical personnel, i.e. 'experts', was given priority, which had important implications for the education system and students within it. The revival by the Party of an old Mao maxim, 'Seeking truth from facts',[3] also allowed for more flexibility in the political sphere and rejection of political dogma. Hua's 'two whatevers' policy seemed doomed as the important article, 'Practice is the Sole Criterion for Testing Truth', was published in May 1978. Deng closely aligned himself with this stance.

The Third Plenum of the Eleventh Central Party Committee in December 1978 endorsed these ideological shifts. This meeting is often viewed as a turning point in contemporary Chinese history, conveniently marking the beginning of Deng's leadership and reformist policies. 'China was henceforth to focus its attention on "socialist modernisation"' (Benewick and Wingrove: 17). Both the new leader and the modernisation programme had previously been on the political scene, but at the end of the 1970s they appeared to be in a much stronger position than ever before. Economic revitalisation and improvements in the people's living standards were put forward as major goals rather than 'class struggle'. But how far would the reform programme be extended beyond the economic sphere?

The prospect of democratisation was suggested once again but Deng had already hinted at his commitment to the traditional version of democracy practised by the Communist Party. Whether the central role of the party and concentration of power at the top of the political hierarchy would be changed as reforms were carried out remained to be seen. The Chinese people watched eagerly for signs of what developments were to take place in China's political life.

One important signal had already been given with the reversal of the 'Tiananmen Incident' verdict. The Communist Youth League magazine, *Zhongguo Qingnian*, was published for the first time since the outbreak of the Cultural Revolution in September 1978. It contained an article positively evaluating the demonstrators as 'heroes' rather than as 'hooligans'. In the complex, indirect manner of Chinese politics, this piece confirmed that the ultra-leftist policies were over and a new political era had begun. Deng Xiaoping was by implication cleared of 'provoking' the disturbances which accompanied the mourning for Zhou Enlai.

The magazine's young audience and other groups seized this opportunity for more open debate about politics in modern China. Discussion on the nature and forms of democracy and how it could be introduced into China was revived. The debate went onto the streets in what became known as the 'Democracy Wall' movement.[4] Like its namesake in Prague a decade before, the 'Beijing Spring' as it was also referred to, had unfortunate consequences. The main activity centred on a large wall at Xidan crossroads in the centre of the capital. Poems from the 'April Fifth' movement of 1976 had been posted there during 1978. The official reversal of the 'Tiananmen verdict' furthered the belief that it was now acceptable for citizens to voice their own views on the events surrounding 'April Fifth'.

Calls were made for people considered wrongfully imprisoned to be released. These included the authors of the 'Li Yi Zhe' document, a 20,000 character *dazibao* which had been posted in Guangzhou on 10 November 1984, some four years before 'Democracy Wall'. The poster had achieved a reputation comparable to the 'Whither China?' essay previously discussed. The three authors, all former Red Guards (Li Yi Zhe was their collective pen name) had been arrested for expressing their radical views in 'On Socialist Democracy and the Legal System',[5] although at first Deng Xiaoping and Zhao Ziyang had suggested that they supported the main ideas of the poster. It can be seen as another outburst of dissatisfaction about the direction taken by the Cultural Revolution and the failure to eliminate what they saw as the rise of a 'Soviet Union type of privileged class' (Brodsgaard 1981: 753). The Chinese state, it was argued, was a rehearsal for 'social fascism' and capitalist restoration was always a possibility without real reform. A truly socialist legal system and democracy complete with free speech and free media were called for. The 'Li Yi Zhe' document was circulated outside Guangzhou and fed an underground debate about China's political system. The sense of liberation engendered when the Tiananmen verdict was reversed led sympathisers of the Li Yi Zhe group to bring calls for their release out into the open.

Various *dazibao* were put on the Xidan wall, which became a public noticeboard. Posters were the main form of communication because of the lack of a direct channel between the party leaders and the people. In a country where the media is state controlled and acts as a mouthpiece for the Party, putting up posters was one of the few forms of communication and free expression. 'Democracy Wall' soon became a popular venue for those with grievances and a focus for the dissent that had been growing under the surface for years.

It cannot be described as a student-led movement, starting as it did on a wall located on a busy shopping street, rather than on one of the capital's many campuses. 'Democracy Wall' immediately attracted a wide cross-section of people. Many of the poster writers were former students, the older generation of educated youth who had returned from the countryside. They criticised the leaders who had deprived them of proper schooling and their adolescent years. Left to languish on the farms, elements of 'rusticated' youth had returned illegally to the cities, without the necessary residence permits (*hukou*). This official document assists the authorities in keeping a check on population movements since no-one is supposed to alter their place of residence without permission. Moving illegally, without *hukou*, means the migrant is not entitled to ration tickets and housing, also they lose other citizen rights. The young people who returned illegally to the cities felt there was little left to lose. By speaking out at 'Democracy Wall' they were addressing the injustices of previous political campaigns as well as calling for political reform.

Younger students did participate but they were less represented. For them, the change in leadership and the promise of reform opened up opportunities denied to the Red Guard generation and they did not want to jeopardise them by becoming too involved in a politically orientated movement. Higher education had only just resumed with some semblance of normality after the disruption of the previous decade. There had been a rush to take part when the national college entrance examination was restored in 1977. Academic ability was to count for more than 'redness' and class background, offering a 'new dawn' (ZGQN 1988 (1): 2) for China's youth. According to official figures, in what was described as 'higher education fever', between February and October 1978 ten million applied to take the examination and 500,000 were successfully enrolled.

Fresh-faced middle-school graduates and 'older youth' clamoured for a chance to become part of China's educated elite, with the prospect of an important role in the modernisation programme and adequate rewards for their skills. 'I never dared to dream I'd have the chance to go to university', said one teacher in his early thirties, remembering his youth in the countryside. 'It seemed quite pointless to hope once I was sent to the farm. But when I heard about the examination being restored, I just wanted to try. It was hard but I succeeded. I was really lucky to have that chance for higher education.' His story was not unusual among the *xiafang* (students sent to the countryside), who found themselves competing with teenagers for college places. Hundreds of candidates were chasing every vacancy in higher education and were ready to take any place offered. They first had to pass the all-important examination.

Many were disappointed in their aspirations. For older youth, this would heighten their existing sense of unfairness in the way their own government had treated them, adding to their discontent. Unofficial journals and pamphlets proliferated during the winter of 1978, often produced in spite of great difficulties and personal risk.[6] 'Democracy Wall' became a meeting place for members of the 'lost generation'. Alongside demands for political reform were specific complaints about individual miscarriages of justice. It was argued that if a proper socialist legal system existed in China, these cases would probably never have happened, or if they did, there would be official channels of redress. There was thus a combination of personal case-history and more general political commentary.

Later campaigns would exhibit a similar mix of individual concerns and social issues. 'Democracy Wall' relayed the message to the authorities that political reform was needed in order to avoid reoccurences of damaging leftist campaigns. Brodsgaard, in his analysis of the 'Beijing Spring', writes that the majority of posters publicised individual cases of wrongful imprisonment, execution, inappropriate class-labels and other detrimental treatment received at the hands of party organisations. Relatives of both survivors and dead victims of the Cultural Revolution and the anti-rightist campaign of 1957 journeyed to the capital. They insisted on the rehabilitation of their relatives and friends, joining the growing numbers gathering daily around the Xidan wall.[7]

Its influence spread beyond Beijing. In other cities, notably Shanghai with its large number of educated youth returned from the countryside, there were similar expressions of grievances. Some people stood up to make speeches and there were rallies and demonstrations calling for greater freedoms and human rights over the winter months. Elements within the party leadership voiced concern at these developments, but others appeared to encourage the people to speak out, notably Deng Xiaoping. He was held in respect by some of the participants who had confidence in his ability to correct many of the injustices and set the country on the path to substantial reform in all areas.

By early 1979, the movement was becoming an expression of popular dissent in the major cities. There were large audiences for the underground journals, like *April Fifth Forum*, *Masses Reference News*, and *Enlightenment*,[8] produced by various pro-democracy groups. Some of the authors were former activists imprisoned after the Tiananmen

Incident who made contacts while in detention and maintained them after being released. Others were dissatisfied rusticated youth and unemployed urban workers with Red Guard backgrounds. Their publications soon sold out, providing an alternative to the state-run media. By February 1979, writes Brodsgaard, 'the underground journals were in full bloom. There were gatherings in the parks where young people read their poetry and sang and danced to the music of guitars' (Brodsgaard 1981: 770).

These were unhealthy developments according to the hardliners Yang Shangkun and Bo Yibo, recently restored to political activity after the Party's Third Plenary Session in December 1978. They feared the decline of the Party itself and another lapse into *da luan*, as during the Cultural Revolution, still fresh in their minds. There were indeed some pro-democracy activists who openly expressed the idea of abolishing the leading role of the party and dismantling the state machinery in favour of creating more democratic structures. They advocated some form of participatory democracy with free elections and a multi-party system. Some views expressed at this time were not dissimilar to those of the 'Li Yi Zhe' document,[9] whose authors were released in February 1979. The leading party officials, however, were not about to relinquish their power and allow centralised authority to disintegrate. Any other form of government in socialist China was out of the question. The 'abolitionists' (Brodsgaard 1981: 770) were therefore on a collision course with the Long March veterans.

Events in Shanghai increased the anxiety of the party elders. Groups of illegally returned 'sent to the country' youth tried to draw attention to their plight with a series of sit-ins and demonstrations. Joined by unemployed youths, their behaviour was labelled as 'riotous' by the local authorities who forbade putting up posters and other activities liable to 'disturb public order'. In a speech on 16 March at a closed meeting of high-ranking cadres, Deng Xiaoping indicated a general crackdown on the pro-democracy movement might take place. He said the activities had 'gone too far' and such behaviour was not in the interest of 'stability, unity and the four modernisations'. Upholding the 'four fundamental principles' of Chinese communism, that is adhering to the socialist road, the dictatorship of the proletariat, the leadership of the Communist Party and Marxist-Leninist-Maoist thought, had to take precedence over the 'four great freedoms' of being able to speak out freely, air views fully, hold debates and write large character posters. As during previous eras, pre- and post-liberation, the rights of the individual were to be sacrificed for the sake of maintaining social stability and avoiding *da luan*. The constitutional rights of the people which exist on paper were withheld for the sake of national unity. On 5 April, two years after the Tiananmen Incident, the *People's Daily* carried an editorial emphasising this message, partly as a warning as well as for information.

One of the leading 'Democracy Wall' activists, Wei Jingsheng, had already responded to the hardening attitude of Deng and his supporters, during late March. He dared to criticise the leader outright. Wei had already become well-known for his outspokenness and his document calling for the 'fifth modernisation' was circulated widely. In a special edition of the underground journal *Exploration*, he referred to Deng as a 'dictator', who was 'no longer worthy of people's trust and support' (Brodsgaard 1981: 771).[10] This was tantamount to sedition. Wei Jingsheng was arrested on 29 March and later sentenced to fifteen years' hard labour. Other pro-democracy activists were also rounded up during the following months. Wei's severe sentence shocked many people; he had become a dissident almost overnight and few believed he had 'passed on state secrets to foreign powers', as accused at his trial. He was obviously serving as an example. It also showed that Deng Xiaoping, despite his intention to reform China's economic structure, was not going to give any ground politically. He would not accept the 'fifth modernisation'.

Xidan Wall was made inaccessible to the public during the summer months and new civic restrictions instituted on putting up *dazibao*. An official 'democracy wall' in another part of the city did not have the same appeal as the original and even that was closed down in September 1980. The 'four great freedoms' were suspended so that public meetings and rallies could not take place. Some of the journals continued for a while until their organisers were arrested. There could be no channels of communication outside state control.

Little could be done to help those like Wei Jingsheng. People threw themselves into their own lives, working hard to 'realise the four modernisations', according to official propaganda. The older student activists were disillusioned once again. Their attempts to bring about political change first of all through breakaway Red Guard factions, then with 'Democracy Wall' had led to repression.

The rising generation of students were more optimistic about the future and did not carry the emotional burdens of the Cultural Revolution. Most had some bad memories of the 'ten black years' but had not been scarred.[11] That would come after ten years of Deng's reforms failed to meet the expectations they had created. The calls for democracy in the meantime shifted back to the campuses.

THE ELECTIONS OF 1980

At institutions of higher education across the country, young (and not so young) hopefuls settled down to study, conscious of the shortcomings within the Chinese political system but prepared to do their best for national reconstruction. Strong elements of patriotism remained a characteristic feature of Chinese youth. The impact of 'Democracy Wall' had heightened expectations for genuine change, however, which were soon to bring many students temporarily out of the classrooms.

In 1980, local elections were to be held, implementing the 'Gengshen Reforms',[12] which allowed for a small but significant element of democratisation at the local level. These elections were the first to be held for offices above the lowest administrative level since China became a republic in 1911 and the first nationwide elections for People's Congresses since the outset of the Cultural Revolution. They were bound to attract wide attention, especially among the 1.14 million students enrolled in China's 675 colleges in 1980 (Nathan 1985: 207).

At Fudan University in Shanghai, a number of students held an election 'campaign', giving speeches, distributing details about themselves and generally trying to rally support from prospective voters. The university authorities encouraged this novel development and three students were eventually elected to the county congress. In some Shanghai factories, once a 'hotbed' of radicalism, there were demands for independent trade unions along the lines of Solidarity in Poland, news of which had reached the Chinese people.

Beijing University was not to be outdone, naturally, by its Shanghai colleagues. A document was produced there by one of the candidates containing concrete proposals for the democratisation of the local elections, including a request for free facilities to assist in the production of campaign materials. Other campuses throughout the country caught the 'election fever'. Putting up posters and shouting slogans about democracy had done little in the past to achieve the students' goal but in 1980, some believed that substantial change could be achieved if the limited opportunities presented by the Gengshen reforms were seized. The overriding power, however, still lay with the party-dominated local election committees. Generally, they did not agree with the style of campaigning witnessed on several major campuses, which they viewed as attempts to copy the 'bourgeois' elections of capitalist countries. These conflicting ideas between party committees and student campaigners nearly led to confrontation at Beida, where the student elected to the local congress was denied his seat.[13]

In November, the lively, open and somewhat controversial manner of the election campaign was seen by the Beida authorities as too 'western'. The eighteen candidates, mostly pro-democracy activists, organised public debates and forums which were packed with interested observers and participants. All sorts of questions and issues were covered, far exceeding what the official election committee felt was in order. The candidates, while not openly supporting dissidents like Wei Jingsheng, nevertheless all favoured democratic reform and expressed only cautious optimism about the Deng-led regime. They went too far in their zeal for election campaigns along western lines and the elections were declared invalid by the authorities. Open conflict was narrowly avoided.

At Hunan Teachers' College in Changsha, the situation worsened. Several of the older students with records of political activism, started campaigning for the local elections in September. Their critical comments about Marxism-Leninism led them into confrontation with the college authorities, who failed to bring the students back into line. Posters appeared all over the campus, which is in Mao's home town, criticising the officials for their interference and treatment of the democratically selected candidates. The students were visibly annoyed by their actions, including attempts to rally support for a more 'suitable' candidate, i.e. officially nominated. Stern warnings broadcast over the student public-address system in the evening of 8 October exacerbated the situation. Thousands of students left their dormitories, enraged by the attitude of the authorities over election procedures and their refusal to permit change.

One central issue here concerned an important aspect of democratic elections in the West, which is the free selection of candidates before actual voting takes place. In China, this was not standard practice. At the higher levels of government, candidates are usually selected by the top leaders themselves, another element of 'top down' power, making the actual election process little more than a 'rubber stamping' exercise. Also, in elections for positions in the National People's Congress, for example, there is often only one candidate for a post, thus unanimous selection is the norm. Given this system of 'democracy', grassroots feelings and preferences have no place. The students, especially the older ones, in the 1980 elections, wanted to change this set-up and introduce real choice at the local level, as one step towards democratisation. The party authorities in charge of the campuses, however, did not feel they could allow these radical developments to take place. Thus the clashes.

In Hunan on the night of 8 October, students marched to the

provincial party headquarters to register their complaints about the handling of the elections at the Teachers' College. Shouting 'Long live democracy' and singing the 'Internationale', they were in some ways evoking the spirit of 'May Fourth' and paving the way for others to take in following years. Their own spontaneously appointed stewards kept the demonstration orderly and on arrival at their destination they won a partial victory. The local cadres recognised their protest as legal[14] and an investigation team was sent to the college to see if their complaints had any substance.

The victory was short-lived. After a few days, the investigators ruled in favour of the college authorities. Another demonstration was called and when the provincial officials refused negotiations, a group of nearly one hundred students began a hunger strike on 14 October. A boycott of classes also began in support of the hunger strikers. The crisis escalated. Activists quickly arranged for publicity material to be sent out so that news of the Changsha situation reached other major cities as well as the outside world. The official media were unlikely to discuss this issue.

The cold and dishevelled hunger strikers gave speeches and 'many people wept as they spoke' (Nathan 1985: 216) which further stirred up emotions. Pledges of support came from other institutions of higher education and there were reports of demonstrations and boycotts else-where. As the crisis came to a head, however, the hunger strikers were persuaded to call off their action before anyone became seriously ill by promises of further investigations into their allegations of 'undemocratic' practices at the college.

The eventual outcome was not favourable to the students who had taken politics into their own hands and tried to realise democratic practices at the local level. Taking the Gengshen Reforms as a sign that political reform was acceptable, they had tried to conduct campaigns along the lines of those in the western world, of which they had some limited knowledge. They took things too far. One of the prominent candidates and activists at the Hunan Teachers' College was eventually arrested and sent for three years to a 're-education through labour' camp. Another left for the USA with his American wife and did not return.[15] The graduate assignments the following year were reportedly very disappointing, with a disproportionate number being sent to rural areas. The 1980 elections failed to secure democratically chosen representatives for the students at the local level in Changsha as elsewhere. Demoralisation rather than democratisation was the immediate result.

Deng Xiaoping made much of this, comparing western-style

democracy unfavourably to Chinese socialist democracy. After the resolution of the Changsha crisis, he warned against 'bourgeois liberalisation' and stressed the need for more ideological work in the colleges. Many students had strayed from the socialist path and needed to be reminded of the superiority of the socialist system. A pattern of events was established which would be observed several times throughout the 1980s: a degree of liberalisation, student activism, then the 'anti-bourgeois' backlash. A flood of media items discussing the problems of youth in general, and students in particular, appeared. The political system was not to blame, but the young people themselves who misunderstood the 'realities' of the Chinese situation. They were naive and easily misled by western ideas, especially since the 'open door' policy had allowed foreign ideas to enter China. In the eyes of the Long March veterans, young people were easily duped by the enemies of socialism and needed to be watched carefully. This patronising attitude of the party authorities towards the young generation of China's intelligentsia only further alienated young people from the party and from socialism. A minority of activists were labelled as 'counter- revolutionaries' and learnt the severity of the party's disapproval. As Carol Lee Hamrin soberly reminds us, 'anti-regime dissidents continue to find room only in the prisons and workcamps' (Goldman *et al.* 1987:276). Calls for democracy along western lines with a multi-party system, free choice of candidates and free elections were not tolerated by the old party leaders, who clung to centralised 'socialist democracy'.

Students, feeling it their duty to point out the shortcomings of policies and personalities in Chinese politics, exercised their traditional custom of remonstrating several times throughout Deng's decade of reform. Each time the demands for democratic reforms to accompany economic ones were ignored. The official attempts to persuade and coerce through propaganda, ideological work and threats contained the problems but never resolved them. The mounting grievances glimpsed during 1979 and 1980 would eventually erupt in spring 1989. There were clear signals, then, from the beginning of his time in power, that Deng would not tolerate serious dissent.

OPEN DOORS, CLOSED MINDS

To avoid a recurrence of the problems experienced in 1980, the electoral law was revised and constitutional amendments made in 1982. No room was left for the sort of 'campaigning' witnessed on the campuses, so that in future the procedures could go ahead smoothly under the party's oversight. Bureaucratic measures could to some extent control behaviour which did not conform to pre-defined socialist standards. But the 'open door' policy attracted many 'unsavoury' foreign imports to China which were more difficult to curb. 'Make foreign things work for China', ran one slogan but it recognised that 'flies and pests' would come in through the open door as well as fresh air to revitalise the stuffy atmosphere in China.

Distinguishing between the good and bad in foreign cultures needed to be carried out thoroughly and those vulnerable to temptation, particularly students in contact with foreigners and western ideas, had to be protected. In reality it was impossible to control the exchange of information and ideas between the newly arriving westerners and young Chinese intellectuals. Slogans alone would not work. The government soon found itself taking an ambivalent stance towards the *waiguoren* (foreigners). They were welcome for what they could help China to achieve in practical terms, but their politics and social attitudes were reviled. There were also splits in the party ranks on this issue. The more conservative sceptics of reform would have gladly closed the door on the outside, non-communist world. The pro-reformers were more aware of the necessity of obtaining modern technology, assistance and financial aid to realise the four modernisations.

The ambiguities and divisions were clear during the euphemistically termed 'spiritual pollution' campaign (*jingshen wuran yundong*) of 1983, when the party elders attempted to keep out the 'flies' they had set free in Chinese society. In the past China had been plundered by westerners eager to exploit large markets and in doing so they brought the nation to its knees. The contemporary open door was to be for the benefit of the Chinese, not their disadvantage. By doing business, inviting foreign experts to work and teach inside China and opening up the country to the world, progress seemed certain. Relationships with foreigners, according to the official line, were to be friendly and co-operative, but based on the contribution they could make to China's modernisation drive. The authorities, however, could not draw the line between official and unofficial contacts and aspects of 'pollution' were noted soon after the open-door policy took effect.

In earlier periods, 'foreign devils' brought with them more than just strange clothes and hairstyles but social and political doctrines as well. Why should their modern-day counterparts be any different? Students were a group already singled out for special attention in the effort to keep out the 'bourgeois liberalism' which had influenced their predecessors at the turn of the century. Young intellectuals eager for knowledge, progress and a better future, were bound to be impressed by new solutions to the problems facing contemporary China. The capitalist 'wind' blowing from the west would also bring pornography, promiscuity and other unhealthy trends destructive to the socialist morality of China.

It was to repel these undesirable side-effects of the open-door policy that the 'spiritual pollution' campaign was started in the winter of 1983. It probably also served the function of reuniting the party against a common threat. In some ways a continuation of the drive against bourgeois liberalism which began after the 1980 elections, it mobilised the media, the CYL and other official agencies in efforts to stamp out undesirable imports. Political thought and social behaviour were to be scrutinised for signs of excessive westernisation by cadres in educational institutions, workplaces and homes. Students had to attend special political classes to remind them of socialist values, the four basic principles and other tenets of Marxist-Leninist-Maoist thought. A brake was applied to the speed of reform. Deng Xiaoping hoped that this would satisfy conservative critics wary of reform and keep in check any unhealthy tendencies among the younger generation.

Intellectuals were perturbed by this turnaround and students, previously urged to 'emancipate their minds' from the fetters of dogma, found themselves once again facing the same old political rhetoric and slogans of former times. 'Firmly adhere to the socialist road' was back in fashion with the party at centre stage. To 'love the motherland' was to embrace wholeheartedly the doctrines of the leadership, even if they were slightly contradictory. Having a western hairstyle or bourgeois political beliefs would attract criticism. The modernisation programme was set back, with China reverting to the policies of class struggle in a diluted form. Fears of a revival of the Cultural Revolution were borne out in some local areas where over-zealous and 'leftist' oriented cadres interpreted the words of the Party directives too literally, trying to eliminate anything new which had come about since the open-door policy was introduced.

One young teacher working in a more conservative college spoke to me of this period with some amusement. 'It wasn't funny at the time, of course, because young people were really getting into trouble for being too westernised', she told me. 'I was severely criticised because my hair was too long and loose, apparently reflecting a loose bourgeois morality! I was also accused of running after foreigners. It wasn't true.' Apart from personal attacks, overseas materials in the English language departments were also scrutinised. 'We had to destroy our copy of *Gone with the Wind*, criticised as decadent and encouraging sexual promiscuity. Many things were lost in the name of socialist purity. It was quite ridiculous.'

It was also quite dangerous. With provincial officials acting in such an enthusiastic manner, the country was once more on the road to chaos. 'Anti bourgeois liberalism' read widely as anti anything since the end of the Cultural Revolution, could have brought back policies which the pragmatists in the government had hoped were gone forever. Consequently, as stories reached the capital of excessive clampdowns and criticisms, the leadership were unnerved and had to halt the campaign before it got out of hand. The success of the modernisation drive was called into question as was the security of party leaders who supported the developmentalist line. Positions might have been changed and the precarious political balance upset by any intensification of the spiritual pollution campaign. It was therefore diluted instead and phased out during 1984, although in some areas, over-zealous cadres were still busy checking bourgeois tendencies well into 1985.

The campaign can be viewed as part of the pattern in contemporary Chinese politics suggested earlier: it was the inevitable backlash against a certain degree of liberalisation. It would be halted only temporarily. It was clear that the Party under Deng still had the ultimate control over defining what constituted 'socialist morality' and democratisation; even 'opening up' in the political sphere was not a priority. The limits of liberalisation were set by the faction within the party which held power.

Economic reforms, however, were set to continue. Since 1979, after the changes in party policies had been accepted by the Third Plenum of the CCP, a number of important measures had been taken. The main trends could be seen in efforts to reduce the role of the state in economic life; to introduce elements of 'free market forces' into previously regulated rural and urban enterprises; to reduce wastage, inefficiency and 'red tape' and to promote the 'entrepreneurial' spirit in order to raise production levels and ultimately living standards across China. Reforms began in selected rural areas, with the introduction of the 'responsibility system' by Zhao Ziyang, at that time a close associate of Deng. Individual families could farm plots of land leased from the state and sell any surpluses in local markets. This implied the eventual disbanding of the rural 'communes' which had been an essential part of Mao's agricultural policy. Farmers were free to use their own initiative more and had an incentive to increase crop-yields, i.e. profits.

The initial successes were impressive. According to Blecher, 'Per capita grain production grew at an average annual rate of 3.7 per cent from 1978 to 1984, compared to 1.2 per cent during the previous thirteen years' (Benewick and Wingrove 1988: 100). Production of other crops also rose substantially – the important oil-bearing crops saw a rise of 13.8 per cent during this period. These achievements were highly praised in the Chinese media and people could see the results for themselves in some localities with more agricultural produce on sale. So-called 'ten thousand yuan households', referring to the high incomes some farmers were now obtaining, were well-publicised and instead of being labelled as 'capitalist exploiters' were held up as models for emulation in the changing rural economic environment.

There were problems with these changes, however, right from the start: not everybody could 'get rich quick'. There were growing inequalities between households, villages and regions. In less fertile and inaccessible regions, introducing free market forces and removing state subsidies brought poverty instead of wealth. The sudden reversal of former Maoist policies was not welcome everywhere and there were limits to the productive capacity of the small plots of land being leased. The advantages, however, seemed to outweigh the disadvantages in the initial period of reform. As the People's Republic of China celebrated its thirty-fifth anniversary in 1984, the prospects for continued agricultural improvement looked good. By the end of the reform decade, though, this situation had changed.

The early success and popularity of rural reforms encouraged the introduction of economic change in urban areas. There were moves towards decentralisation of state-run enterprises. Large factories were made accountable for their own production, profits and losses. Small businesses were encouraged, which brought a rapid proliferation of small privately-owned restaurants and shops on the city streets. Between 1981 and 1985, gross industrial output grew by 12 per cent a year (Benewick and Wingrove 1988: 118). Modern light industries grew faster than the traditional heavy industry. The state's former virtual monopoly of enterprises was reduced with the expansion of the private sector. In retailing, for example, the state's share fell from over 90 per cent to just over 50. The modernisers in the party saw such developments as necessary. Certainly there was more choice for 'consumers'; this itself was a reformation in ideology. But once again problems were recognised, which would only grow worse if not checked. Profiteering, price-hikes, and worsening inequalities between different social groups were the problems which beset Deng's reform programme. Ministers like Zhao Ziyang and Hu Yaobang, themselves committed to extending reform and making China a richer, modern nation, were given the responsibility for easing the difficulties. This task would later prove too great for both men.

All these changes were giving China the appearance of 'turning capitalist'. The leadership strongly denied this was the case; reforms were part of the modernisation drive towards 'socialism with Chinese characteristics' (*Zhongguo tese*). I never met any students who could define what this slogan meant, but usually it brought a look of amusement to their faces. 'It's just a slogan. I don't think even the leaders know what it means', I was often told. More significantly the direction of change was viewed suspiciously by young intellectuals who had hoped for the realisation of the 'fifth modernisation'. 'We have the worst aspects of capitalism developing in China like vast inequalities, corruption and profiteering, but none of the good things such as democracy. The outcome can't be good', one student told me in 1984.

Leaving aside the unsettled question of political liberalisation, it cannot be denied that much has been achieved since Deng Xiaoping took over the Party leadership. By 1984, five years into reform and the open-door policy, the lives of millions of Chinese people had changed greatly. On the streets, the drab appearance of the Mao years was becoming brighter, especially in the main cities. People wore different clothes, shopped in privately-owned shops and were able to talk with the thousands of foreigners living, working in or touring China. Substantial parts of the urban population were better off in material terms and there had been changes in attitudes. During the Cultural Revolution, for example, a woman could be severely beaten for attempting to adorn herself in any way and 'running after bourgeois ways'. In 1984, queues formed outside privately-run hairdressers for the latest fashion in 'perms'.

In the smaller, less accessible towns (many regions were still officially closed to foreigners in 1984), one could catch a glimpse of what China was like before reforms and bulldozers moved in. Luxury hotels, tower-blocks of flats and foreigners were noticeable by their absence compared to the main cities. Locals were wary of any outsiders and cautious about change. Students dreaded being assigned to these small towns where there were few opportunities to develop their talents or lead an interesting life. Most young intellectuals preferred to go to large cities like Beijing and Shanghai after graduation where reforms had made life noticeably more modern. My first introduction to China and its frustrated young intellectuals was in a small town, a cultural 'back-water', still in the throes of a 'spiritual pollution' campaign which was largely abandoned elsewhere. The town was 'backward' compared to the big cities, but according to local Party officials it would soon catch up. In their smart western-style suits and ties (just like the trend-setting party secretary Hu Yaobang) they spoke English, the language of the open-door policy. Appointed more for their academic qualifications and skills than sound political credentials, the new breed of young, educated officials intended to bring their old-fashioned city up to date.

Assurances that a new era was underway were made at a civic banquet to celebrate the thirty-fifth anniversary of the People's Republic.

This optimism was shared to some extent by students, especially those learning technical subjects. Their skills were in demand as China struggled to adapt itself to the age of new technology. They were hoping to have some choice about their future occupation after graduation. The graduate assignment system, in operation since the 1950s, usually placed young people according to national plan and local demands. It was efficient in that most graduates were placed and unemployment rare. The responsibility for students to find their own jobs was minimised. Work units submitted the numbers of new employees required each year and the state officials sent them along. The problems were immense, however, as students had no opportunity to select their own profession or place of work. 'We are just hammered into place', I was told. 'We all dread the day assignments come out. And it's usually for life', a group of graduating students told me.

Economic reform, however, offered the prospect of correcting the system's numerous drawbacks. With the new-found emphasis on efficiency and profitability, the inflexible system had to change. People with different skills and training were to be allocated to places where these could be fully utilised, unlike before. Cases of unsuitable placements were common, but there was very little to be done once the assignment had gone ahead.

Students had high expectations for their future with the renewed emphasis on 'expertise' rather than 'redness'. Those without a technical or scientific background were less enthusiastic, being more destined for lower status posts like teaching. Divisions among different groups of students were clear; they were not a homogeneous group but differentiated along the lines of study area, social origins, gender and so on. These sources of differences affected their overall view of the reform programme since some were set to gain more than others. The interesting point, however, is that divisions within the student body would become less significant as conditions for all students deteriorated throughout the reform decade and optimism gave way to despair. They also shared a sense of growing frustration with the lack of political reform and democratisation.

During the noisy thirty-fifth anniversary celebrations, when Deng Xiaoping and his reform programme were at the peak of their popularity, few voices of dissent could be heard. But they were there. Several students told me of their plans to go abroad to live because the party would never release its tight grip over people's lives. Liberalisation in the economic sphere was not enough to satisfy their demands. They wanted political reform and more freedom. Some reminded me of Wei Jingsheng, in his fifth year of solitary confinement for daring to speak out and discuss the 'fifth modernisation'. Democracy was still an idea in the minds of China's students but their leaders had other priorities. The door was open but minds, it seemed, remained closed.

4 'Deepening the divide'
Student dissatisfaction and demonstrations

OVERVIEW

The material circumstances of life for most students in China failed to improve as economic reforms were extended and strengthened. Their social position also appeared to suffer a decline as education entered a period of crisis. Increasing dissatisfaction among both teachers and students led them frequently to ask the question, 'Why study at all?', with some justification. Although it was usually specific issues which drove groups of students to write *dazibao* and hold demonstrations, as in the mid-1980s, the more general themes of democracy, free speech and human rights were also present. Educated youth were fed propaganda about their leading role in the reform programme, but this contrasted starkly with the realities of everyday life. They were being used to test the limits of reform, also to resolve factional struggles within the leadership, especially between the 'reformers' and 'conservatives'. But they were not just pawns in the political game: students had their own ideas which will be addressed in this chapter on Chinese students in mid-1980s.

THE REALITIES OF STUDENT LIFE IN THE 1980s: MORE DESPAIR THAN PRIVILEGE?

Tournebise and Macdonald in their comprehensive account of student life and protests in China during the 1980s, raise this important question of 'privilege or despair' among the young intellectuals.[1] In a number of ways they are an elite group who have reached the pinnacle of academic achievement by securing one of the scarce places in one of the 1,054[2] institutions of higher education. Since the re-instatement of the nation-wide college entrance examinations in 1977 and the reversal of 'leftist' educational policies which stressed class background and political suitability rather than academic ability, competition had been very keen, as we have already indicated. In spite of the expansion of higher education through the provision of extra places and additional institutions, the demand was still far greater than the supply. Between 1978 and 1982, for example, 117 institutions were added to the tertiary sector, but as Cleverley writes, 'growth in higher education is still far from meeting national needs' (Cleverley 1985: 245).

Data on the proportion of college-aged young people at universities and colleges differ slightly because of the accuracy of statistics available at any one time, the definitions of the group in question and the types of course and institutions included. Thus we have a proportion as low as 1.6 per cent of the age group studying in higher education in 1979 (Gasper 1989: 9), compared to a higher but more vague 'less than five per cent' given by Ethridge in 1988 (Ethridge 1988: 193). Tournebise and Macdonald, writing in 1987, state that of the 19 to 24-year-old age group, only 3 per cent would have the chance to acquire a place in higher education. Whichever figure is accepted, it can be seen that they are uniformly low at below 5 per cent, even in more recent years. This proportion contrasts with that for developed nations such as the USA, where 35 per cent of young people attend college (Tournebise and Macdonald 1987: 47). But even other relatively poor, developing countries fare better than the PRC. India, for example, when measured in terms of the proportion of students in higher education per 10,000 of the population comes out at 58.4 in 1982, compared to only 11.4 in China (Cleverley 1986: 245).

Consequently, secondary-school pupils in China have only a limited opportunity to go into higher education and in this sense, those who do make it can be viewed as a privileged elite. When compared to their peers who fail to pass the entrance examinations, they have the prospect of a better life: four or more years at university (rather than waiting to be assigned to low-skilled, often low-paid work) and the likelihood on graduation of a secure post in the state bureaucracy. There were also opportunities for overseas travel related to study and meeting foreigners for those attending the larger universities and colleges in the major cities. Young people who finish their education after secondary school often viewed their contemporaries in higher education with envy. The competition for places leaves many candidates exhausted after 'cramming' for the examinations and many are disappointed. In 1987, for example, 2,275,000 senior middle school pupils sat the examinations but only 617,000 were subsequently enrolled in the tertiary sector (Ethridge 1988: 193).

During the Cultural Revolution, Mao had attempted to eliminate this 'new elite', largely made up of the children of urban intellectuals and well-placed party officials. His drive towards restructuring higher education along egalitarian lines opened up the colleges to those from less privileged 'proletarian' backgrounds and those who showed the correct political disposition. Susan Shirk describes this as an attempt to create a 'virtuocracy' based on Maoist criteria in contrast to a meritocracy.[3] The abolition of examinations, shortening the length of courses and open criticism of teachers and academic knowledge, among other features of the Cultural Revolution period, led to disruption and chaos rather than Mao's goal of an egalitarian higher education system.

By the mid-1980s, the leftist policies had been reversed and China was operating more meritocratic principles for selecting those entering the educational elite, yet the social make-up of the successful few did not reflect the totality of the whole society. As before the Cultural Revolution, the children from intellectual and professional backgrounds were once more over-represented. As Hooper wrote in 1985, 'China's current educational system is proving to be a highly elitist one. Students at ... university, especially the top universities, come overwhelmingly from privileged urban backgrounds' (Hooper 1985: 55). Parental encouragement and pressure, access to books and other educational materials, useful personal contacts and influence with party organisations, among other reasons, are usually cited for the rapid return to this preponderance of urban, intellectual youth in higher education.

Children from rural areas are less likely to complete secondary education, let alone apply for university places, and comparing literacy rates between rural and urban areas can be illuminating here. The measured total literacy rate in Beijing, 1981, was 85 per cent compared to 53.8 per cent in the poverty-stricken province of Anhui and 52.1 per cent in the southern province of Guizhou. When the dimension of gender is added, we can see even greater disadvantage and inequality for females. Taking the same places given above, the female rates fall to 77.7, 35.9 and 32.6 per cent respectively (PRC Population Data Sheet, Beijing University 1987). Young people in rural areas can expect little more than basic primary school education and the girls may not even receive that. The prospect of a university education must appear as an unattainable dream: some are successful but these are exceptional cases. Children from China's fifty-five minority groups are also at a disadvantage in the competition for higher education places, according to Cleverley. They have to learn the dominant language, Mandarin, and adopt many of the cultural values of the majority Han Chinese in order to make progress in education. In Beijing there is a Minorities Institute where approximately 3,000 students from minority backgrounds pursue various courses of higher education. Back in the regions they come from, such as Xinjiang and Tibet, conditions are 'backward' and often terribly poor.

Therefore, viewing university students as an elite is justified in many ways when considering the low proportion who can enter this group and the usually predictable social backgrounds of the successful candidates. But the 'despair' element is also strongly noticeable. Tournebise and Macdonald believe that the actual conditions of higher education lead to a sense of desperation among the student population which, when added to other grievances such as lack of political reform in contemporary China, create potentially explosive situations. Student protests in 1984, 1985 and 1986, documented by these two authors, were partly symptomatic of these underlying problems and the 'privilege–despair' dilemma.

In December 1984, after the excitement of the thirty-fifth anniversary celebrations had died down, students at Beijing University took part in small-scale, localised protests. An official decision by the authorities to switch off electricity to student dormitories at 11 p.m. led to unrest on campus. The authorities had intended to encourage an 'early to bed, early to rise' regime as well as to save electricity, which is always in short supply in China. The students felt it was another infringement of their already limited freedom and disliked the highhanded manner in which it was carried out.

This unpopular decision added another item to the growing list of complaints about the living and study environment at one of China's top universities. Over a thousand students left their dormitories and protested outside the campus administrative building by putting up posters and calling for the resignation of key officials who had little understanding or sympathy with their plight. In one sense, the 'lights out' issue at Beida was the last straw; when added to other grievances, it drove the students to risk punishment and protest. They were having serious problems with food, to cite one example. The urban economic reforms had led to price increases in basic foodstuffs and the introduction of private enterprise in the university canteens. With the state no longer fixing the price of many basic foodstuffs and the introduction of the profit motive, the cost of eating rose, yet the quality of food deteriorated. Varied and nutritional meals were becoming prohibitively priced for large sections of the student body who had to survive on steamed buns, noodles and low-quality meat and vegetables, and that too usually in very small quantities. Student allowances are often provided by the parents, themselves often low-paid intellectuals and by the mid-1980s, income could hardly keep pace with price rises. Students increasingly complained that they could not afford to eat properly.

Government promises of higher expenditure on education and a greater commitment to improving the life of students and intellectuals after the ravages of the Cultural Revolution had hardly changed the typical campus environment. The Beida students in 1984 were keen to point this out. Although 'privileged' to be studying at this top-level university, living conditions were spartan. China's urban areas are extremely overcrowded and students are not spared from this reality. Housed six or seven, sometimes eight to a room in draughty dormitories, there is little chance for quiet study or privacy. A student's bed becomes their territory, covered not only with quilts but books and papers. Switching off the lights at 11 p.m. would deny many of them their private study-time. Noisy, dark and usually reeking with the smells wafting from the 'squat' toilets and the piles of half-rotten food which students attempt to cook for themselves to save money, the campus dormitories are uncomfortable places to live and study. They are also unhealthy.

In the regions immediately south of the Huanghe (Yellow River) there is no heating available due to fuel shortages. In major cities like Shanghai, Wuhan and Nanjing, where hundreds of colleges are located, winter temperatures can fall below freezing. Students have nowhere warm to complete their assignments and other work. 'We have to wear more clothes. We are used to it', I was often told but their susceptibility to colds and other illnesses indicated otherwise. The low-quality food also exacerbated their poor health. Considered as a 'privileged elite', university students were put in a paradoxical situation. Tournebise and Macdonald describe university life in China as a 'profound deception' (op. cit: 46). Compared to their rural counterparts and unemployed urban youth, students had definite advantages but many felt disappointed with the realities of higher education in the 1980s after the optimistic language of the early reform years.

Even Beida students felt disappointed. They had heating in their classrooms and dormitories, and therefore were more fortunate than their southern colleagues. Apart from food and the 'lights out' issue, why else should they protest on those cold nights in December 1984? There was some dissatisfaction with the curriculum, which had hardly been touched by the modernisation drive. Education had been labelled by some leading party members as the 'fifth modernisation' (not democracy as political activists insisted), yet the lessons remained traditional. Innovation and experimentation in the classroom, both in educational content and teaching methods, were discussed but there were few examples to be seen in practice. What the students learned was 'dry as dust and stagnant as pond water', one young man told me about his studies. Modernisation of the curriculum and teaching methods would, of course, have involved more financial investment which was hard to find. Ethridge writes that although expenditure on education increased during the 1980s, 'the increase in enrolment has been such that the average per-pupil expenditure actually decreased'. (Ethridge: 181) The damage caused by the Cultural Revolution, destruction of books for example, was also costly to repair and swallowed up some of the funds. Any increases in spending on education were seen as insufficient by staff and students alike at major universities.

The universities looked run-down and neglected in sharp contrast to new luxury hotels being built with foreign loans and technology in the large cities. The students felt left behind, living in relative poverty while businessmen, *getihu*, were becoming rich often at the expense of the weaker groups in society. They felt there should be some safeguards to protect less well-off people who lived, like themselves, on fixed, low incomes, from the excesses of profiteering and corruption. These negative trends were becoming more common as people 'looked towards money' rather than socialist moral values, a situation the party leaders regretted but seemed unable to control. Students were experiencing a sense of decline, both in terms of material and social positions, a form of downward social mobility. Young people with little education but the right connections or boldness could make more money selling goods like watermelons on the street than they could hope to earn after graduation. As the gap between the rich and the poor was perceived to be widening, students felt this was bad for them and the country as a whole. 'Knowledge is useless', was a familiar sentiment expressed by downhearted young people.

Those in more technical areas had a greater sense of optimism because they would leave university with practical training. Even these students, however, were dismayed by their living and study conditions. There was also the contentious issue of discipline, which affected all the students. Discipline regulations were considered too strict, with few individual rights and freedoms. Students could be expelled on the slightest pretext and their behaviour was closely observed by class monitors and other officials.[4] Detailed files were kept on every student which could help determine what sort of assignment they received upon graduation. One mistake could have a profound effect later on. But this monitoring was for many students inconsistent with their future leading roles in Chinese industry, commerce and society in general. They were treated like children, not young adults and the 11 p.m. rule imposed on the Beida students without consultation was symptomatic of the authorities' attitude towards them. Tired of this paternalistic and oppressive regime, Beida students aired their complaints over several evenings in mid-December. Students at the nearby People's University (Renda) joined in by chanting, beating their tin wash-basins and foodbowls and setting off firecrackers to make a lot of commotion. It looked likely that the protest would spread to other campuses in the university quarter and even spill out onto the streets of the Haidian district. The authorities promised to look into the complaints in order to defuse the situation. The protests subsided but there was little improvement afterwards.

Some of those who participated in the December unrest at Beida were expelled early in 1985 for 'lax study habits and 'bourgeois thought and lifestyle' (FBIS *China Report* 19. 3. 1985: 61). Officials denied that the 249 students were dismissed because of the demonstrations, but the two events seemed inextricably linked. Colleges and universities were advised to strengthen discipline, already considered too strict by many students, and step up ideological work. Warnings were given about the consequences of this sort of behaviour as there was a localised backlash against the Beijing students. Work-study was presented as a means of solving some of the student problems. Taking on part-time jobs could help pay their way without relying totally on parents and the state for financial support. It would also keep students busy in their free time, keeping 'bourgeois liberalism' at bay. With more ideological education and propaganda, it was hoped the students could be kept in line. But the authorities could not control their minds and many were becoming increasingly disillusioned with developments in contemporary China. The 'lights out' issue in December 1984 was just the tip of the iceberg.

A small-scale survey conducted among 300 undergraduates in Shanghai in early 1985 found pessimism about the government's measures to improve the political and material status of Chinese intellectuals.[5] Twenty-six per cent had no confidence in the ongoing reforms. Overall, however, students had a strong sense of duty to help China develop into a powerful, modern country, but they were uncertain as to how they could contribute given the constraints placed on them. Twenty per cent saw western concepts of democracy and freedom as useful to China, an indication that this issue had not been forgotten. Many other surveys were conducted at this time, employing the newly re-established social science departments, which had been inactive for over two decades. The government was keen to know more about the quarter of a billion youths[6] in the population and the less than five per cent attending higher education institutions. As a social group, youth was viewed increasingly as a 'problem'. Finding out more information had definite policy implications during this stage of transition into 'Chinese-style socialism'.

The old style, however, persisted. Party elders were concerned that the younger generation of intellectuals took no interest in Marxist-Leninist-Maoist thought and were neglecting their political studies. A vice-principal of a teachers' university probably spoke on behalf of many party members in positions of responsibility when he said that some young comrades lacked the 'backbone of Marxism-Leninism', especially those studying liberal arts subjects.[7] Nor did they have sufficient 'team spirit', being overly individualistic and concerned with themselves rather than the collective good. These unhealthy trends needed to be corrected, he warned, and students firmly guided away from the false ideals of bourgeois liberalism. The socialist road had to be adhered to, even though that itself was changing with the ultimate destination now uncertain.

The older 'rusticated' youth from the Cultural Revolution period continued to cause anxiety for the authorities. Thousands were still eking out an existence in China's desolate border regions, their sacrifices and hardships almost forgotten in the new era of reform. Many of them wanted to return to their city homes, but government would not permit this mass relocation of older, educated youth. Severe over-crowding in the urban areas was usually cited as the reason for keeping them in the countryside, but there were probably underlying political motives. These people had been highly politicised during the 'ten years of chaos' and could infect the younger generation, already causing some problems, with their negative attitudes and ideas. A heightening of the students' sense of political awareness was to be avoided. It was declared the best policy was for the 'sent down' youth to remain where they were so that they could make their valuable contribution to the motherland on the 'agricultural front', as in previous decades. A group of over 300 former Beijing students, unhappy with their enforced exile, travelled to the capital and staged a sit-in demonstration outside the city hall in June 1985, demanding the right to return home. They were persuaded after a few days to go back to far-off Shaanxi province and continue to do their duty in their 'adopted rural home'. The sadness and disappointment of this lost generation must have been a salutary warning to younger students not to follow the party unquestioningly, otherwise they too could have their lives wasted.

No one could doubt, however, the students' patriotism, an apparently enduring characteristic right across the generations. The older, rusticated students were moved by appeals to their sense of national duty (as well as by threats), while the younger students wished to revive anti-Japanese feeling because of what they perceived as the 'second Japanese invasion'. Their patriotic zeal developed into demonstrations originating at Beida in September 1985. There had already been a violent expression of xenophobic sentiment earlier in the year when China's football team failed to qualify for the World Cup. Their defeat by Hong Kong in May sparked off serious disturbances in the streets of Beijing, with Japanese cars and taxis being overturned and foreigners attacked.[8] They were quickly brought under control, however, and the 'hooligan element' accused of inciting the 'riot' arrested. Although this behaviour was widely condemned and probably few, if any, students took part, the nationalistic sentiments and feelings of frustration with the condition of modern China were not isolated phenomena. Scores of students I spoke with at that time suffered hurt pride that socialist China, supposedly superior to capitalist states, could be defeated by its small neighbour (and soon to be returned) Hong Kong. The government had to handle these sentiments with extreme caution.

Taking students' minds off China's economic and social problems through nationalistic emotions directed against foreigners was acceptable up to a point. But the open-door policy had to remain intact, thus overseas trading and business partners like Japan could not be unduly offended. The more conservative-minded members of the leadership probably saw the students' anti-Japanese protests as a way of criticising the 'reformist' faction. They may have openly encouraged the students, according to Gittings.[9] A typically ambiguous attitude towards foreigners manifested itself at this point. Former enemies of the nation were welcome for their hard currency, new technology and to some extent their social and political ideas. But, as in the past, the students were concerned at the prospect of foreign domination through trade and financial deals, the modern-day manifestation of imperialism.

The Japanese were particularly disliked because of their past record in China. Beijing University students fifty years before had dared to protest against the first Japanese invasion and Chiang Kaishek's apparent complicity in their designs in what become known as the 'December Ninth' movement. The 1985 demonstrations were triggered off by Japan's intention to commemorate the 'Mukden Incident' of 1931, which marked the beginning of their annexation of north-east China. There was also controversy raging about their attempt to rewrite the account of the fall of Chiang's former capital, usually referred to as 'the rape of Nanking'. Thousands perished, but the Japanese wished to play down the extent of the atrocities committed by their soldiers. The Chinese government had themselves complained about this attempt to 'falsify history'. The students in this respect were merely showing support for the official position and expressing their patriotism, but they went too far in their protest action.

The first demonstration took place on 18 September, with calls for a boycott of Japanese goods and slogans attacking their large trading partner. Highly suspicious of Japan's motives, the students referred to their militarism and ability to bring China to its knees as they did in the 1930s. They put up *dazibao* accusing the government of 'selling its soul' with the open-door policy and doing business with anyone, irrespective of their past behaviour in China. These remarks were highly embarrassing for the government and brought out the different opinions within the party on the open-door policy. Other issues were raised such as the practice of banning Chinese from western hotels in the major cities unless they were on official business or actually accompanying foreigners. This 'mini-apartheid' was reminiscent of the colonial era, when parts of China were out of bounds to its own people. The much-quoted example of the parks in colonial Shanghai with their noticeboards reading 'No dogs or Chinese allowed', is pertinent here. Students did not want to suffer such humiliation even though the new policies were implemented by their government for the betterment of the nation.

Students in other cities quickly followed the lead of their Beijing counterparts. In Xian, a similar demonstration was reported lasting for three days with some violence. Unrest was recorded in Shanghai and Chengdu. The students were rapidly becoming the most vocal critics of reform as it was being implemented by the government led by Deng Xiaoping. It seemed as if the younger generation did not trust the judgement of the leadership. The students in the 1980s were also concerned with the fate of China and their own future security. This was all very worrying for the reformers in the government who though applauding the young people's sense of nationalistic duty rejected their misgivings about the open-door policy.

The September demonstrations appeared very much like a single-issue movement, but I would argue that other concerns were raised, including the lack of political reform in China. Their international position would improve, it was suggested, if there were some form of democracy. After all, Japan had democratic structures and procedures, as well as a far higher standard of living for most of its people. At the end of the Second World War, Japan and China were both rundown but China had become the poor neighbour, a condition the students were not satisfied to accept without questions. It was the questioning aspect of the developing student campaign that most concerned the government. The protest had to be contained and drawn to some form of conclusion without any further loss of face or foreign investment.

With the fiftieth anniversary of the historic 'December Ninth' approaching, students were laying plans for large-scale rallies to remind the government of their traditional role as remonstrators and revolutionaries. Official moves to placate the students with promises that their complaints would be looked into eventually succeeded. The December demonstrations were called off and order on the campuses was restored, but the underlying issues and grievances remained. It was predictable that another important single issue could bring the students back out of their classrooms and onto the streets. The reformers in the government temporarily won a truce, between themselves and the students as well as with the conservatives.

It was an uneasy truce, however, with clear signs of tension persisting. One indication of the deep-seated level of dissent followed soon after the anti-Japanese student protests. Fang Lizhi, a leading astrophysicist noted for his frequent outspoken comments on the Chinese political system was invited to speak to electronics students at Beida on 4 November 1985. These students, like Fang himself, were part of the technocratic elite referred to earlier, but their better prospects and opportunities apparently failed to compensate for other sources of discontent. According to Kelly, Fang's speech, 'displayed all the features which were to lead to his purge in 1987' (Kelly 1987: 133). He was already renowned for his view that 'democracy is something to be struggled for, not conferred from above', and as Kelly points out, this doctrine was voiced during the September protests. Fang told the electronics students that a better intellectual environment would also have to be fought for, with intellectuals taking matters more into their own hands. He was certainly not one of the 'tame' scholars and did not expect the young people to be so.

His November speech was applauded loudly. He declared that 'discipline, order, morality and civilisation are on a higher level out there than in China' (Kelly 1987: 133). His comments inspired the students, but placed him on the list of suspicious intellectuals. He knew this as did other 'leading lights' who spoke out against the regime such as Liu Binyan and Wang Ruowang.[10] Fang appeared prepared to sacrifice his privileges as part of the technical intelligentsia to speak out; otherwise, he believed 'education will remain a master–apprentice affair' (Kelly 1987: 134). His stress on original ideas and individual contributions to the country were a form of patriotic loyalty not in line with what the party laid down. The Beida students were receptive to his ideas, but the leadership were more antagonistic. Fang would play an important role in the next round of student demonstrations at the end of 1986.

Meanwhile 1985 ended with unrest among students from the Uighur ethnic minority. About 800 held a demonstration in Tiananmen Square in mid-December to protest against nuclear testing in their homeland of Xinjiang province in the extreme north-west of China. In Shanghai a little later, about one hundred Uighurs held a similar protest.[11] Nuclear testing was one issue. They were generally concerned about the treatment of their minority by the Han majority. Being mostly Muslim and with a Central Asian cultural background, the Uighurs had been incorporated into China in the nineteenth century (Xinjiang was formerly known as Turkestan). In the mid-1980s the Uighur students called for independence from China, as the Tibetans have been doing for decades. Urumqi (Urumchi), the capital of Xinjiang province, saw thousands of students take to the streets in large demonstrations at the end of the year. The situation in the remoter regions was tense. It appeared that students all over China were on edge and quite willing to express their numerous grievances, encouraged by leading intellectuals and various 'factions' within the party itself.

A SECOND 'HUNDRED FLOWER' MOVEMENT AND THE WINTER OF DISCONTENT

The demonstrations at the end of 1985 brought about a degree of response, although the authorities did not address the main issues raised by the students. The students were, as Kelly tells us, becoming 'a medium of public opinion in their own right' (Kelly 1987: 140). Other people were taking note of what they had to say, including sections of the leadership.

Hu Yaobang, General Secretary of the Communist Party, and Premier Zhao Ziyang were known to be enthusiastic about pressing ahead with further restructuring of the economy and initiating change in other areas of Chinese society. They believed success could win over the students and other intellectuals. The more conservative party members were less convinced of the need to transform China into a market-oriented system with all that would entail. Deng Xiaoping as paramount leader, although officially only carrying out his duties as the Chairman of the Military Affairs Commission, was caught in the middle, trying to maintain a balance between factions in the party which he denied existed. His own popularity had declined amongst the Chinese people and he was seen as too old and unwell for the job. (He was already 81 and had cancer.) It was rumoured that 71-year-old Hu

Yaobang, Deng's long-standing protégé was impatient for his mentor to step down so that he could firmly take the political reins and strengthen the embattled reformist position.

It was against this uncertain political backdrop that the cycle of relaxation and repression in political and intellectual life began again. With the reformers gaining the upper hand, 1986 heralded a new start in the reform programme aimed at tapping the reserves of knowledge and skill possessed by the educated elite in order to boost the flagging economy. The idea of introducing a degree of democratisation in the political sphere, put on the 'back burner' since 1980,[12] was advanced again in the slightly more relaxed and optimistic atmosphere of the new year. It seemed likely that a second 'hundred flowers' movement was in the offing, thirty years after the original one had ended in disaster for thousands of Chinese intellectuals.

Times had changed, people were reminded. The open-door policy was set to continue and China was no longer governed by one all-powerful dictator, but in theory at least, by the 'collective leadership' of the CPC. Class struggle had been replaced by the modernisation drive. Intellectuals were needed to play their role not just in the technical sphere but in many fields of expertise if China was going to build a materially prosperous as well as socialist civilisation. Impatient for change, the intellectuals took the lead in criticism of the party, their dissent having, according to Kelly, 'few precedents in recent Chinese history'. The Shanghai-based *World Economic Herald* (*Shijie Jingji Daobao*), a new and controversial journal, published a number of articles by leading pro-reform intellectuals insisting on the need for greater freedom and 'ideological relaxation' (Wang Ruowang cited in Kelly 1987: 135). Rather than being suppressed, these articles found support in the more mainstream and consequently more orthodox (party) newspapers such as *Renmin Ribao* and *Guangming Ribao*. This rather unusual development may have been due to the influence of Hu Yaobang in the Ministry of Propaganda or to a younger generation of journalists who demanded more honesty in their reporting. Either way, relaxation of media control encouraged further intellectual debate about the problems facing China and alternative solutions to the ones offered by Marxism-Leninism.

There is usually a big 'but', however in these cycles of liberalisation. This contemporary 'Double Hundred' did not have Chairman Mao waiting to apprehend dissidents but there were numerous other antagonists among the 'conservative' camp. It was also true that the reformers were more interested in what practical achievements could be made by a period of liberalisation. According to Saich, 'The main reason for this renewed willingness to talk about reform was the fear among many that the economic reforms were in danger of reaching an impasse' (Saich 1985: 29). If a certain opening up of the political life could reinvigorate the economy, that would be sufficient justification for adding a new dimension to 'socialism with Chinese characteristics'. Liberalisation and democratisation were not so much of intrinsic value as of practical value for the reformist-minded leadership. This pragmatism would later conflict with those intellectuals and students who thought political reform was desirable in its own right.

There was a clear link with past practices of fitting the ideology to the needs of the state rather than its constituent members. A few leading officials believed that free speech, human rights and other concepts embraced by the term 'democracy' were honourable in themselves, but mostly it appeared that support for democracy was based on promoting economic progress. Believing in democracy for its own sake does not seem to be characteristic of Chinese political thought, past or present. Dissenting voices, however, were beginning to suggest otherwise, including young scholars who were tired of 'autocracy'. The danger of going too far was always present right from the start of the renewed intellectual 'blooming and contending'.

As in the past, the students would be the ones to go over the brink, encouraged and inspired by the 'freer' intellectual environment of 1986. The open debate in the media had, according to the intellectual Ding Wang (cited in Kelly 1987: 139), stimulated the students to more reflection on contemporary society. In this sense, the intellectual 'counter elite' were a catalyst of the demonstrations which broke out at the end of the year. The students' own deteriorating conditions and increasing awareness of problems experienced by other social groups also played a role. Food, discipline, standards of living, the curriculum, educational facilities, study opportunities and employment prospects were all examined and found wanting by increasing numbers of students. Some were more fortunate than others and conditions were not totally uniform throughout the country. Science and technology institutes tended to receive more investment than the liberal arts colleges. I saw several brand new technical institutes, complete with Japanese-equipped language laboratories, which no-one knew how to use, and libraries stacked with scientific books.

At the Sixth Plenum of the Twelfth Party Central Committee in September 1986, the leading members of the Politbureau, such as Zhao Ziyang and Hu Yaobang, put forward their views about the effects of continuing to 'open up' intellectual debate and introduce political reforms. The conservative opposition managed to prevent any real discussion of political change. Saich tells how instead of debating planned reforms, the Plenum 'passed a resolution on the needs to improve work in the ideological and cultural spheres, issues identified with those who wish to limit political reform' (Saich 1988: 30). Commentators such as Kelly see this meeting as a 'watershed' where the reformers lost their case. Their opponents linked the negative phenomena in Chinese society with 'bourgeois contamination', as they had done so in the 'spiritual pollution' campaign. It would only be a matter of time, analysts warned, before a conservative backlash would begin with the usual repressive measures against bourgeois liberalism. Hu Yaobang apparently lost the patronage of Deng Xiaoping at this time and for him too the future looked uncertain as China's supreme ruler moved towards the conservative side. Official reports of the Plenum indicated changing allegiances and the victory of those suspicious of reform. Intellectuals who had been encouraged to 'bloom' temporarily knew that the 'harvest reckoning' (Kelly 1987: 127) would follow.

Students were perturbed that their new-found 'freedom' to express themselves was to be revoked by the old men running the country. They had not only been active in discussion among themselves, but had become a source of commentary about the state of the nation. They had come to relish their small but growing role as political and social observers, invoking the spirit of 'May Fourth'. They wanted more reforms, not less, and an active role to play in helping the country rid itself of social ills. Excessive inequalities and corruption were two targets of criticism and the students were ready to speak out.

The largest spontaneous demonstrations since the Cultural Revolution erupted not, as usual, on the Beijing campuses but in the provincial universities. A number of isolated events occurred throughout November and December which culminated in massive displays of 'student power' on the streets of major cities. While not solely triggered by political concerns, they all eventually focused on the need for reform and the lack of democratisation. Details of some of the disturbances were reported by foreign journalists, who were able to see for themselves what was happening. Other actions may have gone unreported. China is a vast country and communications are often difficult. News of some of the events did spread to other districts and had a 'knock-on' effect, with students acting in solidarity. But some of the protests were unrelated and their coincidental timing indicates shared feelings of frustration and resentment among the student population, who were extremely sensitive to official party moves. The warning given by conservative CPC member Peng Zhen in November to those who desired bourgeois democracy 'as if the moonlight of capitalist society were brighter than our sun' (Saich 1988: 31), probably did little to endear the students to the orthodox party leaders.

One of the early scenes of trouble was in Changsha, where students in 1980 protested about the lack of democracy in local elections. In 1986, there were initially small-scale disturbances caused by the forcible eviction of a professor employed by the Teaching College from his accommodation on the Hunan University campus.[13] This was seen as victimisation of intellectuals, already suffering in the changed economic circumstances of modern China. In Shanghai at the Teachers' University, new regulations issued on 10 November made it obligatory for students to do physical exercises before classes. This was formerly standard practice but had lapsed in recent years. Students openly expressed their opposition to these orders. In the following days, many *dazibao* were posted complaining about the low-quality, high-priced canteen food as well as the reinstitution of physical exercise. If the college authorities were concerned about the students' health, it was suggested that they should take action to improve their average daily diet. The real reason for the compulsory exercise, some students believed, was to further intrude into their free time in an already highly regimented day. More freedom of speech and independence would reduce the power of high-handed officials to dictate to the students how they should live.

Canteen food was the initial cause of demonstrations at Shanxi University in Taiyuan, northern China and also at Jinan, the capital of Shandong province. Over in Xian, it was reported that two postgraduates of the Northwestern University were assaulted by the children of a well-placed professor. Friends of the victims demonstrated on the streets, calling for action against the culprits, who had abused their power. The protest in Jinan involved a hunger strike, started on 18 November, and several days later a march through the streets by students, calling on the provincial authorities to listen to their complaints. These were not just about food, but the lack of official concern about declining living and study conditions. Democracy was also raised as an important issue.

The *Beijing Review* carried an article accusing Professor Fang Lizhi of the National Science and Technology University in Hefei of provoking these troubles with 'inflammatory' speeches made at several universities in November. He had, the article claimed, described the students as a 'progressive force for democracy' (Tournebise and Macdonald 1987: 78). Fang would later contest the truth of some of these statements, although he was a self-acknowledged critic of the party leadership. At that time, he was still a Party member, believing it could be reformed from within. There is little doubt that his outspoken views had some effect on the students, and he was a convenient 'scapegoat' for the authorities to blame for the disturbances. They would not accept that the students could act spontaneously and have their own views outside of the party's direction. The factions within the leadership also used the demons- trations to further their own ends in the ongoing struggle for supremacy in the party hierarchy.

Such isolated incidents of student unrest rapidly became a mass movement. On 4 December, several hundred students at Fang's university in Hefei held a demonstration as part of their campaign to organise a boycott of the campus canteens. Also on the agenda at this time were the elections for the local People's Assembly and the imminent anniversary of the 1935 anti-Japanese student movement. Thus there was a combination of potentially explosive contributory factors. The students criticised the official methods of selecting candidates as in 1980, claiming it was totally undemocratic. The authorities then appeared to back down, accepting the students' own nominees. Feeling euphoric at having won this 'victory', they decided to extend their actions in a campaign to bring about more liberty and democracy in other areas of social life. As the important date of 'December Ninth' drew near, the atmosphere in Hefei was tense, a city already marked as a potential centre of trouble because of Professor Fang Lizhi. Now it became a 'hotbed' of student protest as thousands went onto the streets, carrying banners and shouting slogans like 'Long live democracy', 'Down with despotism', and 'No modernisation without democratisation', a direct reference to the words of imprisoned Wei Jingsheng.

Wuhan, a large industrial city on the Changjiang River was next to see students march in defiance of the local authorities. Complaints about food and living conditions mingled with calls for free speech, a free press and democracy. Reform, the young protesters stressed, was good but should be extended into the political sphere, as their predecessors had demanded many times before. Students in Nanjing, further down the river, soon jammed the streets, supporting their colleagues elsewhere. In other major cities, students came out to voice their grievances, worries and hopes about reform. There were inconsistencies in their views, the students having inherited some of the contradictions of the past. They were, however, strongly patriotic in outlook. But as posters went up on campuses in the populous city of Shanghai, the situation became more critical and was fraught with behind-the-scenes manoeuvring.

The student demonstrations were 'clear evidence', according to the conservatives, of the undesirability of unleashing capitalistic-style market forces in Chinese society. 'Great chaos' loomed large, they warned. Deng had to act to defuse the conservative challenge but also rein in the reformers. He did so by using the students. Rather than condemn them, he offered implicit support in the columns of the *People's Daily* (11. 12. 1986), declaring that political reform was the rightful concern of the masses. Since everyone wanted reform the students could not be ruled out of order. It was necessary to be both 'bold and prudent',[14] a phrase which played a large role in the student movement that winter. By putting 'boldness' before 'prudence', Deng was seen to be wearing his reformist hat, a blow to the more cautious-minded in the party leadership. Many students felt Deng was on their side, for they were not politically sophisticated enough to realise that he was using their movement to attack his opponents and thereby strengthen his own position. Like the 'Democracy Wall' activists, they would learn that Deng Xiaoping, the survivor, was on his own side. But for the month of December, the students felt that they were riding a well-placed political movement.

The foreign media were very interested in these events. The 'Voice of America' radio station, popular among young Chinese, broadcast news of students blockading the train station in Wuhan. Telephone lines to the city were jammed and messages of support flowed in from other student bodies. The official media carried no details of the demonstrations, but made announcements about proposed reforms in the electoral code. This should have satisfied the students, but it was too little, too late; a course of action had been set into motion which was difficult to reverse. The authorities, hoping to contain the situation, appeared almost paralysed by the students' actions. They were not prepared for the thousands of young people demonstrating on the streets, apparently with Deng's blessing.

The centre of activity by mid-December was Shanghai, where students listened eagerly to the VOA reports about Wuhan and elsewhere. An open letter written by a group of Hefei students calling for solidarity was passed around the campuses, as well as tapes of Fang Lizhi's Shanghai speech, outlining the need for democracy and the importance of intellectual development in China. Several small incidents, one revolving around a pop concert, incited more students into action. The local party leader in Shanghai, Jiang Zemin, attempted to deter the first demonstration by personally addressing thousands of students at the Jiaotong campus on 19 December, Jiang was a technocrat and moderniser whose future success in the party seemed certain. His meeting with the students, however, did not achieve its aim. There was good deal of heckling and questions thrown at him about the nature of democracy, free speech and freedom of the press. His mainly orthodox replies did little to satisfy the young audience. 'Why had the 1980 Constitution abolished the right to put up posters?' 'Why couldn't people select their own mayor and other local officials?', students asked angrily. The mayor continued his address, but he did not have the right answers.

After the meeting, six to seven thousand students marched on the streets, reaching People's Square (Renmin Guangchang) in the centre of the crowded city before proceeding towards the municipal government offices. They shouted 'Long live democracy!', and sang the by-now familiar 'Internationale'. Attempts by police to halt their progress and warnings from the authorities did not deter the students, who continued their demonstrations over several days. An eyewitness told me of her surprise, when emerging from the Peace Hotel (Heping Fandian) on the Bund, at being confronted by a 'mass of bodies, wave upon wave of students, marching down Nanjing Road in unison and chanting slogans. They took up the whole of the street and nothing could move until this sea of humanity had passed by.' Traffic was halted and people could not get to work, a point emphasised by the authorities in their condemnation of the protests. There seemed little support for the students from the workers at this time, who were more concerned with their own problems than abstract calls for democracy. The students appealed to Deng to assist them in their struggle, maintaining that he was the father of reform. He did not come forward on their behalf.

Elsewhere in China there were demonstrations, but Beijing was uncharacteristically quiet. Students there were either not concerned or just waiting to see what happened next before becoming involved. The authorities feared the spread of disorder to the capital, but the Beijing students took a backseat role while their Shanghai counterparts held the world's attention. The 'movement' seemed to lack organisation or clear direction as the end of the year drew close. Large-scale demonstrations were difficult to sustain and there was an increasing risk of confrontation with the authorities. After they had virtually controlled the city for nearly a week, the Shanghai students scaled down their actions. It was left to the capital's campuses to take up the baton. They did so but not before their counterparts in Tianjin to the south east of Beijing had their turn.

On 24 December a number of *dazibao* appeared at Tianjin and Nankai universities supporting the Shanghai students. One poster criticised local students for being 'late' to wake up to the realities. 'We have forgotten the duty which history has compelled us to carry out. We must wake up the masses and found a truly democratic and free society'

(Tournebise and Macdonald 1987: 106), read the message, with clear links to students in the past and future. It was signed by the 'Statue of Liberty'. Later that day, approximately 3,000 students gathered at 'Tianda', Tianjin University from where they set out for the city centre shouting the familiar slogans of the movement. When the demonstrators reached the municipal government offices, there were some scuffles with a public security unit waiting for the students. The incident was filmed, as others had been, so that student leaders could be later identified. The outcome of this demonstration is unclear because little information was passed on and most foreigners were busy with their Christmas celebrations. Reliable sources, according to Tournebise and Macdonald, claimed that the Tianjin students were the only ones during the 'winter of discontent' to experience serious confrontations with the police and receive violent injuries. The official media claim that nothing happened.

The posters at Tianjin displayed the most open hostility to the communist regime. They were highly critical of leaders who acted in despotic, feudalistic and corrupt ways. The protest in Tianjin was perhaps yet another indication of things to come over two years later when respect for the Party had declined still further and Deng Xiaoping had little support left among young intellectuals.

Meanwhile, Beijing students were on the move. On 23 December several thousands marched from Qinghua University to nearby Beida, calling for independent student organisations. There was some feeling that Beijing had been left behind while the rest of the country had marched for democracy. Beida was slow to become involved, but their ultimate participation completed the final link in the nationwide protest. An article in the *People's Daily* on 25 December describing *dazibao* and demonstrations as quite 'undemocratic' and causing chaos similar to the Cultural Revolution angered students. To make such a parallel was an insult to these young people who considered themselves more sophisticated than the Red Guard generation. The *China Youth* newspaper also ran an article calling for moderation, written by the well-known academic Professor Fei Xiaotong.[15] He stressed that democratic reform could not be achieved overnight but would take time. Prudence as opposed to boldness now seemed the keyword. Fei advised the students to cease their actions and work quietly for reform.

Just in case they did not heed these articles, the Beijing Public Security Bureau issued the 'Ten Article Regulations' on 26 December in an effort to deter student protests. Public marches and rallies were banned in the city centre, including Tiananmen Square and the road to the airport. Putting up posters was illegal. Anyone wishing to organise a rally had to seek permission five days beforehand, giving the numbers of participants, purpose and route. The regulations were intended to prevent the sort of scenes witnessed in Shanghai which had been broadcast across the world. They failed. The students were enraged at these new rules and on 29 December a crowd of between two and three thousand from several Beijing campuses openly defied the authorities by holding a demonstration in the university quarter. The intention was to march onto Tiananmen, but they never reached there on this occasion. The *People's Daily*, attributing the disturbances to a small group of 'hooligans', said that all 'enemies of the people' had to be punished. The conspiracy theory was revived in the media. The students could not be said to be responsible for their own actions and thoughts. The language used was familiar, but the explanations were not acceptable to the Beijing students.

Preparations were made for an 'assault' on Tiananmen Square, over fifteen kilometres away from the university district. The aim was to celebrate the arrival of a new year in the heart of capital and draw further attention to their movement. The situation was tense with appeals and threats to students not to go ahead with their march. Police were waiting on the streets and the square was turned into a dangerous, slippery 'ice rink' as water was sprayed over the hallowed ground in an effort to deter the demonstrators. These measures may have unsettled the crowds gathering on the campuses but did not stop them. Braving freezing temperatures, the bitter Beijing wind and threats from the authorities, thousands reached the square in the early hours of New Year's Day. There was a temporary sit-in on the icy ground by euphoric students, chanting and singing pro-democracy slogans and the 'Internationale'. On the steps of the Great Hall of the People and under the portrait of Chairman Mao, thousands voiced their disapproval of the government which would not allow the freedoms they desired. The police on duty could do little to stop them and, losing patience with the situation, arrested over twenty students. This further provoked the students, who resumed their march along Changan Avenue, halting the early morning traffic and disrupting the centre of Beijing. The year 1987 had arrived on a high note, but possibly a dangerous one.

Returning to the campuses in a state of excitement, they sensed victory over the authorities, but had to secure the release of their arrested colleagues. They planned a 'second Long March' (Tournebise and Macdonald 1987: 119) with around 5,000 prepared to join in. The preparations were halted by the news that the arrested students had been released. Jubilant, most gave up the idea of protesting in the freezing temperatures again, but approximately 1,000 persisted with their plan. Outside the gates of Zhongnanhai, where China's top leaders reside, they shouted for political reform and democracy. Once at the square, they sat down by the Monument to the People's Heroes in the early hours of a bitterly cold Beijing morning. When special buses provided by the universities arrived to take them back to the campuses, most took up the offer. The cold and tired students had made their point.

At the universities, the released students were treated like heroes and paraded around triumphantly in scenes probably akin to 1935, when arrested students from 'December Ninth' were set free. The students had called the authorities' bluff with their protests and shown solidarity across the country. The roar of a student movement had been heard again in China but there was little to gain, it was believed, by further mass demonstrations. The pro-democracy student demonstrations subsided, but the issues raised had not been addressed or resolved by the party. The leaders would have the final say in the winter of discontent.

THE ANTI-BOURGEOIS BACKLASH

On 4 January illegal posters appeared at Beida appealing to Deng Xiaoping to reinstate the basic right of putting up large character posters, which had been banned by the 'Ten Articles'. There was no other channel of communication since the state-controlled media would not give the students a hearing. The authorities, however, reacted predictably. A campaign against 'bourgeois liberalism' was launched with exemplary action against some of the 'troublemakers'.

Several 'workers' were arrested and accused of inciting the students and 'poisoning their minds'. Students objected to being portrayed as naive, immature and easily-led innocents. In a ceremony designed to attract publicity and express their anger about the official media, students in Beijing burned copies of the *People's Daily*, the *Beijing Daily*, the *Red Flag* and some other journals on 5 January. This provoked further criticism from official quarters with more comparisons with the 'bad old days' of the Cultural Revolution. Students could not win a fair hearing it seemed, but they did not pursue the matter any further at this time. The semester was coming to an end and there were important examinations to pass. The final act of the winter of discontent had been played by the students.

The government, however, had only just begun their punitive measures against excessive liberalism. Deng Xiaoping, it was stated, had never supported demonstrations since these were a disorderly and unsocialist method of making a point. The young people had been misinformed and misled. The Party had to be cleansed of those who had stirred up the students and caused trouble. Obvious victims were people like Fang Lizhi, who was dismissed from his post as vice-president of the Science and Technology University in Hefei, on 12 January. Several days later he was expelled from the party. It was claimed that he repeatedly called for the 'total westernisation of China' and incited people to 'change the true colour of the party' (*China Now*, Winter 1986/87: 6). Other leading intellectuals were also told to leave the party and their job. The 'harvest reckoning' referred to earlier by Kelly, came near the end of the winter.

Perhaps the most dramatic fall from grace was the case of Hu Yaobang. He had not been seen in public since 29 December, an indication that he was in trouble. Rumours of his imminent eclipse were confirmed on 16 January when Hu's resignation was announced. He had committed 'grave errors' in political decisions and strayed from the socialist road. Ill health was also given as another reason for his resignation, but there was no doubt the student demonstrations, which he had failed to control, had caused his final disgrace. Deng now had good reasons for losing his former close colleague and fellow reformer. The students were partly to blame, it was implied, but they did not intend to cause his demise and would not forget Hu Yaobang.

Intellectuals young and old were apprehensive, wondering how far the conservative backlash would extend. The 'blooming' of 1986 had turned into the 'weeding' of 1987, thirty years after Mao Zedong's campaign against 'rightist' intellectuals. Young people were dismayed at the trouble the demonstrations had caused. Democracy was further away than ever as censorship and propaganda were intensified. Strict adherence to the 'four basic principles' and the socialist road were stressed once again. The official messages and the students' despair which resulted were familiar to those of previous periods of liberalisation and backlash.

There were signs of hope, however. Zhao Ziyang was appointed to take over Hu Yaobang's former post, signifying that reform was not over. Sixty-nine-year-old Zhao, described as a 'classic moderniser', had pioneered economic reforms in the rural areas starting in 1978. The early successes of the 'responsibility system' had helped to make Deng, Zhao's mentor, a popular figure.

The introduction of economic reforms in urban areas also bore Zhao's hallmark and he was committed to reform and the open-door policy. He advised caution in the anti-bourgeois backlash, recognising the damage it could cause to the already frail economy. With Zhao as Deng's new 'favoured son', political analysts felt the anti-liberalism campaign would be short-lived.

There had to be punishments, however, not just in the party but in the student body, before the campaign could be concluded. A few students were arrested and there was little chance of their being treated with the 'human rights' demanded during the December demonstrations. The case of Lin Jie in Tianjin is one we know about. He was accused of passing on 'state secrets' to the Agence France Presse reporter Lawrence Macdonald, whose account of the student protests has been referred to several occasions. Macdonald was himself expelled from the country, while Lin Jie was imprisoned for his alleged 'treason'.

His was an extreme example, but the Chinese state has other ways of punishing its wayward, educated youth. Political study classes, considered as a 'boring waste of time' by many students, were intensified and large doses of Communist ideology had to be learned by rote. Some students identified from police videos were expelled from their colleges. Others were sent for spells of 're-education' in the countryside, but the easiest way for the state to gain its revenge was through the graduate assignment system. The end of the academic year in 1987 brought many disappointments for graduating students. According to reports, large numbers were allocated to rural and border regions where conditions would be hard and opportunities to develop their talents scarce. Official bodies insisted that these disproportionate 'difficult' placements had nothing to do with the demonstrations and Chinese students were 'happy to serve wherever the motherland needs them'.

Visiting a number of campuses throughout China at graduation time, I found the official explanations difficult to accept. There was a general atmosphere of despondence after the euphoria earlier in the year. 'The demonstrations were mostly started by first- and second-year students', I was told several times, 'but the government are punishing the graduates. We are being made an example of'. The scenes I witnessed and conversations I had with students supported the idea that the graduates were the 'victims' of the conservatives' anger.

One bright young man who some years before had been a 'star' pupil, and assured of a successful career in technology said he had ruined his chances by joining the demonstrations. He told me his motives were purely patriotic; he loved his country and was worried about its future. For daring to speak out, he was assigned to a menial post unrelated to his speciality and skills. This was extremely unfortunate for him and the nation which needed his sort of talent and enthusiasm. His disappointment was by no means an isolated example. He·was being sacrificed along with hundreds of others for the sake of an ideological principle.

On another campus, I saw a young woman crying uncontrollably.

When asked what the problem was, her friends told me she had just been assigned to teach in a distant, rural middle school. Far from home, with low pay and poor conditions, I wondered how this frail girl would survive. 'We are all disappointed', I was told. Their fate had been sealed, irrespective of participation in the winter demonstrations and there was nothing they could do about it. The articles I read in *Zhongguo Qingnian* about the brightest graduates turning down good jobs to volunteer for rural middle schools had a hollow ring to them.

The government's efforts to wipe out bourgeois liberalism abated during the summer of 1987 but many had suffered, from Hu Yaobang at the top to graduating students at the bottom. Leading intellectuals had been purged but were treated more leniently than in the past. Few suffered physical degradation and hardships. (Hu Yaobang and his family, for example, were allowed to carry on living in the privileged conditions of Zhongnanhai and Fang Lizhi was still allowed to travel abroad.) The student demands for democratic rights and freedoms had not been achieved, but China was not plunged into an extremist political campaign. Perhaps things had really changed and progress in human rights had been made. But the instability of the political structures and other weaknesses were obvious in the struggles between the factions within the party. Deng Xiaoping remained the supreme leader, but his popularity had slipped further. What would happen when he died?

The emphasis shifted gradually back to reform. In this uncertain political environment, the less than five per cent of the 19- to 24-year-old group, the 'privileged elite' who attended institutions of higher education, returned to their studies. New students were aware of 1987's punitive assignments. Would they take that as a lesson and conform to the party's expectations of educated youth? The following academic year would prove decisive.

5　Dilemmas and diversions
Student strategies at the end of the reform decade

OVERVIEW

As the reform decade drew to a close, China appeared to be approaching a crisis situation, with rising inflation, food shortages, official corruption and other economic and social problems becoming more apparent. As Chan writes, 'the reforms had begun turning sour in people's minds by the mid-1980s' (Chan 1989: 68). Intellectuals initiated a number of urgent debates about the state of the nation in an effort to find the root cause of the difficulties and propose new solutions. The 'Heshang' ('River Elegy') television series broadcast in June 1988 was an example of intellectual exploration whose conclusions caused controversy among party and non-party members and called into question how far criticisms of official policy could extend. Although 1988 was characterised by a freer, more open intellectual atmosphere, it was clear that the Party still held ultimate authority and would not tolerate criticism that bordered on political dissent. Students actively participated in these discussions, but also sought solutions to their own personal problems arising from their socio-economic position. Applying Shirk's concept of 'adaptive behaviour' (Shirk 1982: 5), their enthusiasm for a number of major student 'tides' such as going abroad to study, doing business and having love affairs, can be viewed as strategies for escaping from the depressing reality of everyday life in contemporary China. After analysis, these strategies will be seen as having their own associated difficulties. The student generation of the late 1980s was attempting to improve their position and find forms of diversion as well as being concerned about the underlying social problems which beset China in the period immediately before the outbreak of the 'patriotic democratic movement'.

ADAPTIVE BEHAVIOUR OR ESCAPISM? THE MAJOR STUDENT 'TIDES' OF 1988

Shirk's work, already alluded to, focused on the ways high school students in the 1960s pursued their own objectives within a highly politicised social setting. She claims that the systematic patterns of individual behaviour were explicable as, 'personal attempts to increase benefits and reduce costs in an environment where the rewards and penalties associated with various actions are established by regime policies' (Shirk 1982: 5). This does not assume, she claims, that people are always completely conscious of their efforts or that they clearly articulate the reasons for trends of common behaviour. The task of the social scientist is to try and make some sense of any observable patterns and the motivations, whether unspoken or not, behind them. This perspective is also useful when examining patterns of behaviour among university students in the late 1980s.

A number of student 'tides' were underway which can be seen as forms of adaptive behaviour or strategies for improving their social position, either temporarily or on a more permanent basis. These 'tides' can also be viewed as forms of diversion, even escapism, as the problems of the reform programme became more difficult to contain. The *chuguo chao* (going abroad tide) was an example, causing concern among the authorities because of the increasing numbers of young intellectuals taking part and more importantly, failing to return.

A reference to the Chinese word 'chao' is necessary here. The common translation is 'tide', as employed here, but 'craze' is also used and sometimes 'chao' is substituted by 're', also translated as 'craze' or 'rush'. Referring to these social phenomena as student 'crazes' detracts from their seriousness, but it is necessary to be aware of the different words, their translations and colloquial usage in the contemporary setting.

A Chinese social scientist studying student behaviour told me that since the demonstrations at the end of 1986, many had become less interested in education. 'Each year seems to bring a new craze, anything but study', he continued, as I was told of the 'talking about reform' craze in 1985, before the student unrest; that of democracy in 1986; falling in love in 1987; and in 1988 the preoccupation with 'doing business'. What was clear from my own research and experience was that all of these 'crazes' or student 'tides', along with a few others, existed side by side in 1988. They had all become part of campus life but the *chuguo chao*, the 'going abroad tide', was probably the most noticeable and was certainly a 'hot topic' (translated from the Chinese 'redian') among students.

Going abroad to study usually involved extremely complicated and difficult procedures. Success required dogged determination, academic ability, money, plenty of patience for dealing with the state bureaucracy and some useful contacts or 'guanxi', i.e. connections with people in positions of responsibility who could help, which was becoming an increasingly important way of getting things done in China. The competition was fierce and only a few could obtain the valuable passports, visas and tickets to leave the confines of China. The motives appeared to be mixture of low living standards in China, the prospect of personal advancement and gain overseas and also patriotic sentiments. Many prospective overseas students told me they wished to return to China to help the nation in the modernisation drive, but they may stay away 'a long time' before doing so. There were some contradictions in their stated motives just as in a previous 'chuguo chao'.

The following comment could be just as easily applied to the 1980s as to earlier this century. 'In this particular decade an unusual movement took place ... the great exodus of Chinese youths, the flower of the nation, to foreign countries with the fixed determination to learn what the world has to teach' (Wang 1928: 61). Dissatisfaction and despair regarding domestic crises were strong motivating factors on both occasions as young intellectuals sought solutions to personal and national problems outside of China or as Wang wrote, 'looked eagerly to the west for the magic which would solve the problems of their country' (Wang 1928: 60).

The original overseas trend had a slow beginning because the Chinese at that time were very wary of anything foreign. The intrusion of foreigners onto Chinese soil in itself was difficult to accept; to send the youth of China to the lands of the 'foreign devils' as the Chinese referred to them, was almost unthinkable. It was also an 'unfilial' thing for a Chinese son to do. The first known Chinese student to go abroad was Yung Wing, who in 1847 went to the USA. He persuaded the government to allow a group of students to be sent to the USA in 1872, but they were recalled for fear they might become 'too gay (morally loose) or western' (Wang 1928: 44), a comment which would not be out of place in more recent times. But by the turn of the century, the trickle had become a tide. In 1898, only six known Chinese were studying in America; by 1922 there was 2,600, while in Japan there was an estimated 15,000 by the 1920s.[1] Great Britain and other European countries were also receiving Chinese students motivated by similar reasons as their 1980s counterparts. The doors of the country had been opened and the outside world beckoned.

Most scholars viewed the acquisition of advanced knowledge and skills across a wide spectrum of academic fields as extremely beneficial once taken back to China. By doing this, they could fulfil their special duty as intellectuals, making an important contribution to the nation. Such motivations took students to colleges throughout the world to learn military science, railway engineering, medicine, etc., at the beginning of the century just as contemporary *liuxuesheng* (overseas students) learn about computers and technology at American universities.

Patriotism, however, was tempered to varying degrees by the personal considerations as already stated. I was frequently told of the necessity for study overseas in order to do anything worthwhile in the academic field because facilities in China were so 'backward'. Talented people could not advance themselves and their position, let alone make a worthwhile contribution to their field. 'We only waste our time here', was the common complaint of those who were aware of what prestigious western universities had to offer. Their heightened expectations for educational progress had not been realised because of low investment and poor management.

Unsatisfactory living conditions, poor salaries and low status were also frequently mentioned as justifications for abandoning China, temporarily or more permanently. Chan makes the point that in recent times academics have fared better than the average urban worker. 'Among the eight occupational groups in the civil service pay-scale, academics rank second highest, after state-organ officials' (Chan 1989: 71). Yet average figures often cover up cases of hardship and even if in real terms salaries for some academics appear generous, others feel disadvantaged and discontent. Chan acknowledges that the state is 'reluctant' to raise salaries by substantial amounts. The young intellectuals, i.e. those still in full-time study or newly-appointed to their posts, were worse off than their seniors and saw going abroad as a way out.

According to a number of articles which appeared in a special series devoted to the 'chuguo chao' in *Guangming Ribao* early in 1988, young intellectuals generally felt oppressed by their circumstances. Some had nowhere to live apart from crowded dormitory rooms, even after getting married. Housing was hard to obtain, good accommodation almost impossible. Salaries were not keeping up with the rate of inflation, which in the cities was estimated to be running at 20 per cent. A *Far Eastern Economic Review* article in June 1988 quotes a 'disgruntled' intellectual: 'Fifteen years ago there was a saying, "the more knowledge, the more reactionary", but now people say, "the more you study, the poorer you are"' (FEER 16. 6. 88: 34). This summed up the view of many: in previous decades intellectuals were frequently punished for being politically 'reactionary', i.e. rightists. Now that label had gone but they were relatively poor and worse off materially. The rise of the money motive served only to devalue knowledge even further. Teachers and students perceived themselves to be a low-status group, looked upon with increasing scorn by other sections of society, whatever the absolute figures for incomes and position were measured to be. Having to take on part-time jobs or 'moonlighting', was not viewed by academics as an acceptable solution to their problems.

These negative trends were discussed in the *Guangming Ribao* series and in other newspapers. The authorities expressed their concern but promises to improve conditions seemed only *konghua*, (empty words). For younger students, the complaints of their older colleagues were all too evident. 'I don't want to struggle all my life for nothing. If I can get out, things are bound to better', a young man told me. His view was fairly typical of his generation. There were elements of what the Chinese call the 'green-eye disease', and the 'moon being rounder', what we would describe as the 'grass being greener'. Idealised versions of life in the USA, for example, were often presented to me by young people who had watched many films and television programmes, as well as talking with foreigners. 'Life is good there for anyone who works hard', I was told by students intending to go to the USA. The students may have been naive about the realities of life abroad, but they wanted to see for themselves what life was like elsewhere rather than being told by party officials and foreigners. As the students in the major urban areas became more familiar with foreign teachers, their desire for overseas travel increased.

Some candidates for overseas study told me in all honesty that the acquisition of consumer durables, the modern-day trappings of success, was the main motivation for their efforts, although they also hoped to help the 'motherland' in the process. It is difficult for them to buy foreign goods because of the large sums of money involved, usually in foreign exchange, and the necessity of good connections. By going abroad and eking out their scholarships, the successful candidates could save money for buying televisions, cassette players and other items. Some Chinese students abroad will scrimp and save every penny, not wishing to spend any more than absolutely necessary. For them, this would perhaps be a unique opportunity to make some money. This again reflects social trends in Chinese society: the poor living conditions of the young intellectuals and the increasing concern with material rather than political or ideological matters.

Did any of these would-be overseas students wish to leave for political reasons? In the broad sense of the term 'political', the answer must be in the affirmative, but it would be difficult to describe these intellectuals as 'dissidents'. Many have, in fact, refused to accept this label; it has overtones of being unpatriotic. Disillusionment with Marxism-Leninism and the party's continued centralised control over the political sphere were causing a sense of dismay as well as confusion among young intellectuals. But it is difficult to equate their negative feelings about politics in China with the desire to go abroad. Few young people I spoke to put politics first, as the main reason for the 'brain drain'. Their ambivalent attitudes were described in a number of social science surveys as a 'clash of values'[2] rather than dissidence. Any expressions of the desire for democracy in China were usually inspired by their patriotism and their wish to improve the nation's standing rather than to over-throw the system. It is, of course, highly unlikely that anyone who diverged too far from the Party's orthodoxy would even reach the TOEFL examination room let alone be awarded a government scholarship. Any serious opponents of the system would end up in prison.

This is not to say that no one who has left China since 1980 has had dissident tendencies, but they would probably keep these concealed before being allowed out. Some Chinese students did set up pro-democracy groups overseas on a very small scale and took some risks in doing so, facing possible arrest and imprisonment on their return to China. These political activists, however, were in the minority. Most Chinese students overseas put their education first and politics second. The events in Beijing during early June 1989 may have changed this situation in a number of important ways, as will be discussed in the final chapter.

Living abroad would naturally influence young scholars, as in the case of their nineteenth-century predecessors, causing further disillusionment with the political order back home. Political considerations may have made them less inclined to return to China, but it was generally not a major reason for leaving in the first place. Many of the students I spoke with in China wanted political freedom, but were not prepared to become compulsory exiles. Once again, 1989 may have altered this, but the queues to go abroad grew longer throughout 1988.

The first stage in the procedure to apply for study abroad is to learn a foreign language, preferably English. The 'English craze' was a concomitant part of the 'chuguo chao' and was increasingly noticeable throughout the 1980s. A recognised level of proficiency had to be attained, usually tested by the TOEFL examination. According to figures given in the *Guangming Ribao*, when the examination was first held in Beijing in 1981, there were 285 candidates. In 1983, this had risen to 2,500 in 1985, 8,000 candidates registered; and in 1987, an estimated

26,000 people applied (GMRB 22. 2. 1988). Test centres exist in other major cities as well, consequently the total figures for TOEFL candidates on a national basis would be far higher. Not all of those who want to apply can do so because of various regulations and procedures. (These have since been tightened as a result of the events in June 1989). Of those who take the tests, few score high enough marks to enable them to apply for assistance from their own government or overseas institutions.

I have seen queues of students, many of them learning English through 'self-study' forming outside the test centres in Beijing just in order to gain an entry form for the next sitting of the TOEFL examination. On several occasions, there were slight public-order disturbances as people pushed and shoved to the front to get a form before they were all gone. If they were successful at this stage, they would then have to find the fee. In 1988, this was over $US 40, payable in this currency only and not the equivalent in Chinese 'people's money' (*renminbi*), which is approximately one month's salary for a young teacher. Finding a foreigner to change money with was one way of obtaining the necessary dollars or changing money on the black market, a very expensive option. There were always hundreds of students asking their foreign teachers for this 'favour' to get them over the first hurdle of the going abroad process. It was difficult to refuse and thereby block their chances, but helping one student set a precedent; any foreigners were plunged into moral dilemmas by their students who wanted help to go abroad. This sometimes went further than raising the TOEFL entry fee and involved putting up guarantees for thousands of dollars for candidates.

Those who found the fee then had to cram for the multiple-choice examination, learning words and grammatical phrases even native speakers would find difficult. Foreign teachers of English often joked that they could not pass TOEFL, but for the Chinese students it was no laughing matter. While engaged in this intensive study of a narrow range of the English language, the students had little time for anything else. I often found it necessary to reprimand students for learning their TOEFL words during classes. But I had to accept that this examination was far more important to them. 'TOEFL is the key for going abroad', I was frequently reminded. Groups of students complained about their Chinese teachers failing to conduct lessons properly because of their preoccupation with TOEFL. People would stop and ask foreigners in the streets to explain obscure phrases. At times it seemed as if most of the students and young teachers were preparing for TOEFL and the major topic of conversation was 'going abroad'. Success in the examination did not secure by itself a study position abroad, but it was the minimum requirement. It was also obvious that other aspects of their education, employment, and even family life were suffering because of the 'going abroad craze'.

More worrying for the government, however, were the large numbers of *liuxuesheng* who once out of the country failed to come back.

It is impossible to give exact figures for non-returners for a number of reasons. Some may change their status from 'visiting scholar' with a year's stay to Ph.D. candidate and plan to go back at some uncertain time in the future. They overstay their time, but may not be genuine non-returners. Others are impossible to locate and drop out of the statistics in due course; therefore accurate figures are difficult to obtain. The State Education Commission does have records of those sent abroad by the state and those who return, but has incomplete data on self-financing or *sifei* students. Informed sources state that there is always a large percentage of those due to return in any one year who failed to do so. I was quoted 80 per cent by a source within the State Education Commission. It is more difficult to keep track on those *sifei* students who left in increasing numbers in the mid-1980s. Out of approximately one hundred prospective overseas students I spoke with, the majority said they had little intention of returning to China unless conditions improved in all aspects of life in the near future, but they were vague about what they would do overseas once their initial period of advanced education was complete.

The incidence of high rates of non-returners is borne out in a *Far Eastern Economic Review* report which suggested that out of the 50,000 scholars sent abroad since 1978, at the start of the reform decade, only 20,000 have returned. Out of the self-financing students, 'virtually no one in this category has yet returned' (FEER 1. 6. 1988: 33). In another category of younger, government-sponsored students working towards postgraduate degrees, only 200 to 300 out of 12,000 have returned home. Some may have plans to return later rather than sooner. The impact of the Tiananmen massacre is bound to be detrimental in this respect.

It is almost inevitable that many would stay away, even disallowing for the events of 1989, but China needs experts in all fields of knowledge. This 'brain drain' must have been viewed by the authorities as acute, otherwise there would not have been so much coverage of the issue in the media. Concern about the plight of young intellectuals was mixed with promises of improvements. Meanwhile the regulations applying to overseas study were tightened, especially for the USA, where the largest numbers of young Chinese overstayed their official visit. Those deemed to have 'immigrant tendencies' (the phrase used by the Chinese officials) such as single people' or those married but without children or people with close relatives already settled abroad, were simply refused passports even if everything else had been arranged. I knew of young people who would rush into marriages, even parenthood, in order to further their passport and visa applications, such was their desperation to get out. Visa restrictions brought in by foreign governments in co-operation with the Chinese authorities in March and April of 1988 did little to reduce the queues of hopefuls in the embassy districts of Beijing and Shanghai. Waiting day after day, many said they would 'keep trying' because it was their only hope. The goal was becoming more difficult to reach but the 'tide' continued.

Returning to the perspective of 'adaptive behaviour' discussed earlier, we can call into question the extent to which going abroad can legitimately be viewed as a student strategy for maximising opportunities in China when by necessity it implied turning away from the 'motherland' in favour of foreign countries. Leaving behind low living standards and poor conditions in work and study seems more like rejection than adaptation. My own investigations, however, suggest that the option of going abroad, open only to several thousand young Chinese intellectuals each year,[5] is a strategy of maximising opportunities and benefits. Although it appears as a contradiction, just like some of the stated motives of those leaving, I believe it is a form of adaptive behaviour. These young intellectuals in the TOEFL examination queues are seeking overseas what they cannot obtain in China under the present circumstances: money, material goods, higher academic training and qualifications, and advanced technical skills, which they may, at a later date, take back with them to China. Not all of those applying for scholarships or assistance from foreign universities wish to stay away indefinitely. Many are vague. Others realise that it will be difficult to extend their stay overseas without becoming an illegal immigrant, an added burden they may not wish to take on. Conse-quently, it can be seen as a strategy for improving their social position and 'market' position, i.e. being able to offer more skills in the labour market in the future. Whether that would be in China or another country depended on the unknown factors of what they would actually find overseas and the outcome of developments in China. The events of June 1989 will certainly influence their decisions, as mentioned before.

In 1988, the country was seen to be losing some of its best and brightest people, which further demoralised those who could not leave. According to a *Zhongguo Qingnian* article, the 'dream of the generation' had changed (ZGQN 1988, 1: 2). Young people were looking forward to a modern China in which they would play an active role. They wished to be 'good socialists', working hard for their country but without the burden of excessive, leftist political campaigns. Dreams and desires may have changed during the reform decade, but the conditions of society had not altered accordingly. 'Looking towards money' had become a key phrase, but young intellectuals were aware of its adverse effects. There was little chance to look towards democracy or any political liberalisation, moreover, while the party remained the central authority. The 'going abroad tide' with its mixture of motivations, sentiments and contradictions was set to continue as long as the leadership refused to address the major reasons behind it.

Many students realised they had little hope of going abroad and sought instead other escape routes from their situation. The 'doing business' ('jing shangre') tide or craze swept through the campuses, motivating the students to make money and improve life for themselves within the confines of Chinese society. Initially encouraged as a way for both students and teachers to become financially independent, using their own efforts to earn extra money, the tide had many negative side-effects. By selling various items from computers to eggs, offering consultative services and home tutoring, young intellectuals showed their ingenuity and flexibility in trying to improve their economic situation. Some universities insisted that departmental offices made business their primary concern in order to boost finances, especially since the government could not promise increased investment. Chan gives the example of Qinghua University in Beijing, which through a 'create income' scheme was able to distribute a 600–1,000 yuan bonus to staff members at the end of 1987 (Chan 1985: 72). This amount was approximately equivalent to half of their annual salary, depending on age and position held. It was certainly a substantial sum. But Qinghua was something of an exception, being China's top technological university, with better facilities than other institutions and a high level of prestige.

Other universities could not expect to fare so well in operating 'create income' programmes, and within certain institutions some departments are in favourable positions to offer lucrative services such as computing. Other subjects like philosophy and history have fewer opportunities. Staff were more likely to be reduced to selling snacks during break, which was much less profitable than computing services and much more demeaning for academics.

The government at first thought the business trend embodied the pragmatic spirit of the reform decade and was a way to raise much-needed finances. Intellectuals were called on to transform their knowledge into hard cash. By 'doing business', students could be in contact with society rather than live the sheltered campus life which was frequently blamed for their lack of realistic social knowledge. It was implied that working part-time could disabuse them of naive and mistaken ideas about modern Chinese society. The 'bourgeois liberalism' dreaded by the authorities would also be less likely to have an impact. Students would be too busy with real life to be bothered about social problems and conditions. There were thus political and ideological reasons for promoting this student tide, not just economic ones. In the days of the 'socialist commodity economy'[6] (a slogan that described the expected outcome of party policies), 'doing business' seemed to be a suitable pastime. Even the CYL became involved with the tide, setting up small businesses to help raise money (ZGQN 16. 7. 1988: 15). The problems, however, did not remain unnoticed for long.

By the start of the new term in the autumn of 1988, the negative aspects of the 'tide' were uppermost in the authorities' minds. At the beginning of October, the State Education Commission issued a statement calling on all provincial education departments and universities under its jurisdiction to forbid students to 'engage in business on or off campus for the purpose of getting rich' (CD 7. 10. 1988). Students were expected to be 'hardworking and thrifty', only earning small amounts to help meet their study expenses or setting up shops to improve business practice and skills. If such extra-curricula activities were well organised, they could be useful and educational, but they should not detract from study or emphasise the 'get rich quick' ideology.

Academics were always worried that young people would be spending too much time 'looking towards money' rather than their studies. Increasingly, the authorities became concerned about the adverse effects of this trend and viewed it in a dimmer light. Stories of students too tired to study and teachers selling boiled eggs during classes were common, bringing into question the value and role of education and its intellectual workers. The money motive was perhaps not quite the panacea it was once believed to be, as some departments became relatively well off while others could barely afford to pay their salaries. In a socialist society, it was asked, were such gross disparities and inequalities permissible? The undercurrent of dissatisfaction with the business craze surfaced during 1988, although there were some intellectuals who unabashedly enjoyed the benefits of this trend.

An article in *Zhongguo Qingnian* summarised some of the main criticisms of 'doing business'. The author wrote that during reform, it was 'admirable' for students to do 'creative' things but the results were 'worrying' because, 'it will probably lead to a vicious circle of everybody doing business'. This would congest an already overcrowded circulation of goods. 'When college students set about doing business, they can do little to help provide raw materials and consumer goods at fair prices for thousands of people'. But they can exploit people. The author asked, 'if they lose money in doing business how can they calm down to do their studies?' (ZGQN 1. 9. 1988: 1). The dangers were clear and ultimately no one benefited, least of all the students.

It was difficult, however, to stem the tide since the party leadership was committed to extending economic reforms and intent on reforming education to make it more self-financing. Economic dependency was frowned on, but there was no question of political independence. Students in the late 1980s, described as the 'fourth generation' (since the communist revolution) in a popular book of the same title,[7] could not be 'relaxed'. They were facing too many contradictory features in society. According to the book's author, Zhang Yong Jie, himself a young man in his twenties, they were forced to find short-term solutions to long-term problems and they lacked well-established beliefs and values because of the rapidly changing nature of Chinese society. 'Doing business' was one of the contradictions. It was not possible suddenly to change direction, yet the damage being done to education was obvious as campuses sometimes resembled market-places rather than institutions of higher learning. Teachers were out 'moonlighting', while their students were trying to make some money in what was officially described as the 'primary stage of socialism'.

The young people also wanted to have some enjoyment in their scarce free time and escape from the contradictions of their 'privileged' position. 'Falling in love' was another student tide considered as improper, even immoral if sexual relations were involved, by the authorities. In the years before 1980, it was difficult for romance to develop given the strict socialist morality which stressed politics rather than personal relationships. Privacy was virtually non-existent as the local 'cadres' knew all the details of people's lives. Students living in crowded dormitories under the watchful eyes of their 'banzhuren'[8] and monitors could be kept in line relatively easily. To 'talk love' as it is described by the Chinese, was strictly taboo before the relaxations in the social code during the reform decade. The authorities warned young people about the 'unhealthy winds' blowing in through the open door, such as sexual promiscuity, pornography and prostitution, homosexuality, alcohol abuse and drugs. It was implied that socialist China was 'pure' and liable to be infected by these 'evils' if people were not wary. This is, of course, a point of contention which will not be pursued here but is useful to bear in mind.

During my first stay in China in 1984, it was very rare indeed to see young people holding hands in public and I clearly remember the expressions of shock when a student dared to ask, in a packed lecture hall, if students in Britain were allowed to 'talk love'. He implied that Chinese students did form relationships, but these were frowned upon by the college authorities. The nervous laughter from the young audience suggested that he had raised a 'hot topic'. Four years later, more open displays of affection both on and off campus were common. Students were eager to develop relationships even in the restrictive university environment. Some roommates had special arrangement with each other so they could all spend time alone with their 'special friend', even sleeping with them. This behaviour was unmentionable a few years before, although it probably did take place. It was still risky, however, and anyone found in the wrong dormitory outside of hours faced expulsion. Announcements on college noticeboards often gave details of students who had been involved in 'inappropriate conduct' and dismissed from their studies.

There were other manifestations of this 'craze' such as 'love suicides'. In 1988 there were several well-publicised cases of young people committing suicide apparently because of unrequited love. There were probably other factors such as pressures caused by examinations and the competition for jobs. At Qinghua University, I was told of a 'suicide building' where thirteen students had leapt to their death that year, mostly because of failure in love. Young people were already feeling insecure because of the far-reaching changes going on around them and the uncertainties about the reform programme. Seeking personal satisfaction through secure relationships was 'adaptive behaviour', a strategy for making the most of the situation. But it had obvious difficulties for many students who found they could not manage both love affairs and study.

There were few places where young people with personal problems could seek help. The authorities in Beijing realised that 'many college students ... suffered serious mental problems because of loneliness or anxiety over their studies or love lives' (CD 23. 2. 1988) and several major institutions were talking of the possibility of setting up advisory bodies for students with emotional problems, but few actually existed. It had only been recently acknowledged by official bodies that psychology could offer some understanding of young people's problems. In the past, the predominant ideology insisted that psychology and sociology were 'bourgeois' subjects which had no place in a socialist system. People only had political problems, which could be solved with the proper application of Marxist-Leninist-Maoist thought. In the changed social environment of the reform years, this solution was no longer seen as adequate because there were new problems. But new solutions were still being developed and meanwhile students with personal problems had to seek each other's help. The discussions of youth problems on the pages of *Zhongguo Qingnian* did not offer realistic advice according to many students. 'It's out of touch with our lives', they said.

Females were particularly vulnerable in the 'falling in love craze' and could suffer more than the males as a result of their romantic encounters. The reasons, I would argue, are not just due to any innate biological features of females, but have social causes just as the 'craze' itself. The 'myth' of sexual equality in China had been shattered during the reform decade with women facing discrimination in the workplace on a greater scale. 'Go back to the kitchen', was the plea of the male-dominated management and administration in commerce and industry. The workforce in many work units was being trimmed in order to improve efficiency and save money. Female graduates facing ever-increasing competition were often passed over in favour of their male classmates even when they possessed better qualifications. A newly emerging Women's Studies movement in major universities[9] saw this discrimination as a particularly negative effect of reform. 'We don't want girls', prospective employers were reported as saying, 'unless they are pretty'. In such a highly discouraging environment, female students were tempted to spend their college lives looking for 'Mr Right', who could offer them companionship during the years of study and secure a good future afterwards. 'Falling in love', therefore, was more than just a trivial pastime but a serious business. It reflected to some extent the failure of reforms to provide sufficient opportunities for graduates of both sexes and was indicative of the devaluation of knowledge already referred to. 'Be practical and be quick', was the advice given to many girls when entering higher education. It did not refer to study technique but to finding a husband, a potential breadwinner, because realistically speaking, females were increasingly unlikely to obtain satisfactory employment on graduation.

Given this situation, some girls were more likely to spend their time cultivating romance than academic qualifications. Rejection by a boyfriend could be disastrous, especially if sexual activity had been involved. The 'double standard' exists in China as elsewhere. Sexually experienced females are viewed in derogatory terms. 'Problem pages' in the women's and youth magazines carried letters from unhappy girls who had 'given themselves' to their boyfriends subsequently to be abandoned and labelled as a 'package of dirty linen'. For those females who had concentrated on love affairs rather than their studies, graduating with low grades and low status was bound to be distressing, giving rise to depression and even thoughts of suicide. There seemed to be little hope for the future, just a mundane job and low pay and fewer prospects for meeting the opposite sex once university days were over. 'Falling in love', therefore, reflected social realities. It may have sounded like good fun, and obviously was for many young people, but this pleasurable diversion had a very serious side which went beyond romance. Unsuccessful affairs could lead to personal disaster. They could also lead to unwanted pregnancies and venereal disease, both on the increase among young people.[10]

Contraception is usually not freely available to unmarried couples in China, therefore sexual activity between students involved added risks other than expulsion. Abortion is normally mandatory for unmarried females and of course is a clear sign of their 'immoral' behaviour. There was something approaching a 'moral panic'[11] taking place in China during the last few years of the reform decade, exacerbated by the 'falling in love craze' and some of its unhealthy results. The authorities were anxious not just about the state of students' political thought but their physical and mental health as well since they were increasingly prone to fall foul of temptation. Even middle-school students, a number of articles declared, were doing more than merely 'talking love'.

This increasing concern was behind a number of social surveys conducted among students by official bodies, and a greater official vigilance on the campuses during 1988, according to informed sources. I was told that only about one-quarter of the students at institutes of higher education in Beijing were actually getting on with their studies and many of these were motivated solely by the desire to go abroad. It is not clear how this estimate was reached or what the terms of reference were, but it is an indicative view borne out by widespread apathy among students for their lessons. Many were simply too busy doing other things, and although not all were involved in the student tides discussed, a majority of them were devoting their energies to extracurricular activities.

The government was in an ambiguous position because its policies had created a social environment almost detrimental to study, yet the success of the reform was partly dependent upon academic research and development. 'Without the participation of educated youth, the reform programme will fail', became a frequently uttered warning. But the conservatives within the party were more alarmed by the decline in 'socialist morality' which they attributed directly to the reform and open-door policies. The so-called 'fourth generation' were caught in the middle and it is no wonder they suffered from a 'clash in values' described in a number of articles discussing youth 'problems'. The students were being fed contradictory messages and did what they could to lead their lives in the best way possible, given deteriorating conditions and mounting ideological and political debates. They were, therefore, exhibiting adaptive behaviour in these various 'student tides.'

The 'Heshang' controversy was one important debate which provided intellectual substance for those who believed that the contemporary situation could not continue indefinitely with all its dilemmas and difficulties.

YOUNG INTELLECTUALS AND THE 'RIVER ELEGY'

This important six-part television series was shown for the first time in June 1988, and in itself was an indication that freedom of intellectual debate had indeed been extended, but it also forewarned of the type of strong criticism to be expected from the conservatives in the party. 'Heshang', translated as 'River Elegy' was written by three intellectuals, Su Xiaokang, Xia Jun and Lu Xiang, who wanted to address the question of why the Chinese civilisation, once a world leader, declined so rapidly after the seventeenth century.

Even in its planning stages there was intense opposition to the series. The conservative 'faction' in the party denounced it as sheer 'bourgeois liberalism' and dangerous provocation. Its pro-western stance brought into doubt the very legitimacy of the Chinese Communist Party, and its multitude of criticisms of the Chinese civilisation were akin to attitudes of the Cultural Revolution. In spite of attempts to stop their transmission, the programmes went out on CCTV, watched by millions and caused a great deal of lively, heated debate.

The complex, sometimes obscure series certainly was provocative, as it probably meant to be, waking the Chinese people up to harsh realities. The authors argued that the huge cultural wealth of China which had once made it such a powerful nation had become a massive psychological burden, weighing the people down, oppressing and stifling free thought. This stunted any development and modernisation and kept China in a backward state. Tracing the origins of Chinese civilisation back to the Yellow River (Huanghe), the 'cradle' of the nation's culture, a basic contradiction was noted which continued to have a profound effect on the people. The river was not only the root of civilisation but also of China's 'sorrow' with its predilection for flooding and catastrophe. The moods of the river affected the people and ultimately the culture which was bound to it. The river was despotic and barbaric, ruling over its subjects without mercy. This unequal relationship was reflected in the autocratic, all-powerful state headed usually by one person. The people had to be obedient to the ruler and not question his government, just as the

Yellow River was feared and respected. 'How could concepts of democracy take root in such a system?', asked the author. While western or 'blue' cultures were moving towards modernisation and democracy China was left behind, trapped in its own feudalistic culture of subservience.

There was no middle ground, the programme stressed, between absolute power and obedience on the one hand and chaos and 'banditry' on the other. This traditional system was inherited by the communists who, by implication, continued to rule in an autocratic manner. This point had been raised before by intellectuals and they usually suffered for their lack of 'loyalty'. The 'Heshang' authors were on a collision course with the conservatives by taking this stance. They were also too 'pro-western'. These cultures, viewed as being more outward-looking and less insular because they had very early on been maritime powers, were referred to as 'blue' cultures. While China turned inwards, European countries were involved increasingly in overseas trade and exploration of new territories, always looking to the horizon and the future. Feudalistic China remained locked in the past and bore the seeds of its own decline, eventually being overpowered and nearly destroyed by the 'blue' cultures.

Modern China retained these problems which stemmed from its massive cultural heritage and as a consequence could not move forward. The hope, according to the programme authors, lay with the intellectuals, described as an oasis in the midst of this desert of feudalistic subservience. In the past they had spoken out and would do so again, drawing inspiration from the ideas of democracy and science to help China modernise. This was a vital necessity, otherwise the nation would remain backward, introverted and its people remain in a state of psychological subjugation. Thus an important role was envisaged for those with enough education to see beyond the 'yellow' culture. The main failings of the nation lay within its own boundaries, not in the outside world or such phenomena as 'bourgeois liberalism', which the authors did not view in the same threatening light as did the more conservative party members. If China was 'backward', it was its own fault and it was up to the people, led by the intellectuals, to do something about it.

Many of the ideas included in the series, only a few of which have been mentioned above, were not original. But presented in this systematic and visually effective manner, they provoked viewers into consideration about the state of the nation. It offered answers for frequently raised questions about China's relatively low level of development not just in comparison to western nations but also to other eastern states such as

Japan, South Korea and others. The main value of 'Heshang', I was told by a number of commentators, was that it did 'wake people up' and shake them out of their apathy. Viewers tended to be either for or against the main thrust of its argument; few were able to take a neutral stance and discussions were often quite heated between students and their teachers, academics and party members. The fact that the programmes were shown reflected a degree of openness on the part of Party authorities, with the reformists having the upper hand. But there were heavy criticisms during the period it was broadcast and in the following months. 'It speaks for all of us intellectuals, but will upset some people', one class of students told me during a 'Heshang' discussion. Others, however, described it as a form of 'intellectual carping' which failed to say anything of originality or significance.

Several newspapers carried extracts from the series, including *Guangming Ribao*[12] and *Wen Hui Bao*[13] throughout June and July, which kept the debate going. Numerous articles elsewhere offered analysis and comments on 'Heshang'. Demand was so great that a commentary of the programmes was published.[14] Thousands of viewers wrote to CCTV insisting that the series be repeated. Some Party members, however, were calling for it to be banned. They drew parallels with the Cultural Revolution because of its criticisms of Chinese culture. The glorification of the west was at the expense of China's own cultural heritage which could not be viewed in a totally negative light. CCTV had to weigh up the demands for the series to be repeated with the views expressed by some Party members that 'Heshang' was subversive and dangerous. The controversy deepened with obvious pressure coming from various quarters being put on the authors and the television network.

The series was eventually re-run in August but with several revisions. In an interview in *Zhongguo Qingnian Bao* on 16 August, Su Xiao Kang, one of the writers of the series, talked about the concerns which were expressed by the authorities and the pressures to make some changes before the repeats. While on Hainan Island, he received a telegram from Beijing urging him to return to the capital. He said that after 'Heshang' was shown, there were different reactions. A meeting of university presidents was taking place in Beijing, prompted by student unrest in June (which will be looked at in the next chapter), and they were considering the effects that 'Heshang' might have. 'They were afraid that "Heshang" would arouse radical reactions among college students', Su Xiao Kang told the interviewer. But he continued that this concern was quite natural because whenever something new emerges in the cultural/ideological area, those who are concerned about the future of

China become nervous. Basically, he believed, 'many people saw 'Heshang' as positive.

On the question of the revisions in the series, he said that the management of CCTV agreed that the series could be reshown but with some alterations. The parts of the programmes which might cause 'misunderstanding' should be revised, but not the parts related to academic opinions which can be discussed within society. He stressed that 'Heshang' was mainly intended to raise questions and some of the reactions were bound to be critical. But if the audience could receive 'Heshang' with tolerance, then the programme should accept criticism with tolerance. 'After all, one of the goals of "Heshang" is to advocate criticism, assessment and discussion' (ZGQN 16. 8. 1988).[15]

The clear danger was, however, that certain factions within the party leadership would not be so tolerant as Su Xiao Kang hoped and that the freer intellectual atmosphere of 1988 might be drawing to an end. According to some critics, the 'Heshang' authors had gone too far and there were signs that a backlash might be imminent. The programme had been linked to student unrest in June and it had indeed become a focus of attention among young intellectuals on the campuses. 'Heshang' became another 'tide' as debates continued and articles in the media proliferated. Discussions in student dormitories were often dominated by the 'Heshang' series at this time. The series encapsulated many of the important social and political issues of the time and therefore was not just an academic analysis. 'Heshang' tested the intellectual water and the limits to which the debate could be taken. By the end of 1988, the boundaries were becoming more obvious as the situation became more tense. The writers of the series, like other intellectuals, were aware of the ever-present possibility of backlash and apparently were advised to 'keep quiet'. Increasing anxiety about the state of student thought and the prospect of disturbances added to the 'Heshang' controversy.

The student unrest of 1988 needs to be addressed next. It is obviously linked to the dilemmas and strategies of contemporary students, and itself was a form of adaptive behaviour. It also contained all the features of the protest which would break out in 1989 as the 'patriotic democracy movement'. The signs were already there on the campuses, particularly in the capital, that 'something' would happen sooner or later.

6 1988

The writing on the wall

OVERVIEW

At several points during 1988, the underlying tension of the students' position intensified to the point of open unrest on several campuses. At Beida there were two major poster campaigns in April and June, the latter being provoked by the 'murder' of a postgraduate student. The posters contained the major elements of student grievances and demands which were to reappear in 1989. The end-of-the-year demonstrations appeared to be caused by 'racial' conflict between Chinese and African students, but it will be argued that these were once again expressions of the Chinese students' general discontent and disappointment after ten years of reform. A few other small-scale but significant events will also receive attention in our discussion of this period. The message was being clearly expressed that the students were increasingly dissatisfied with the Deng-led regime and were ready to speak out.

APRIL AND MAY: POSTERS, THE SHOESHINE PROTEST AND A UNIVERSITY CELEBRATES ITS BIRTHDAY

The brief but significant poster campaign at Beida in early April took place against the background of one of the most open National People's Congresses (NPC) ever held. Normally a rubber-stamping exercise, representatives from all over the country come to discuss an agenda largely set by the party. Unanimous voting on all issues was the rule. In 1988, the procedures were more open although still far from what could be described as 'democratic'. Members of the foreign press were allowed as observers for the first time and 'dialogue' was the stated aim of the congress and also of the CPPCC to follow.

The animated debate amongst students and intellectuals before the Seventh National People's Congress in April indicated that the anti-bourgeois campaign of 1987 was over and that a renewed period of liberalisation was under way. But there was also the realisation that the economy was in trouble and the country was facing many problems. The small 'democratic' parties at the NPC[1] were invited to speak freely and offer their opinions for the party to consider. Professor Fei Xiaotong of Beijing University was the chairman of the biggest Democratic party called the Democratic Alliance and he claimed that this party represented the interests of intellectuals and especially intellectuals involved in teaching (Chan 1989: 83).

A section of the intelligentsia watching the development, however, were less than enthusiastic about this appearance of liberalism, being well aware of the cyclical pattern of development in China. Fearful of yet another backlash, some kept quiet while congress members spoke out about the reforms, the problems being experienced in the economy, social problems, the crisis in education and other topical issues. Many delegates were concerned about increasing numbers of young people leaving schools and colleges before completing their courses. According to official statistics, between 1980 and 1987 30 million primary and middle-school 'dropouts' had been recorded with the numbers rising more rapidly during the previous few years (CD 7.12. 88). Some pupils, especially girls in rural areas, were withdrawn by their parents who considered it a 'waste of money' to send girls to school. Other young people left voluntarily to seek work and earn money, viewed as more important than education. Increases in school fees and charges for 'extras' also discouraged parents from keeping their children in education for the required nine years, thus making a mockery of the 'compulsory' education system in China. But pupils were not the only ones 'dropping out'. Teachers were leaving the profession in growing numbers because of poor pay and conditions, especially in country areas.

These problems, among others, were aired during the 1988 NPC. Outspoken speeches were given which received spontaneous standing ovations. There were even some members who abstained from voting, a quite unprecedented phenomenon. The lively debate spilled out onto the Beijing University campus where students and young teachers eagerly followed the proceedings.

The noticeboard area at Beida, so often the source of student movements, became busy after 6 April when several *dazibao* were posted.[2] One took the form of an 'open' letter to the NPC telling the representatives about their hopes for reform but their disappointment with the results. The congress was called on to consider the 'educational crisis' in particular, referring to the 'backward' and 'miserable' conditions for students and teachers. The *dazibao* also expressed the desire for freedom of speech, stating that, 'intellectuals cannot be silenced any longer'. Political reform had not kept pace with economic changes and some form of democracy was considered necessary to improve education and government. The state bureaucracy, it was claimed, could be reduced to save money and time, as well as to allow direct contact between the Party and the people. Bureaucracy was becoming a major issue in contemporary China. The *dazibao* writers regretted the fact that they had to resort to this medium for making their opinions known. Free speech was still a 'dream', yet to be realised.

Over the next few days, more posters went up and as I read them, students whispered that 'something might happen'. Beida has its long historical tradition of student movements and the foreign press, sent to Beijing to cover the NPC, were diverted to the poster sideshow. The BBC World Service reported that this campaign appeared to unite both students and staff, particularly the younger teachers, a worrying trend for the authorities. The posters were not removed however and education was certainly one of the main topics of debate at this unusual NPC. Representatives from the State Education Commission accepted that funds were insufficient but argued that the state could not be expected to provide for everything. Self-sufficiency was recommended since the 'doing business craze' still had the official blessing at this time.

The poster campaigners at Beida picked up this point, that academics were becoming financially independent and seeking ways of making money. A group of young teachers wrote new posters calling on their colleagues to descend on the Great Hall of the People and offer to shine the shoes of the representatives to raise some cash. The cynicism of this was obvious, along with the underlying sentiment. A small group actually went to Tiananmen, sat down and made the 'shoeshine protest' for a brief period. Police were put on alert in case larger groups of demonstrators joined in. It remained a small, symbolic gesture of anger at the official policy on education. A few new posters appeared as students from other colleges went to Beida to have a look at what was happening.

The appointment of Li Peng to the post of Premier at the congress did not impress the student protesters. Although highly educated and a 'technocrat', Li was not a popular figure, and was viewed as an extreme example of 'guanxi', i.e. advancement by personal contacts. Li was the adopted son of former Premier Zhou Enlai, yet he lacked the charisma and popularity of his 'father'. Also at the meeting, Zhao Ziyang, who had held the post of Premier temporarily since the downfall of Hu

Yaobang, was appointed to the position of Party General Secretary.

Apart from making fun of Li Peng, the main message of the posters was that reform could not succeed without a sound education system, a view widely supported among intellectuals, especially those in the Democratic Alliance. They saw conditions at all levels of education worsening. In the media, stories about primary school pupils 'dropping out' to take on jobs were common. Spending per pupil averaged out over one year at less than what would be spent per person at an official banquet, it was claimed. This bitter complaint and reference to lavish party practices and official corruption was to grow louder over the year. Meanwhile, tension mounted at Beida with students becoming increasingly restless. The university authorities did not wish to provoke the students by forcibly removing the posters. Instead they tried to take their minds off the poster campaign by providing weekend entertainment. In the middle of the campaign, there were several films and dance parties for the students. Some were obviously more interested in break-dancing than poster writing, as I witnessed for myself. Not all Beida students were activists or radicals. Some told me that it was 'useless' to put up posters. Several 'veterans' of the 'winter of discontent' told me that it was mainly the younger students who got together with their teachers to protest. 'They're excited now but will learn later'. The young teachers, recently assigned to their posts, perhaps felt they had little to lose by openly expressing their grievances because their salaries and living standards were low. The poster campaign lasted just over one week, serving as a strong reminder to the party leadership of the underlying current of discontent among students and teachers. On 17 April, several days after the conclusion of the protest, the government announced its intention to raise teachers' salaries and spend more in the next year on education. This was probably related to the Beida poster campaign, but a 'victory' could not be claimed until the promises were actually fulfilled. Sceptics greeted this news as yet more 'empty words'(*konghua*).

Several days later another interesting event took place, again at Beida. The large statue of Chairman Mao which had dominated the quadrant outside the library, where he had once worked in his youth, suddenly 'disappeared'. I had noticed the scaffolding placed around it the week before and thought it looked an odd sight, with the Chairman's head just visible over the striped plastic sheeting. I intended to take my camera to take a few pictures of the Mao under wraps, apparently for a 'spring cleaning'. Next time I went to Beida, however, it had gone, having been demolished overnight. This act provoked intense discussion in the dormitories among students who were scarcely teenagers when he died.

Some sang, 'Where have all the statues gone?', to the refrain of 'Where have all the flowers gone?'. Why should they be so concerned with the statue's removal when most other similar monuments erected during the height of the Cultural Revolution had already been demolished? Few Beijing campuses still possessed these reminders of the 'cult of personality' which had led China to the brink of civil war. Beida was just falling in line by removing the large statue, it was argued.

The issue was about more than the Chairman's statue, however. His memory may have been tarnished over the previous decade with the acknowledgement of his serious policy errors. But for many Chinese people he remained a great leader who, in spite of mistakes later in life, had led China into a new era. His frugal life-style contrasted starkly with that of some of the more contemporary Party officials who seemed to relish soft living, at the nation's expense. No one, it was argued, could accuse the former Chairman of corruption. To remove his statue in such a disrespectful manner was an insult not only to Mao Zedong but also the Communist Party. If the authorities could allow this sort of 'vandalism', what else were they capable of? Indirect criticisms were made of the incumbent leadership who were themselves struggling to maintain legitimacy during this period when the reforms had run into difficulties. The 'closet Maoists', even among this young generation of students who hardly remembered the Chairman, came out temporarily to air their views.

Others were not as concerned about Mao as the manner in which his statue was removed: by night, under cover and without any consultation. 'The statue was ugly, sure, but no one asked our opinions', some students complained. 'I think it should have been left alone', one young man told me. They were not Maoists, but recognised his special association with Beijing University, the home of 'May Fourth' and to some extent of Chinese communism. For these reasons alone, they felt the statue should not have been demolished. Others were pleased to see the 'old man' gone for good. 'He was a dictator, just like an emperor', they said. The differing views on the 'statue affair' reflected deeper political opinions and divisions among the student body. What they did seem in agreement on was their criticism of the university authorities and the government which allowed such actions to go unchallenged.

The next major event which could have ended in unrest was Beida's ninetieth anniversary on the historic date of 4 May. This month had ushered in substantial price rises on basic food items like rice, oil, pork and flour. Although students had a small subsidy, the increases represented a further erosion of living standards, for them as well as other urban residents.[3] Price rises of 30–50 per cent were not uncommon at this time. People were feeling the 'pinch' of economic reform and were not convinced by official explanations of the necessity for hardships while some private businesses were making huge profits. Large, somewhat extravagant celebrations were planned at Beida, perhaps to take students' and teachers' minds off the immediate economic situation and to focus attention instead on the university's great traditional heritage.

Apart from dance parties and fireworks, there were several major meetings held during the week of the anniversary. On 4 May, at one of these meetings, the minister of the State Education Commission, Li Tieying, addressed the Beida students. He said that students should develop 'morally' as well as intellectually and referred to the historic legacy of Beida. He apologised, however, for the fact that 'funding for education cannot increase greatly because the country remains poor' (CD 5.5.1988) and appealed to the students to work hard for their country. When he spoke of developing Beida as a 'truly socialist university', there were jeers and laughter from the students. By contrast, when the university's president, Ding Shisun, spoke of developing Beida as a 'pioneer of democracy', the applause was loud and long. The message was clear: Beijing University had a special character and wanted to go its own way, as it had done in the past, and lead other universities in the process. The president's speech also indicated a degree of unity between staff and students.

Meanwhile, the CYL was holding its Twelfth National Congress in Beijing, but most students were more interested in social get-togethers than League policies. They were viewed as 'stuffy' and 'out of touch with reality'. Many students told me that they only joined the League because it was the correct thing to do at middle school and at university they maintained their membership for the social functions the League organised, such as outings and dances. As a political organisation it was generally considered defunct. The CYL meeting attracted little attention apart from that of the official youth newspaper.

Meanwhile, the atmosphere on the Beida campus grew more excited as the celebrations continued. It was a 'celebration of youth by youth'. The university authorities seemed to trust the students. They provided many of the resources for the celebrations and allowed the students to proceed as they wished with few officials presiding over events. The education and economic crises were temporarily forgotten as the Beida students, joined by others from nearby campuses, celebrated loudly and energetically. I sensed they were trying to make a statement with their carefree attitude: if we can't do anything else, we are going to enjoy this anniversary. It was clear that this privileged student body with its energy and antagonism to the central authorities could one day be involved in a serious confrontation with the authorities.

All the pop songs in vogue at the time were sung communally – songs such as those from the award-winning film, *Hong Gaoliang* (*Red Sorghum*)[4] and the virtual national anthem of youth during 1988, 'Yi Wu Suo You', 'The One Who Has Nothing'. The hero in this song is pleading with his girlfriend to go with him, to love him in spite of his being poor and having nothing to offer. He offers her his freedom, his only possession with his open hands. It is a very emotional song made famous by the popular popstar, Cui Jian. Many students identified with the character in this song and the sentiments behind the words. 'We too have nothing, not even the freedom he sings of which we would like. We enjoy this song.' It was sung over and over during the parties. The enthusiasm and energy of the Beida students were obvious, but there were few outlets for them and little prospect of doing anything with their love of life and of their country. They threw themselves into the celebrations, a temporary release from the daily routine, but the problems would still be there once the party was over.

THE JUNE STUDENT MOVEMENT AT BEIJING UNIVERSITY

The June poster campaign was described as a 'xuechao', student movement, in one analysis carried out at the time, although there were no demonstrations.[5] It began only one month after Beida's ninetieth anniversary with the 'murder' of a postgraduate student, Chai Qing Feng, at a nearby snackbar. This incident, on 2 June, enraged the dead student's classmates and friends, who demanded immediate official action to be taken. They put up *dazibao* which at first mostly mourned Chai, but the contents of the posters soon became more politically oriented. The situation at Beida became tense as demonstrations were called to protest not just at the student's death but the poor conditions of intellectuals in China, the lack of free speech and human rights, excessive bureaucracy in the party's structure and rampant corruption within party echelons. These issues were all becoming 'hot topics' of discussion and were later to form an integral part of the 1989 student movement. The tragic death of Chai Qing Feng gave rise to small-scale protest which signalled clear warnings to the leadership of the serious problems they would have to face. A brief 'diary' of the tense days in June 1988, when a full-fledged 'xuechao' was narrowly avoided, is given below.

2 June   Beijing University postgraduate student Chai Qing Feng dies as a result of wounds received during a 'brawl' at a snack bar near to campus where he had gone with some friends to buy drinks. The assailants were 'unemployed youths', apparently all with records of hooliganism.

3 June   'Hundreds' of Beida students march on the local Public Security Department to protest. Calls were made for immediate action and 'justice'. The Vice Mayor of Beijing came to address them and appealed for calm, assuring them that the 'murder' would be dealt with speedily and according to proper legal procedures. *Dazibao* appear at the university.

6 June   The noticeboard area on campus becomes an *ad hoc*, outdoor 'funeral parlour' for the dead student, with poems, posters splashed with red paint, photographs and portraits of Chai and wreaths. Funeral music is played continually. Friends of Chai act as stewards as hundreds come to see the spectacle, including foreign correspondents.

7 June   The university authorities are reported as saying only posters that support the government and reform are allowed and not those which incite trouble. All the 'mourning' items, wreaths and so on, are removed to a specially designated memorial room, leaving the noticeboard area free for a 'poster fight'. Late night discussions held in an 'open political forum' around the noticeboard area. The Party, reforms, democracy and other topics debated freely.

8 June   Foreign reports based on student 'rumours' of demonstrations bring hundreds to the campus. Tension mounts as temperatures soar on one of the hottest days of the year. Thousands of police put on alert on all main roads leading to Tiananmen. Attempts to organise demonstrations fail.

9 June   University authorities warn that the poster campaign 'should stop'. No new posters appear. Students are worried about the activities of 'plain-clothes police' mingling with the crowds on campus.

11 June   All the posters are washed away under the orders of university authorities. There are calls for a strengthening of 'ideological work' among students with a stress on 'social practice', i.e. doing work in the community during the forthcoming summer vacations.

The 'xuechao' died out after just over one week but at its height both the university and state authorities were concerned that demonstrations could occur involving not only the Beida students but those from nearby campuses and even disaffected workers. The recent price rises and the subsequent decline in general standards of living had left whole sections of the urban population dissatisfied with the results of reform. Corruption was also an important issue which became very prominent during 1988. For students, corruption and the use of 'guanxi wang' – relationship networks – by those who had them, meant that their job prospects were further worsened. It was not so much 'what you know' as 'who you know' and this heightened their already serious sense of unfairness. Among the general population, corruption was a big issue. According to a survey cited by the FEER, over 83 per cent of China's urban population believed that the state bureaucracy was corrupt. Worse still, over 63 per cent of the cadres surveyed admitted that they were involved in some form of corrupt practice.[6] This ranged from the fairly trivial practice of holding too many banquets and offering 'gifts' to customers to the more serious misappropriation of state funds and reselling of state supplies on the free market for large profits.

While education and other social crises deepened, state officials were seen being driven around in expensive foreign cars and eating lavish banquets. The CPC had released a statement from its three-day conference at the end of May strongly condemning corruption and excessive expenditure and promising to tackle these problems. But students and many of their working counterparts no longer trusted the Party, which was seen to be 'feathering its own nest'. Their behaviour contrasted starkly to the more traditional image of Party members as simple-living, self-sacrificing people. Even young students were aware of how things had changed. 'We can no longer trust these people', many told me quite openly. June 1988 gave them an opportunity to express their grievances, seriously unnerving the struggling pro-reform Party leadership. The disparities between rich and poor were becoming greater and they were not successfully justified in the official media. Using terms like the 'primary stage of socialism', and the 'socialist commodity economy', did little to placate students and other low-income groups who were struggling to make ends meet.

There was genuine fear that demonstrations could erupt. In an effort to contain the June 'xuechao' on campus, the authorities issued warnings to major Beijing work units. Employees were told not to support the students and to reject any form of illegal protest (demonstrations and posters fell into this category). The warning may have had an effect, but did nothing to dispel feelings among various groups of workers that the Party was not dealing with reform correctly. They were quietly seething. June 1988 may not have been the right time for demonstrations, but parts of the student body and some sectors of the urban population appeared to be contemplating some form of action to let the government know of their intentions.

The students at Beida, some of whom were on the verge of taking to the streets, probably feared the possible repercussions and with the end of term imminent, they decided that open protest was not worth the risk. I spoke with many students during this period from several major universities and the majority were sympathetic to the poster campaign. They considered it was 'useless', however, remembering the protests of 1986–7 and the backlash that followed. Those approaching graduation had even more to fear. Already job prospects had deteriorated because economic reforms had led to reductions in the labour force at many state organisations, where graduates hope to obtain positions. The negative effects of the 'guanxi wang' reduced career opportunities still further.

The government had made serious proposals during 1988 about reforming the graduate assignment system because of its glaring inefficiencies. The move from 'arranged marriage' to 'marriage based on free choice', as described in a *Zhongguo Qingnian* article (1988, 5: 27) was to be welcomed in many ways because a large number of graduates every year were wrongly placed. But the problem with allowing free choice during the period of economic reform was that there were not enough suitable jobs available, and the prospect of graduate unemployment was very real in spite of official denials of graduate 'surpluses'. According to a State Education Commission investigation, various work units across the country had refused 5,500 graduates in 1987, indicating that there were too many coming from the universities. The SEC, however, explained that in reality many ministries did not have their quota. Beijing municipality, for example, required 9,000 graduates but only received 6,000. In 1988, 460,000 students were graduating nationwide, but there was a demand for 700,000 a shortfall, not a surplus. The commission pointed out that compared to developed nations, China was deficient in college-trained personnel. In the USA, out of every 10,000 people, 524 were college students, compared to 60 in China (ZGQN 30. 7. 1988). The main problem was that many graduates did not want to go to units where conditions were not seen as 'suitable' to their requirements. They all wanted to 'crowd into beneficial units and enterprises so there is a contradiction' (ZGQN 30. 7. 1988). An apparent surplus was a shortage, according to this official line of argument, which was disputed by a number of students and teachers alike. Some of the jobs on offer in the assignment process were not 'good' jobs, suited to graduates' fields of study or expertise, and some involved very little real work, being 'employment' in name only. The statistics mentioned by the authorities could not be accepted at face value. It was not surprising that students tried to find places in the 'good' work units which offered decent conditions along with a chance of self-development and advancement. The prospect of 'underemployment' was not appealing, let alone finding no job at all. Taking part in protests could jeopardise any existing opportunities of securing a decent employment position for those coming up to graduation. The government still had this vital hold over many of its educated youth.

Consequently the June 'xuechao' was contained, but not before it had seriously worried the leadership and the students had made a number of important points which would resurface less than a year later. The two student movements were both triggered by a death: in 1988, a student; in 1989, former party secretary Hu Yaobang. The unfortunate death of Chai Qing Feng, labelled as a 'murder' immediately in the media, without a proper investigation into the circumstances, symbolised for the students just how low their social position had sunk. The fact that the people involved who killed Chai in the snackbar fight were mostly 'unemployed youths', seemed to emphasise for the young intellectuals the disrespect for knowledge prevalent in a money-orientated society. Educated people had become a despised group, just as during the Cultural Revolution, when they suffered verbal and physical abuse. Reports of beatings and verbal attacks in and around other campuses were becoming common, according as local reports. Students did not feel safe, yet the authorities did little to protect them. Their pleas for greater security had gone unheard, and this murder in their view was the 'inevitable' outcome, raising the whole question of the social position of intellectuals in contemporary China.

There were obvious inaccuracies in the reports of Chai's death which, if investigated properly, would have shown it as a case of 'manslaughter' rather than 'murder' in my own view. But passions were aroused. Students were feeling threatened from all quarters, their social position deteriorating, living conditions worsening and prospects for the future looking fairly dim. They wanted something to be done, quickly, to redress the situation. The public security bureau provided the immediate action called for by the students. Within forty hours of Chai's death, the six criminals had been arrested, their capture even conveniently filmed and shown on the television news. They were pronounced 'guilty' even before their arrest, let alone the trial which was the usual brief process typical of Chinese legal justice. The fact that most of them already had criminal records was widely publicised and used as evidence of their guilt in the Chai Qing Feng case.

The *Guangming Daily* had carried an article on 4 June, stating that, 'a gang of ruffians violently beat a Beijing University postgraduate to death.' (GMRB 4. 6. 1988) The case, it was said, was 'basically cut and dried', thus publicly condemning the six before they were even tried. Other newspapers carried similar articles in an effort to show to the Beida students that something was being done quickly about the case. After the speedy 'trial' and a statutory appeal, which was dismissed, as is usual within a few hours, one of the six was executed and the others started long prison sentences. There had been little investigation or calling for witnesses. They had little chance to ask for the type of 'human rights' being demanded by students in the Beida posters.

Were students satisfied with this summary justice? The ones I spoke with believed that the authorities had failed to address the real issues. The fate of the six people involved in the snackbar death reflected some of the bad practices which they said should be corrected through the institution of a truly socialist legal system which had human rights incorporated into it. This would involve freedom of speech, another demand in the posters, and was reminiscent of the 'Li Yi Zhe' document of 1973. The ideal of 'democracy' was also discussed during the 'xuechao', with the leadership being strongly criticised for their feudalistic autocratic manner of ruling the country. Some slogans and ideas from the 'Democracy Wall Movement' of 1978–79 received another brief hearing during these days.

There were disagreements among poster writers and speakers at the political forums held at night. Some insisted that the reforms were naturally problematic and they had to support the Party in its efforts to modernise China. Others were pro-reform but disapproved of the way the reforms were currently being implemented. A minority of activists raised more radical ideas for change in Chinese politics and society, such as the abandonment of socialism and doing away with Party domination. Some posters were probably written by officials and there is no doubt that a few 'agents provocateurs' were active on the Beida campus, drawing out the activists so they would be recognised later. Once it was clear that no demonstrations would take place, the students became nervous about the 'xuechao' and began to withdraw from any action which could have been construed as political activism. Consequently, the 'xuechao' came to end, but not before the 'hope of China' as young people are often referred to had declared that, 'we have no hope'[7] They insisted that they were supportive of reform, 'but these are not the reforms we want'.[8] The demands for better conditions for young intellectuals, for action to be taken on corruption, for political reforms to match those taking place in the economic sphere, and for free speech had become familiar by now. These grievances and demands remained and although they did not drive the students out onto the streets of the capital this time to demonstrate, it was clear that they certainly could at some time in the near future.

THE YEAR WINDS DOWN, STUDENT DISCONTENT RISES

The authorities were becoming increasingly concerned by the unhealthy state of student activism. Top-level meetings were called in the summer in which university principals and State Education Commission officials discussed the problems on the campuses and possible solutions. Thousands of students, particularly from Beijing, were sent to undertake 'social practice' during the summer vacation in the hope that contact with 'real life' would bring them down to earth and give them a more realistic assessment of society. Returning to the universities for the new academic year in September 1988, this objective appeared to remain unachieved. Dissatisfaction, apathy, the desire to escape and the other manifestations of the student 'problem' appeared to be intact. Some of those who had been out to the countryside or into factories to do their 'social practice' were even more critical of the existing regime. They had been shocked by the 'reality' they had come across and were more committed to action.

Beneath an apparent calm on the campuses were all the unresolved and unaddressed issues of the time. Various isolated examples of unrest acted as reminders to the authorities. A few of these incidents can be cited in support of this view. On 17 November, for example, about 200 chemistry department students held a sit-in outside the main administrative building at Beijing Normal (Teachers') University. They were objecting to having to travel by bus everyday to their laboratories and classrooms located on another site. Those familiar with the bus arrangements in Beijing could understand their annoyance. Despite year-long complaints nothing had been done about the problem. Tired of being ignored, they demanded some immediate response from the authorities. Many teachers appeared to support this action because their complaints taken through the proper channels had gone unanswered. The sit-in at Beishida (shortened form of the university's name) caused some tension, but eventually the college principal promised to look into the matter. The sit-in appeared to have scored a victory, but the ultimate outcome, i.e. whether the laboratories were moved, was not clear. The students had, however, taken a fairly bold action to call attention to their grievance.

The day after their sit-in, some *dazibao* appeared on another Beijing campus, complaining about poor security. People from outside the college had been coming in freely, causing trouble, stealing and even beating students. This had also happened elsewhere, for instance at Beishida. The residents were worried about this trend of increasing violence towards intellectuals, symptomatic, it was claimed, of their low status in society. The authorities seemed to be doing little about tackling this social problem. There were two sides to the campus security issue, however. Most colleges are walled or fenced with guards at the gates. The gates are usually locked at night and it used to be fairly standard practice that people going in and out had to identify themselves. Non-residents would have to register their names at the gate as well as the time of arrival and their business. I noticed in recent years these practices becoming more lax, which was supported in some ways by both students and staff, who felt an increased sense of freedom. It was also easier to bring in friends without involving the college bureaucracy. The negative effects, however, were the less welcome members of society coming and going quite freely. By tightening security, 'hooligans' could be kept out by students and other college residents would once again feel as if they were 'prisoners'. (One campus I knew of in a large industrial city used to be so strictly guarded that the students referred to it as the town's 'second prison'.) Locking the gates, however, could do little to reverse the social trends which the *dazibao* complained of.

As December approached, there were fears that the historic 'December Ninth' might be marked by student unrest. I was informed that a group of young teachers at one college were planning a boycott on the day to protests against their poor living conditions and low pay. They did not want their gesture to be viewed as part of that historical movement but as a genuine protest with genuine grievances. But they felt 'December Ninth' was a good day to attempt to gain sympathy for their cause. They were finding it hard to make ends meet and life had become very miserable. One of them told me, 'We are the victims, the victims of reform.' Although worried about the consequences of their boycott, they went ahead and were offered a pay rise as a result. But they were all told to attend political study meetings and make self-criticisms about their actions. They feared further repercussions at a later date because their participation in the boycott would almost certainly go into their files.

Any pay rises were quickly swallowed up by further price increases and unofficial estimates of inflation were as high as twenty-five per cent in the cities. Some goods rose by more than this average percentage. The general economic news for December was bad with forecasts of poverty, even starvation in the countryside. Many farmers had given up working the land because of low rates of return and had turned to producing more lucrative goods. There had also been a 'drift' to the cities of unemployed rural labour who were creating a new social problem in communist China. Some as young as eleven and twelve, these 'migrant labourers' went looking for work and did not always find it, turning to other less than legal ways of earning their bread. There was not enough food being grown on the farms and the government could not afford to pay for all of the grain it had requisitioned from the farmers. There were rumours of anger among the grain farmers, who were being given IOUs instead of cash for their crops. Comparisons were being drawn between the party leadership and the 'bankrupt' Nationalist government of Chiang Kaishek in the 1930s. The student population was well-informed of the economic and social crises facing the country, but their own problems remained uppermost in their minds.

The trend of devaluing knowledge went on, leading to a drop in numbers applying for postgraduate study in 1989. During the five-day application period that began on 1 December, only 5,700 young people applied for 8,600 postgraduate places available in Beijing.[9] The waning of enthusiasm for higher education had begun several years before, but this was the first time there had been fewer applicants than places offered. There were also high drop-out rates from postgraduate study, with disillusioned academics applying for employment at the foreign hotels as waiters, porters and chambermaids. They could earn far more money in these positions than if they remained inside the universities, be assured of good meals daily and sometimes also have accommodation provided. Compared to dormitory life and low student stipends, even what was once considered demeaning work could offer a much more comfortable life. Those who persisted with their postgraduate study often did so purely in order to go abroad. Optimistic academics and enthusiastic students were in a minority. Most were exasperated by their own position and that of the nation in general.

The end of the year saw thousands take to the streets in order to demonstrate their anger and resentment, ostensibly with the African students in China but more indirectly with the party's failure to tackle the problems of reform. The trouble began in Nanjing, as reported in the *China Daily* on 27 December. Two African students refused to register their Chinese girlfriends at a Christmas dance. This regulation of registration often causes bad feeling because it means that Chinese people friendly with foreigners are easily recognised and traced. The outcome of their refusal to follow the rules was a scuffle, apparently caused by the Africans not the Chinese. 'African students attacked university employees who came to the spot to maintain order', wrote the *China Daily*. Eleven university staff were injured, one seriously. This all took place on Christmas Eve. By the next day, hundreds of Chinese students gathered at the Nanjing campuses calling for the African students to be punished and marched on to the municipal offices. Several days of unrest followed which spread across the country and involved thousands of students.

It is impossible to know exactly what happened that evening. Although criticising the Africans, whom many Chinese do not like because they have more money because of higher scholarships and a greater degree of freedom, there is a legitimate case to be made for the view that the students had found another excuse to bring attention to their own problems and views about conditions in China. There is even the suggestion of a 'conspiracy', that the authorities manipulated these troubles, realising the existence of conflicts between Chinese and African students and hoping to divert attention away from the disastrous economic forecasts for the coming year. Whipping up nationalistic sentiment is not difficult to do with Chinese students because of an underlying layer of patriotic sentiment and if there is any substance to this 'conspiracy' theory, the African students may indeed have been used as a diversion.

Certainly, a good deal of anti-foreigner sentiment was unleashed, first of all in Nanjing and then other major cities, and traditional prejudices were allowed to run riot for the Christmas period. The Africans were described as 'noisy' because they liked to party and sing and dance. They were also accused of being sexually promiscuous and of leading young Chinese girls astray. The spectre of AIDs was raised. Their general behaviour offended Chinese morality and also showed how 'ungrateful' they were to China – a special friend to Africa.[10] Some of the African students taken into custody by the police claimed they had been beaten up. Accusations flew back and forth for several days. Chinese students in Beijing did not march as their counterparts did in several provincial cities. One student told me that they were watching and waiting. 'We don't have any real grievances against the African students.' The whole affair, however, failed to gain the status of a diplomatic issue and started to calm down after the New Year holiday, leaving bad feeling between different groups of students.

Was it all a stage-managed event by the party leadership in order to distract their own people and foreign observers from the real issues facing China? There are strong suspicions of implicit backing for the anti-African demonstrations. Whatever the truth is of the 'Christmas clashes', the situation in China could be seen as highly volatile.

Another small but significant outburst took place in Beijing on Mao Zedong's birthday, 26 December. A group of around one hundred people stood outside his mausoleum in Tiananmen Square and chanted 'Long Live Chairman Mao!' This could be viewed as another indirect criticism of the embattled leadership and their poor record on corruption. There were also several minority group demonstrations in December. Students from Tibet studying in the capital held a brief demonstration against the Han Chinese treatment of their nation and people, as did a group of Uighurs from Xinjiang province.

The year 1988 ended with unrest, tension and uncertainty about which 'faction' was controlling the party's central committee. According to official messages, the 'modernisers' still had the upper hand and the reform programme was set to continue in spite of the economic and social problems which had troubled the leaders throughout 1988. Ten years before, in December 1978, Deng Xiaoping had given his support to reforming the economy first in the rural areas then in the cities. The early successes of the responsibility system in the countryside had encouraged Deng and his close allies to propose further changes and China's population appeared happy with the developments. Ten years on, the situation was different but, according to a *People's Daily* editorial entitled 'A Great Decade' (22. 12. 1988). 'China's reform, the trend of history and the choice of the people, should be carried out without wavering.' It referred to the previous centrally planned economy as 'unimaginable' in the changed circumstances brought about by reform. The editorial contained strong words of commitment to Deng's modernising policies, but was probably intended to convince an uncertain population that reforms would continue, despite apparent problems and doubts. The *China Daily* wrote, 'Decade-old reforms are destined to go on', but not everyone was assured by these media messages. In their existing forms, reforms looked likely to lead to social unrest and further disturbances.

The new year, 1989, opened with the government barely keeping a 'lid' on the situation. I left China feeling that the state of affairs could not continue for much longer without serious public disorder, possibly started by the students. Things were becoming intolerable, with many sections of the population holding serious grievances. The government had admitted that as the reforms 'deepened' there would be signs of inequalities and economic problems which the people had to accept with patience. Once the 'primary stage of socialism' had been passed through, everything would get better, according to the official propaganda. But few people were listening any more. Just in case they were not convinced, the authorities had broadcast messages of their improved ability to cope with any public disorders. The police, it was suggested, were prepared to tackle any outbreaks of 'hooliganism' or 'counterrevolutionary' activity.

The scene was set for an eventual conflict with the question being 'when' rather than 'will' a protest movement break out.

7   The Outbreak of the 'Patriotic Democratic Movement', spring 1989

OVERVIEW

A new semester began for the nearly two million students at China's 1,064 institutions of higher education, but for them the old problems persisted. The educational and social crises highlighted not only the difficulties facing the pro-reform leadership but their failure to bring about any substantial degree of democratisation in the political sphere during the reform decade. The sudden death of former Party secretary Hu Yaobang brought thousands of students onto the streets of the capital calling for Hu's rehabilitation and for action to be taken on China's pressing problems. Their implicit criticisms of the government quickly became open and direct as the campaign, which was later known as the 'patriotic democratic movement', quickly spread across the country. The origins of this student-led action have already been traced back to the ancient and more recent history of student activism in China. This chapter will outline the actual outbreak of the spring protests from the start of the new semester and Hu Yaobang's unexpected death in April. The development of the movement will be described and discussed up until the publication of the significant *People's Daily* editorial on 26 April which further aggravated an already uneasy relationship between the students and the authorities and made the likelihood of conflict much greater.

A NEW SEMESTER BEGINS, OLD PROBLEMS PERSIST AND A FORMER LEADER DIES

At the end of February 1989 a new semester was just beginning after the annual 'Spring Festival' vacation. The majority of students in higher education returned to their campuses after a few weeks at home celebrating Chinese New Year with family and friends. 'Spring Festival is our most important holiday', numerous Chinese friends reminded me, 'like your Christmas'. The parallels are clear when considering the over-consumption of food and inactivity in front of the television set, which in recent years has become the modern manner of celebrating this ancient festival.

Tendencies towards over-spending and wastage of food were causing concern throughout the country, particularly as neither the state nor the people could really afford these forms of conspicuous consumption. The authorities had repeatedly warned officials not to squander state money on lavish banquets and to make cut-backs wherever possible.[1] But good food and drink at the state's expense were considered a 'perk' by many high-ranking officials, who persisted with the practice of entertaining business colleagues for New Year in an extravagant manner. This misuse of power and funds was constantly criticised by students and teachers, as well as ordinary people because they realised it was, in the end, their money being wasted.

For individuals, social customs dictated that a good show of delicacies and hospitality had to be on offer when friends and family dropped by to pay the traditional New Year visit. Keeping up with appearances and not 'losing face' were still considered important in spite of economic difficulties in the urban areas. The feasting and festivities probably gave little pleasure to those on fixed, low incomes including the majority of academics and other intellectuals. With a monthly wage of about 100 yuan (less than £20), many young teachers, for example, would have been struggling just to make ends meet, let alone buy extra luxuries. Students, largely reliant on their parents for an allowance, would also have felt the economic 'pinch'. Many of the younger generation were questioning these negative aspects of the vacation, although they enjoyed the break from the boredom of daily campus routine. Spring Festival was a brief respite from the problems and anxieties of the academic environment but entailed unwelcome expense for the families of many students.

Returning to the campuses there was little hope of improvement in the conditions, pay or status of those involved in the advancement of knowledge. The State Education Commission had, it is true, promised changes but scepticism was rife about whether they could actually implement them. Educational expenditure was set to double over a three-year period, according to an announcement made at the end of 1988 (*China Daily* 23. 12. 1988). It was not clear, however, where this extra money was coming from and even with such an increase, China would still be spending only four per cent of its GNP on education, one of the lowest levels in the world.

The extra funds, if found from various sources, would also have to be spread around the system thinly, with higher education receiving only 15 per cent increase in its budget (barely offsetting inflation). Out of that, a minimum amount was destined for the much-publicised salary rises (*Times Higher Education Supplement* 31. 3. 1989). In March 1989, Li Peng, who had been the SEC's first chief when it was established in 1985, now addressed the Seventh National People's Congress as Premier and apologised for this budget. He admitted the shortfalls but said it was the best they could do, given the prevailing adverse economic situation. The reform programme had run into some major problems and state finances were in short supply. Farmers had to be paid for their agricultural produce and there were also loans from foreign countries that had to be serviced.

Education minister Li Tieying stressed that educational establishments should not always look to the state for funding but think of ways they themselves could obtain the much-needed finance for projects and research. Many had already achieved a degree of financial independence with the 'doing business' tide but not all institutions could be successful in such ventures. The task of raising funds, however, was being laid more firmly at the doors of the universities themselves. This reinforced the tendency of the state to withdraw its backing from what was formerly considered a public service. Education was plunged into even greater difficulty, according to concerned academics. How could the extra money be found without further jeopardising the system? Raising fees was one obvious solution for the colleges, but the wisdom of such a move was called into doubt. Increased tuition would drive prospective students away at a time when the value of higher education was already questioned. Those currently in the system would suffer even more and see yet more deterioration in their living standards. Li Tieying's address at the congress did little to settle nerves within the field of education. Turning the educated elite into paupers could do little to further the government's modernisation programme. The very base from which to launch the needed new economic initiative was unstable. But the leaders seemed to lack the political will or capacity to do anything about these problems.

This was the setting for the start of a new semester. Education remained a 'hot topic' both inside and outside the Great Hall of the People and feelings ran high. A number of posters calling on the government to improve conditions for intellectuals and criticising those in the party who only looked after their own interests appeared on campus at Beijing University early in April. Similar posters had been put up one year before. All those involved in education, from first-year undergraduates to senior professors, were anxious about their future. They were also very tired of 'kong hua', empty words.

The new 'Year of the Snake' did not, therefore, have an auspicious beginning but entered on the back of the despair left by the 'Dragon Year', 1988.[2] Generally speaking, the atmosphere in the institutions of higher learning was depressing. Another semester began with complaints and frustration with the economic and educational crises. 'The leaders continue to hold large banquets, while our education system collapses around us', one young man wrote in early April. 'This spring will not be a quiet one', another student warned. In the dormitories throughout China students were no doubt discussing what they did in the vacation, their love affairs, favourite pop stars and other topics, but China's social problems were never far from their minds.

The controversy surrounding the astro-physicist Fang Lizhi was also prominent in discussion. Professor Fang had in previous years made known his opinions about the party leadership and their policies and was dismissed from the party after the student demonstrations of the winter of 1986–7. In 1989, Fang 'opened the new year on an uncompromising note', according to Kelly (Kelly 1990: 13). He had already sent a letter to Deng Xiaoping in January demanding the release of 'Democracy Wall' activist Wei Jingsheng. In an open letter to the leader on 13 February, a group of 33 intellectuals called for human rights for all political prisoners. Professor Fang had set a trend calling for reform in China's political and legal system which other intellectuals followed. For this Fang was not allowed to attend a reception on 26 February given by President Bush in spite of having an invitation. This triggered debate about China's leading dissident.

THE SIGNIFICANCE OF HU YAOBANG'S DEATH

A sense that nothing could be done to change the situation had prevailed for a long time. Demonstrations and posters had been considered as 'useless' actions, but suddenly and almost without warning thousands of Beijing students were out on the streets. The event which put them there was the death of Hu Yaobang from a heart attack on Saturday 15 April. At seventy-three, Hu was somewhat youthful when compared to others in the party hierarchy still in active service. But Comrade Hu had not been among those making decisions in China for the two years prior to his death. After his resignation in early 1987, he had been spending his last years in comfortable but enforced early retirement, before finally 'going to see Marx', the phrase often used in China when top leaders die.

The news of his death quickly reached the major campuses in the capital. Beijing University students appeared to be the first to respond in their customary manner by putting up *dazibao*. In these they praised the dead man and called for his 'rehabilitation'. Other colleges quickly followed over the weekend and another potentially explosive poster campaign was under way. This time, unlike 1988, the students dared to come out of the universities. Even those who doubted the value or wisdom of demonstrations joined their more active classmates in making their opinions known to the Chinese public and, indeed, to the rest of the world. This act of leaving the campuses to march on the places that matter in Beijing, i.e. Tiananmen Square and Zhongnanhai, where the party leaders live, was significant in several ways. It was the first time since early 1987, the 'winter of discontent', that large numbers of students had held spontaneous demonstrations. This was also, strictly speaking, illegal and the participants were well aware of the possible dangers awaiting them. Some were probably encouraged by the earlier 'open letters' of leading intellectuals, already mentioned, calling for human rights. Police failed to stop the march. Shouting slogans such as, 'Down with dictatorship!' and 'Long live democracy!', the students poured out of the university quarter. These chants were interspersed with calls for Hu Yaobang's record to be corrected and his name cleared of the criticisms he had received after the last round of student demonstrations in 1986–7. The cry for democracy, heard at sporadic intervals during the ten years of reform in which Hu had once played a prominent part, was again out in the open. In the enclave of Zhongnanhai, the leadership was caught off guard, facing an unexpected challenge from the angry and grieving students on the streets. Why did Hu's death have such a profound effect on these students, shaking them from their uneasy apathy and inspiring them to action? Why did this dead man suddenly become a 'hero' in their eyes, and worth taking risks for? They could have met them with force right from the start before their actions developed into a full-fledged 'xuechao' .

The answer will involve untangling several main strands of thought, for it was not simply the case that the students saw Hu as the 'champion of reform' as some commentators declared. The prevailing, if not overbearing, economic and social conditions on that April day were also important, as previously discussed. The students were ready to adopt a cause through which they could air their own more general grievances. They did not merely use Hu's death as an excuse for demonstrating, but neither were they going to let the opportunity for expressing their discontent pass by. Once Hu Yaobang had been cremated and his memorial service completed, the 'xuechao' came to be dominated by other issues, with the former party secretary as a secondary factor.

In my contacts with a wide variety of students in and around Beijing up until a few months before Hu's death, I hardly heard his name mentioned let alone referred to as a 'champion of reform'. When questioned specifically about prominent Chinese leaders past and present deserving of respect, no one cited Hu Yaobang. There are several possible reasons for this. It could have been that since his forced resignation from office and political inactivity, he was not eligible to be classed as a person worthy of respect. Out of sight, out of mind: his absence from the public eye had perhaps reduced him to the status of a 'non-person'.

Another possible reason is that my informants were not willing to align themselves with a political outcast, at least not while he was still alive. This may have reflected badly on their own standing or even have created the impression that they were politically unsound and given to excesses of 'bourgeois liberalism', an official criticism levelled at Hu Yaobang.

It may also have been that he was judged quite simply as a 'failure', having made little impact on Chinese political or social life while occupying the post of General Party Secretary. The students' comments about his 'great historical achievements' made after his death, however, would appear to belie such a negative view.

There is also a cultural point that in China a public figure is often more respected when dead than alive. Free from worldly failings and human weaknesses, their essential goodness can shine forth and those who wronged them during their lifetime can be called into question. This partly explains the rush of people to Beijing in an attempt to have the record of their dead relatives cleared after the Cultural Revolution. Hundreds still wait around the official areas in a state of semi-vagrancy, hoping for a chance to clear the name of loved ones. The phenomenon of martyrdom perhaps also has a role to play here, and in China honour can be bestowed even if the person's death was not directly attributable to the pursuit of a noble cause or ideal. Indirect association with the ideal will often suffice. The murdered Beida student in 1988 is a case in point. He did not die fighting the cause of downtrodden intellectuals but in an unfortunate bar-room brawl. Never the less, he became a martyr.

Hu Yaobang did not die because of his political convictions. During his time in office, he behaved cautiously and pragmatically. He was outspoken, but not always. During the 'spiritual pollution campaign' of 1983, for example, he largely acceded to the wishes of Deng Xiaoping, probably to ensure that he had a continued role to play in the Party leadership. Jonathon Mirsky wrote in 1986 that 'loyalty to Deng will be no problem for Hu. The older man has been at his elbow for more than 40 years, helping him up some of the same rungs on the perilous career ladder which Deng had climbed years earlier' (Mirsky in The *Observer* 8. 6. 1986). Hu's eventual downfull was partly due to the need for a 'scapegoat' rather than because of his independent political behaviour.

Neither did he die as a campaigner, although rumours circulating among the students at the time linked the fatal heart attack to a heated argument in which Hu defended his commitment to reform. This is how students preferred to picture him and it certainly facilitated their post-humous elevation of Hu Yaobang's status. Once raised into the position of a semi-martyr and publicly declared as their 'champion of reform', he commanded the respect denied him during the previous years. His knowledge and expertise had been wasted, a condition students could readily identify with. Hu's political impotence was not unlike their own powerlessness. The former leader, now dead, was a 'victim', like them-selves, wronged by others in power and with little recourse to justice. The added irony here lies in Hu's downfall being related to the previous round of student demonstrations. Perhaps some of those who came out to mourn his death two years on thought of this. The fortunes of the students had been in some ways linked to those of Hu Yaobang. On his death they felt sufficiently moved to say something out loud: the consequences were far-reaching.

Presenting images of Hu as both hero and victim prepared the ground for an attack on the existing leaders who had wronged him. The students also blamed the government's shortcomings for their own difficulties and warned that the future of China was in danger because of their inadequacies. 'Sincere men have died while hypocrites live on', claimed one poster, possibly implying that the despised Premier Li Peng should have died instead. There were many calls for Hu's rehabilitation which would have necessitated an official reappraisal of his work and, by implication, of the Party's own policies. To reverse the criticisms levelled at Hu Yaobang at the time of his resignation would indicate that mistakes were made by the paramount leaders, particularly Deng Xiaoping. It is difficult to imagine Deng and his associates undertaking such a procedure and indicting themselves for a long list of policy errors and mismanagement. But the students had the nerve to suggest that those in power should put the record straight, not just for Hu Yaobang but for the whole country. They wanted something akin to the reversal of the 'Tiananmen Incident' verdict of ten years before. In 1989, the students were invoking a traditional practice by calling for the official, posthumous recognition of Hu Yaobang's contribution to the Party and state and the restoration of his political standing.

Deng Xiaoping did not intend to restore Hu's reputation. He was to be given the proper funeral service in the Great Hall of the People with sufficient honour befitting his status. But there was to be no rehabilitation. Deng's inflexibility at this stage of the nascent 'xuechao' was a trait which would endure throughout the movement. It won him no praise from the students on the streets, who showed their own determination by refusing to return quietly to the campuses and forget the issues raised in their posters and demonstrations.

These young people eventually earned for themselves the inglorious label of 'counter revolutionaries', even 'hooligans', as did the Tiananmen demonstrators after Zhou Enlai's death in 1976. One wonders if there will be a reversal of this judgement in later years, after Deng himself has gone to 'see Marx'.

A brief timetable of events will be useful here to show, at a glance, the development of the student movement in its first major 'phase', i.e. up until the response to the *People's Daily* editorial.

THE LIFE HISTORY OF THE STUDENT'S PATRIOTIC DEMOCRATIC MOVEMENT: PHASE ONE

13 April   Hu Yaobang dies. Students in Beijing put up 'large character posters' calling for his rehabilitation. Start of a week of protest centred mainly in Tiananmen Square and outside Zhongnanhai.

16 April   Students march to Tiananmen to mourn Hu and call for freedom and democracy. Corruption also an issue.

17 April   Demonstration outside Zhongnanhai with students asking for a dialogue with the top leaders. Chanting 'Long live Democracy', and 'Down with dictatorship', they also call for the publication of leaders' incomes and business interests. A sit-in begins outside the walled compound. More wreaths for Hu are laid around the Monument to the People's Heroes in the square. Comparisons made with 1976 after the death of Premier Zhou Enlai.

19 April   University quarter in Beijing sees more demonstrations. Protests in other cities reported. Government issues stern warning that demonstrations are illegal and participants will be punished.

20 April   Clashes between students and police outside of Zhongnanhai. Reports of injuries. Students in Shanghai also come out to protest.

21 April   Student numbers in Tiananmen continue to grow with around

100,000 keeping an all-night vigil. Some workers join in while others give food, money or verbal support. Official orders and threats to clear the square are ignored and the government backs down, 'allowing' the students to remain.

22 April   Memorial service for Hu in the Great Hall is broadcast to student crowds, who afterwards chant for Li Peng to come out and address them personally. He fails to appear.

23 April   Reports of unrest in other cities. In Xian, some violence and injuries as 'unemployed youth run riot'. Also clashes in Changsha. Beijing student leaders meet to co-ordinate a boycott of classes.

24 April   Boycott begins in Beijing with widespread support. Teachers speak out in their favour. Leaflets handed out to the public explaining their actions and money collected for the growing campaign.

26 April   *People's Daily* prints an editorial attacking the students, accusing them of causing 'chaos' and calling for the proper handling of the situation. Deng Xiaoping allegedly in favour of a hardline approach to restore order, with bloodletting 'not a bad thing'. Anger and resentment among the student body.

27 April   Massive march of tens of thousands of students from the university district in Beijing to Tiananmen. Crowds of people line the route and cheer the students. Open support for their demands apparent as jubilant scenes are witnessed on the streets. The police road blocks fail to stop the students. Demonstrations reported in other places. Boycott of classes continues.

THE STUDENTS COME OUT AND STAY OUT

Throughout the week following Hu Yaobang's death, students deserted their classrooms and poured into the centre of the capital. Wreaths and poems were carefully prepared and taken to Tiananmen Square in a spontaneous display of public mourning. Observers speculated about how far the comparisons with the 'Tiananmen Incident' of 1976 would go and whether the new outbreak of veiled protest would lead to a similar crackdown.

Certainly the numbers of demonstrators were reckoned to be the largest in thirteen years. The Party leaders were faced with an obvious dilemma in dealing with the sensitive situation because there were early signs of support from the general public for the students' action. Often in the past, the workers could be played off against the intellectuals because of their different 'class' interests. The student demonstrations of the winter of 1986–7 drew little support from the urban workers, but the situation had changed. More people were disappointed with the reforms and nursing grievances. Inflation affected everybody except for those in privileged positions and they were now tainted with corruption as well. Always fearful of an alliance between intellectuals and workers, the government had to tread cautiously in order to avoid creating more serious social unrest. Thus, the authorities largely tolerated the students' actions, even attempts to enter the hallowed offices of Zhongnanhai and the Great Hall of the People, although they severely criticised the students in the state-run media.

On 18 and 19 April, several thousand students assembled at the Xinhuamen Gate of the leadership's enclave, clamouring for their demands to be met. These already included the declaration of top leaders' incomes and business interests. This was a direct reference to the use of 'guanxi' (relationships) and corruption by party officials to feather their own nests at the expense of the nation. 'What hope is there for China?', one poster asked. Some students wanted to put this and other questions straight to the leadership, in person. Their attempt to break into the compound to seek face-to-face dialogue with the government led to scuffles, but security guards foiled the attempt to 'storm the palace'. The Chinese authorities stressed that 'very few' people took part in this direct action, not all of them students and that no one was detained (*Beijing Review* 32 [26. 6. 1989]). This conflicted with foreign media reports such as the 'Voice of America', which claimed there were serious injuries and hundreds of arrests. (They were later criticised for 'irresponsible rumour-mongering', along with the BBC World Service reports.)

A 'sit-in' was quickly organised outside the gates in order to maintain pressure on the leaders at the centre of Chinese political life. The spontaneous leadership of a young Beijing Teachers' (normal) University student, Wu'Er Kaixi, was apparently largely responsible for this continued presence outside Zhongnanhai. The rest of the capital looked on with concern. They had been aroused by the corruption issue, a card played by the students in their favour. Money which could have been spent on better education, housing and public amenities was seen to be squandered by those in power. 'They are too busy holding banquets. We have to wait for the left-overs', was not an unusual sentiment expressed both before and during the Spring campaign.

The city centre was not the only scene of protest. In the northwestern district of Haidian, where several of the major universities are located (see Figure 1), posters were appearing on noticeboards and street

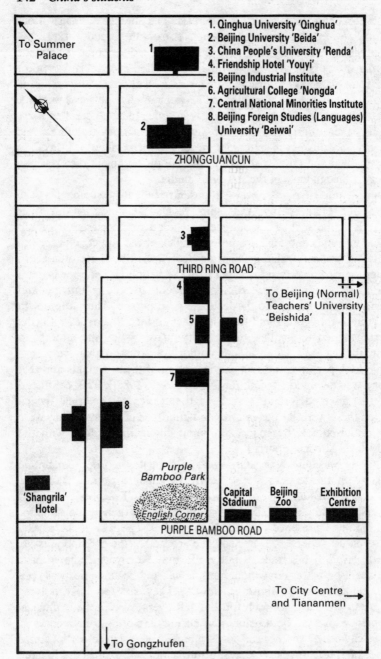

1. Qinghua University 'Qinghua'
2. Beijing University 'Beida'
3. China People's University 'Renda'
4. Friendship Hotel 'Youyi'
5. Beijing Industrial Institute
6. Agricultural College 'Nongda'
7. Central National Minorities Institute
8. Beijing Foreign Studies (Languages) University 'Beiwai'

To Summer Palace

ZHONGGUANCUN

THIRD RING ROAD

To Beijing (Normal) Teachers' University 'Beishida'

Purple Bamboo Park

English Corner

'Shangrila' Hotel

Capital Stadium   Beijing Zoo   Exhibition Centre

PURPLE BAMBOO ROAD

To City Centre and Tiananmen

To Gongzhufen

Figure 1   Sketchmap of Beijing's University Quarter

corners with political forums and speeches held by students, attempting to sway public opinion. Meanwhile, the numbers of wreaths and poems dedicated to Hu Yaobang continued to grow.

Demonstrations also took place in other cities, such as Shanghai. Slogans calling for democracy and an end to corruption echoed throughout the major urban areas, tentatively at first but then more confidently as support became more widespread. Government orders for the students to return to campuses and workers not to get involved were openly ignored. Over the successive weeks the young people would test their strength against the authorities, scoring a number of victories before the ultimate confrontation and crackdown.

The first significant breakthrough came during the weekend of the funeral service for Hu Yaobang in the Great Hall of the People. The large numbers of people who had gathered in the square during the preceding days were threatened with force by the authorities and there was even talk of martial law being imposed to clear the area, an option believed to be favoured by Deng Xiaoping. But the crowds did not move, risking the consequences of the first head-on confrontation with the party leaders. Armed police around the square did not prevent the build-up of students and a vigil began, planned to continue throughout the night of 21 April. In other parts of the city people came out in defiance of the authorities both to mourn Hu and show their contempt for threats of force.

This peaceful vigil was permitted to continue, an apparent victory for the students. The government must have been aware that any violence perpetrated by them would lead to further disturbances. In another move to placate the students, the ceremony was broadcast across Tiananmen, in the hope that afterwards they would all quietly return to their colleges. This strategy did not succeed because the students had other demands. They wanted Premier Li Peng to address them personally, and chanted, 'Li Peng, come out, come out!' His refusal to do so added further to their resentment. As a supreme example of 'guanxi', Li, the adopted son of Zhou Enlai, was mocked and criticised in posters and jokes being passed around the square. He was considered a 'coward' for not facing the students directly and a disgrace to the memory of Zhou Enlai, a highly respected former leader whose own death had been mourned in this same place thirteen years before.

Inside the Great Hall, the funeral ceremony for Hu was rushed through, further angering the protesters outside on the streets. Since no leader had dared to come out and speak with the students, they wanted to present a petition containing their major demands to a senior leader of the Central Party Committee, still hoping to initiate a dialogue about the serious issues at stake. Three student leaders, including Wu'Er Kaixi, were allowed to present their petition, which they did gracefully, kneeling on the steps of the Great Hall. This poignant scene moved many onlookers. Like their petition-bearing predecessors of 1895, they were bitterly disappointed. No one in authority came to take it from them; it was effectively rejected. Chai Ling, a student in the crowd, later said this rejection moved her sufficiently to want to take a more active role in the movement. She later became 'Commander in Chief' of the Tiananmen Square student headquarters.

The student mood was of hurt and rejection. 'They do not care about us', was the general sentiment. The leadership had turned their backs on the youthful demonstrators and possibly on the whole country. If they had accepted the petition, there is a possibility that the movement would have developed differently.

On the days immediately after the extraordinary funeral ceremony in Beijing, there were some violent scenes in other major cities. These were not welcomed by students who wished to keep their protests peaceful. In the ancient city of Xian, thousands of demonstrators went onto the streets to commemorate Hu's death and criticise the surviving leaders. Feelings ran high as anger and violence erupted, mostly directed against symbols of the state's authority, including government buildings and police vehicles. Several thousand mostly 'unemployed youth' it was claimed, went on a rampage, smashing and burning along the way. The local 'friendship store', where luxury goods can be purchased by officials with enough 'guanxi' to obtain the required Foreign Exchange Certificates,[3] was also a target. Armed police tried to restore order, but a number were injured before the situation was brought under control. The figures for injuries and arrests are not reliable.

In the southern city of Changsha, the 'worst outbreak of violence in forty years', according to the official Xinhua news agency (24. 4. 1989) took place with rioting and looting. A number of people were detained. Other cities also saw some form of protest action. These incidents of 'beating, smashing, grabbing and burning',[4] could easily have been turned into useful propaganda, invoking the 'ten black years' in order to discredit the students. The threat of 'da luan' (chaos) has always been dreaded in China and throughout history, autocratic regimes have used it to justify their suppression of political opposition or dissent. A great deal of brutality has been employed in the name of restoring law and order, with the communist regime being no exception. Fortunately for the student movement, the violent outbursts appeared relatively isolated incidents amidst the numerous peaceful actions taking place across the country.

In Shanghai, China's most populous city, around 10,000 students tried to converge on the People's Square to show solidarity with their Beijing colleagues. A large police presence prevented their entry, with the local party leader Jiang Zemin, determined to keep the city orderly. He would later be rewarded by Deng for his efforts. Also in Shanghai, there was controversy brewing about the *World Economic Herald* journal published in this city. The editor had permitted publication of articles sympathetic to the students and critical of the party's treatment of Hu Yaobang. This journal has had a history of 'dissidence'. Copies of the offending issues were confiscated by the police and the editor dismissed. This provoked angry responses from students and intellectuals who were demanding a free press in China. The Shanghai incident further underlined their cause and their desire for a fair hearing in the media.

Back in Beijing, a boycott of classes had been called in order to maintain the pressure on the government. Although their demands still included the rehabilitation of Hu Yaobang, the corruption-democracy related issues were becoming more crystallised. There was a certain vagueness about calls for 'more democracy', but others, like a free press outside of the state's control, were clearer. At Beida, the official student union was being dissolved in order to form an autonomous body to represent students. The 'All China Student Federation', along with the CYL had long been considered 'useless', good only for rubber-stamping party policies and arranging leisure activities. It was considered politically defunct with no power. The idea of an autonomous union was to have fair and powerful representation. Elections were called to select democratically the new representatives. On other campuses similar moves were underway, amidst rousing speeches and frantic *dazibao* writing. Collections were organised around the city for funds to set up a student newspaper which would publish the 'truth' about their campaign to counter the official media propaganda. Citizens and workers appeared to be donating freely.

The speed with which the young activists organised the boycott took many observers by surprise. Kelly writes, 'After the failures of 1986 and 1988, the student's ability to stage the moral dramatic street protest came as a shock' (Kelly 1990: 14). They had possibly discussed such action before, perhaps even laid contingency plans during many dormitory discussions on what was needed to reform China. But they never had the opportunity or daring to put them into action before. 'They just needed organising', claimed Wu'Er Kaixi, somewhat arrogantly. The party elders, however, could only be critical of this grassroots movement, with people organising for themselves rather than being directed from above.

Many lecturers at the affected universities such as Renda, Beida, Qinghua and Beishida, spoke out in favour of their charges. They agreed it was high time to bring out into the open the anxiety about the underfunding of education, the poor treatment of intellectuals and the growing despondency about China's future. A petition was being circulated among the university staff and many were adding their signatures. From young teachers to senior professors came messages of encouragement along with concern as the boycott was put into effect on 24 April. Some of the older academics remembered their own youth, when they suffered as a result of unfavourable party policies. From the 'Hundred Flowers' to the short-lived 'anti-bourgeois liberalism' campaign of 1987, they had experienced criticism and punishment. The firm stand taken by the younger generation appeared as a brave presentation of their case which had been repressed for so long. 'They will not be pushed around as we were', commented one middle-aged teacher I had spoken with earlier that year.

Others were more cautious and worried about the fate of their students. Reflecting on their own bitter experiences, they insisted the boycott could only bring trouble and advised the students not to challenge the great might of the Party. This was not a safe way to institute change, they believed. Few spoke in outright opposition to what was now seen as a pro-democracy campaign.

Both on and off campuses, students were busy with everything apart from their studies, now considered even more irrelevant and useless than before. They were organising and co-ordinating the largest pressure group in communist China's history and putting years of political study into practice. With leaflets to write and distribute, money to collect and discussion groups to lead, their time was fully occupied. At last, young intellectuals had found a prominent role to play in their country's development. As agitators for democracy, they believed they could rescue the motherland from the 'abyss of history', as one leaflet read. By showing the way to the masses of Chinese people and remonstrating about the mistakes of the leadership, the students could finally occupy their rightful place as social leaders after decades of obscurity and repression. They were in the midst of shaking off their 'victim' status and becoming the harbingers of the type of reform the government refused to undertake. The 'Democracy Wall' adage of 'No modernisation without democracy' was widely accepted.

Growing in confidence, some of the poster writers were openly critical of the leaders, Li Peng in particular, and there were already calls for him to 'xia tai', resign. Party Secretary Zhao Ziyang was treated carefully. Although probably as guilty as the others of misusing his position to further family business and financial interests, he was seen as more of a reformer and some hope was placed in him. The obvious absence of a new 'champion' was a sad reflection on the state of Chinese political life.

The best they could hope for, in realistic terms, was the reshuffling of people already in power, most of them over seventy, in order to facilitate further reforms and bring in some degree of democracy in the long term. Deng Xiaoping, like Mao Zedong before him, had effectively stamped out any real opposition to his strong hold over the party. Dissent had either been successfully incorporated or harshly repressed, even if it came from Deng's own hand-chosen favourites such as Hu Yaobang and later Zhao Ziyang. A poster at Beishida described him as, 'a man with a wolf's heart and a dog's tongue' (*Guardian* 25. 4. 1989). The system allowed for his supremacy and ultimate repression of anything considered as 'dissent'.

While free-market forces had been let loose in the economy, the ossified political structures remained largely intact. The party was to remain in control, the hardliners claiming that there was no other way to rule the vast dominions of China and keep the dreaded 'da luan' at bay. In fact, forty years of communist rule had ensured that there could be no alternative, no fledgeling parties to challenge the communists apart from the ineffective 'democratic parties' of the NPC, no autonomous pressure groups with aspiring politicians who could replace the ageing leaders, and no conception that there just might be another way of running the country. The students dared to disagree. Out of turn and without permission to do so, they were initiating a search for realistic alternatives which other social groups were joining in.

Deng and his colleagues were faced with a growing dissent they had neither instigated nor could control. Workers were putting up posters in Tiananmen Square supporting the students' ideas. Perhaps they would also go on strike and the leadership could thus be faced with a serious crisis. They needed to act to curtail the development of the student-led, pro-democracy movement.

THE IMPORTANCE OF THE *PEOPLE'S DAILY* EDITORIAL

At a meeting of the CPC on 24 April, top leaders discussed the crisis. Zhao Ziyang, the man who may have spoken in favour of the students, was conveniently on official business in North Korea. The inevitable outcome, therefore, could not be conciliatory towards the students but only more 'hardline'. The official view was clearly expressed in the *People's Daily* newspaper on 26 April: the students had to cease their activities or face the consequences. Couched in language more reminiscent of the 'class struggle' 1960s rather than the 'open door' 1980s, it talked of a 'counter-revolution' being plotted by a small 'handful' of 'hooligans' who were poisoning the students' minds with their anti-party propaganda. The fearsome reminder of the harsh side of the regime ran true to form, with its criticisms of 'bourgeois liberalism' and the weakening of the 'true' form of democracy which lay in the dictatorship of the proletariat. Only the Party could save China and not the rumour-mongering conspirators, who had to be stopped.

The editorial was threatening because it showed that the hardliners were maintaining the upper hand and were not about to compromise their power with more reform-minded party members let alone with the students. The pro-democracy movement was not viewed as a spontaneous outbreak of popular discontent but merely the work of a few conspirators. The students were not, therefore, responsible for the actions witnessed so far but could suffer the consequences if they did not return to their classes. It was hoped that this editorial would force them back into acquiescence.

The editorial aroused more contempt for the government and the students' resolve remained firm, if nervous. Talk of army movements around the capital appeared to support the threats of an imminent crackdown but these were not sufficient to end the class boycott. More speeches on the campuses rallied the students as well as the communal singing of China's national anthem and the communist anthem, (the 'Internationale'), which were to become the theme songs of this movement. They stressed their patriotism and denied charges of being counter-revolutionaries. The accusation that the students were 'unpatriotic' had really touched a raw nerve and they strongly rejected this label. In their eyes, they were the true patriots because they had the interests of the nation at heart. For this reason they could not end the movement but had to carry on, calling for democratisation of political structures and action to be taken against corruption. A free press would report fairly on their aims and not allow editorials like the one printed in the *People's Daily* on 26 April to misrepresent their case.

Sympathy appeared to be on the side of the students. Large numbers of intellectuals and teachers spoke in their favour and warned the government not to take drastic action. The workers were waiting on the sidelines, giving clear signals of support. What would the leaders do in the wake of this threatening editorial?

The harsh words were not matched with an iron fist, at least this time. Possibly due to wise counselling, inefficiency, an ongoing power struggle in the party or a combination of all these factors, there was no crackdown in April. The students took their disapproval of the editorial onto the streets, where they were greeted enthusiastically by Beijing citizens and workers. An estimated 150,000 people gathered in the university quarter on 27 April, while police attempted to cordon off the campuses to prevent further crowds amassing, but the human waves broke through almost effortlessly. The destination was over ten miles away: Tiananmen Square. The largest demonstration of the communist era in China was under way amidst a cheerful atmosphere on a bright spring day. 'The people just kept coming and coming'. remarked one observer of the sight, 'it was incredible'.

Television pictures transmitted across the world showed workers rushing out of their factories to greet the students, offering snacks and drinks or just a hand raised in support. 'We love the students!', onlookers shouted. 'We love the people', was the reply. Doctors and nurses ran out of their hospitals to meet the demonstrators, shouting encouragement and advice about not staying out in the sun for too long, and to drink plenty en route. If the government had shown signs of not caring about the students' welfare, the people of Beijing certainly compensated for it. The police simply had to give way to the flow of humanity they were supposed to be controlling. No violence, no fights and no crimes were reported. Tiananmen was reached easily and another victory over the leadership was won.

The old men in Zhongnanhai must have been taken aback by the massive and popular protest and the sheer affrontery of the student demonstrations. Other cities also saw student protests over the *People's Daily* editorial, but the focus was on Beijing where the Party leaders had agreed to hold talks with student representatives. There were many problems, however, as the government stressed the need for a 'calm' atmosphere and an end to the 'turmoil' caused by protests. Students naturally rejected the view that they were creating disorder. They wanted their own representatives from the newly formed autonomous student union to speak on their behalf at any meeting with party officials. There was doubt, however, about the wisdom of talks because they could be merely a ploy to distract the students and wear down their movement.

Heady with the success of the 27 April demonstration and mistrustful of the leadership's real aims, student representatives attempted to control the agenda of negotiations. The resulting attempts were televised, as insisted by student leaders, but the first real contact between the two sides was not a success. The government still refused to accept the students' own union as legal and would not permit them to meet with top officials like Li Peng. Some students dismissed the abortive talks as a 'media trick' with no substance. They were set to continue their actions with the important seventieth anniversary of 'May Fourth' only a few days away. The gestures made by the leaders did not go anywhere to meeting the student demands and only served to upset them still further. The half-hearted attempts at talks failed and the students left the Great Hall of the People to consider their next move.

8 The Beijing Spring

OVERVIEW

The unprecedented scenes in Beijing and other Chinese cities during April 1989 created even greater expectations for the seventieth anniversary of the historic 'May Fourth' movement. The students made sure they celebrated the day in their own way and used the occasion to advance their criticisms of the Li Peng government. Afterwards the direction of the student movement was unclear with different opinions put forward about what should be done. Several smaller demonstrations kept the campaign for democracy alive and in the public eye but a real turning point came with the start of a hunger strike at the time of President Gorbachev's arrival for the first Sino-Soviet summit in thirty years. The stakes were raised as Tiananmen was occupied by students and supporters, much to the embarrassment of the Chinese leaders. After Gorbachev had left China, Premier Li Peng attempted to crack down on the students by declaring martial law, but the incredible scenes which followed caused further loss of face. The people of Beijing poured onto the streets and repeatedly turned the army back, to protect the students and prevent the hardliners from having their way. After mass euphoria with millions of people demonstrating openly and even the press being 'free' for several days, the movement appeared to be over, but the ultimate conclusion was still unclear.

THE PATRIOTIC DEMOCRATIC MOVEMENT: PHASE TWO

1 May   International Workers' Day. Student leaders present an ultimatum to the government: proper dialogue or more demonstrations.

3 May   Zhao Ziyang calls for stability and moderation, but does not condemn the students. Leading intellectuals issue a declaration supporting the students.

4 May   The seventieth anniversary of 'May Fourth' marked by a large demonstration. Members of the autonomous student union hoist their flag onto the People's Monument. Zhao addresses the Asian Development Bank in the Great Hall and refers to some of the student demands as 'reasonable'.

10 May   Journalists sign a petition in favour of the pro-democracy campaign and a free press. Leading writers join in rallies in Beijing.

13 May   Thousands of students march to the square with hundreds sworn to go on hunger strike for democracy. 'Give me democracy or give me death', becomes a new slogan.

15 May   Arrival of Mikhail Gorbachev for the Sino-Soviet summit upset by the student occupation of the square. Welcoming ceremony shifted to the airport. Hunger strike attracts more volunteers. Workers and citizens join in the protest activities.

16 May   Further alterations to Gorbachev's itinerary because of the hunger strike. Up to 3,000 students now refusing food. Support becoming more vocal and open.

17 May   Gorbachev leaves for Shanghai, where he is also greeted by demonstrations. Beijing is in 'ferment' as the city authorities appear to lose control. Some hunger strikers in a critical condition.

18 May   Gorbachev leaves China. Protests in many major cities.

19 May   Over one million people on the streets of Beijing to demonstrate. Zhao Ziyang and Li Peng visit hunger strikers with Zhao apologising for coming 'too late'. Workers of the newly-formed autonomous union call for a general strike. Few people are at work.

20 May   Li Peng declares martial law in Beijing. Troops converge on the city, but are stopped by the capital's residents. A weekend of mostly peaceful confrontations between the PLA and the public. A news blackout is attempted. The hunger strike is called off by a narrow margin but students remain in the square. Demonstrations continue elsewhere.

The following week sees almost daily demonstrations.

'MAY FOURTH' REVISITED

The seventieth anniversary of 'May Fourth' was certain to have been a big event by any standard, but the escalating pro-democracy campaign added a greater degree of significance to the celebrations, which mark the birth of China's first modern-day student movement. There were different opinions among the student body about how best to mark the occasion and not all were agreed on holding another massive demonstration. Their basic demands, however, remained the same: a free press, free speech, democratic reforms, human rights, more expenditure on education, publication of top leaders' incomes and assets, elimination of corruption, the rehabilitation of Hu Yaobang and apologies to the students for the *People's Daily* editorial. How best to advance these safely and surely was now debated among the student groups.

There was much behind-the-scenes activity on both sides. The government stressed the need for calm and order as they prepared to receive important guests for the Asian Development Bank meeting. China needed to increase foreign investment and the leaders did not wish to 'lose face' in front of important visitors. But 'May Fourth' was imminent as well as the arrival of President Mikhail Gorbachev not long afterwards. Deng Xiaoping kept a low profile at this time but added to discontent with his uncompromising attitude and comments. He upheld his criticisms of Hu Yaobang and the students. He did not appear to take the attempts at negotiations with them seriously.

On the 'May Day' holiday, the student leaders presented the government with an ultimatum. This was taken from Beishida, one of the leading universities of the pro-democracy movement, to the NPC by students on bicycles. It contained twelve preconditions which needed to be met before real negotiations could begin between students and leaders. If a favourable response was not met by the deadline on 3 May, the 'largest demonstration the capital has ever seen', according to activist Wu'Er Kaixi, would take place. By presenting 'concrete demands', the students hoped for a 'concrete reply'.

1 May, International Workers' Day, passed by with pro-democracy activities continuing. Noticeable by their absence along Changan Avenue on May day were the 'four beards': Marx, Engels, Stalin and Lenin, whose portraits are annually erected to remind the capital's population of their political heritage. Only Chairman Mao whose portrait is there permanently, and Zhong Shan (Dr Sun Yatsen), the father figure of the first republic, were on display. This may have been due to the volatile situation in Beijing. Putting up the portraits might have sparked off more accusations of the government being deceitful, preaching socialism on one hand while practising corruption on the other. The nature of socialism with 'Chinese characteristics' was already a subject of heated debate. Consequently, the old portraits remained under wraps.

At this time, a group of leading scholars met at the request of a senior

Beida professor to discuss the situation with the students. The group wanted to appeal to the government to recognise the autonomous student union and accept their request for a dialogue. They believed the young people had the interests of China at heart and were not 'counter-revolutionaries'. Some of the participants wept, fearing the students would be meted out with the same type of recrimination they had known in their own lives with more problems for China if the leaders used force to squash the movement. They expressed their hopes about the possibilities raised by the students, but also gave voice to their anxieties, knowing quite well the nature of the communist state, which had shed blood before in the name of restoring 'order'.

In Shanghai a large demonstration took place on 2 May when about 70,000 students and supporters marched to the People's Square in the city centre. Official figures from Xinhua claim that only 6,000 participated (*Guardian*: 3. 5. 1989). Students occupied the river embankment (the Bund) where the local government offices are located and demanded to see Jiang Zemin. He was not a popular figure with the students because of a hardline approach which endeared him to the leaders in Beijing. The *World Economic Herald* was still closed down and the students were demanding that it be reopened as well as calling, more generally, for a free press in China.

The issue of press freedom was never far from the minds of those most directly affected by Party censorship, the journalists. On 3 May a group of around one hundred journalists met in the capital and decided to support the students. They wanted to be able to report freely and fairly on the extraordinary events happening in China at that time rather than carrying the party leadership's version. They joined in the students' 4 May demonstration, which took place after the failure to receive a satisfactory answer from the party leaders.

It did not turn out to be, as promised, the biggest demonstration ever seen in the capital, but it was still considerable with about 60,000 students marching to the square which they had 'taken' the week before. Beida, home of the original 'May Fourth' protesters, felt a certain sense of historical mission and proudly headed the procession, following in the footsteps of their predecessors along the familiar route. Crowds lined the streets, cheering and returning the students' slogans. The snaking mass of demonstrators easily broke through police lines, crying 'Long live democracy!' One banner read, 'We have waited seventy years, how much longer?' The national anthem and 'Internationale' were the main songs for the day. Food, drink, ice-cream and money were donated by the people along with offers of free bicycle repairs for those cycling the long distance to the city centre. Delegations from Hong Kong and

Taiwan joined their mainland compatriots along with the group of journalists. They shouted out about not wanting to 'tell lies' any longer.

Tiananmen belonged to the students once again and the marchers started to celebrate with singing, cheering, even dancing, while speeches were made through makeshift tannoy systems. Plenty of banners were carried to the square and leaflets, some making fun of the leadership which seemed unable to stem the tide of popular enthusiasm engendered by the pro-democracy movement let alone run the country. Students chatted, exchanging ideas and stories of their campaign activities, or just milled around in the sunshine, enjoying the feeling of success. A group of students climbed onto the Monument to the People's Heroes in the centre of the square and hoisted the blue and white flag of their illegal but popular union. Student leaders declared the demonstration as a 'great victory', but suggested that the class boycott be ended and other ways found of continuing the campaign. This was not a unanimous view and there were some jeers. The student movement had grown in size and divisions of opinion were unavoidable. During the lifetime of this spring campaign there would be several periods of disagreement on strategy which the government hoped would pull the whole thing apart. But even with divisions and different views, it remained as one movement.

On 4 May, however, nothing was going to spoil their special day as the celebrations continued in the square and later, back on the campuses. The colleges remained lively although the next move was not clear. Should the students back down while they were still ahead? Or, as others suggested, should they persist in their actions while onto a 'winning streak'? They seemed to be enjoying the support of the people, which the government could no longer command. Zhao Ziyang also offered tacit backing in a speech in the Great Hall where he was hosting the Asian Development Bank, by not condemning their actions and demands outright. Demonstrations were not a good way of achieving their goals, but some of their demands were 'reasonable', according to Zhao. While the students were in a good position, he was too but should they fall, they would bring him down as well.

Would they fall or be pushed by the hardliners in the party? To some extent this depended on what action, if any, they took next. The demonstrations had been a great success in attracting attention to the calls for democracy all over China. Some commentators felt that 4 May was the last massive turnout, suggesting that the movement was winding down. Some students did drift back to the classrooms after Tiananmen was deserted again, but the original 'May Fourth' movement did not end so abruptly and the indications were that this one would not do so either.

The next week was relatively quiet in comparison with the early phase of the movement, but several incidents reminded the people and party that it was not over. There was probably a core group of students at most major campuses who were committed to keeping the struggle for democracy alive until tangible results had been achieved, starting with the genuine dialogue insisted on by student leaders. But they could not carry on with massive demonstrations which ran the risk of serious confrontations and were tiring for the young people. Some decided to begin the summer vacation early since the term had been severely disrupted. Heading home early made sense for several reasons, notably the avoidance of possible recriminations by the authorities later on in the year.

The government hoped the students had spent their energy and would settle down since the arrival of Russian President Gorbachev was only days away. The leadership, keen to impress, did not wish to see the first Sino-Soviet summit in thirty years marred by students choking up the streets with banners and protests. For a number of reasons the Chinese wanted to put on a good show and let their former allies witness the 'miracle' of economic development that reform had brought about. They did not want their problems to be put on public display. The Chinese officials were also planning to increase trading and financial deals. Signs of social unrest could endanger future agreements and cause economic setbacks. The students could ruin the plans and spoil the image the party leaders were seeking to put across during Gorbachev's visit. The world's media would also be watching events with interest and any 'loss of face' would be broadcast all over the globe.

The government were quite aware, on the other hand, of the appeal of the Russian leader to young Chinese intellectuals, which contrasted sharply with their own low standing. The political reforms initiated by the charismatic President included limited but free elections and this was known to the Chinese. Russia had gone some way towards democracy: why not China? Impressed by these moves towards reforming the Stalinist structures in the neighbouring communist state, the students considered Gorbachev as a leader worthy of respect. The old Long March veterans running China would not consider similar reforms and appeared as old-fashioned and out-of-touch with what other communist states were doing politically. Economic reforms were not enough on their own. To the students, Deng Xiaoping looked particularly 'past it' compared to Gorbachev and his dynamic style of statesmanship. 'Why don't we have such a leader?', complained some young people, wishing their country were in the hands of younger, more open-minded politicians.

If the students turned out to welcome Gorbachev in some way other than according to the official programme, it would be highly embarrassing to the Chinese, especially Deng, who had put a lot of effort into bringing the summit about. It was to be the 'jewel' in his 'crown', but already there were danger signals, with the social unrest caused first by Hu Yaobang's death and then by student demonstrations. Scare tactics had apparently been unsuccessful and attempts at negotiations had not met with the approval of the young people. But top party officials were adamant that the power structures were to remain intact. The situation was therefore at an *impasse*.

To show they had not abandoned their struggles, a group of activists organised a 'bicycle demonstration' through the streets of Beijing, aimed specifically at focusing attention on the lack of freedom in the mass media. Several thousands cycled to the offices of the country's leading newspapers, magazines and broadcasting stations, calling for fair reporting on their actions and demands. This followed a day of action by a group of leading journalists who presented a petition to the government calling for open debate about censorship and the general restrictions on the Chinese media. The Shanghai-based World Economic Herald was still a contentious issue. The treatment of its editor was not considered acceptable in a modern society but more fitting to the 'bad old days' of class struggle. His reinstatement was a specific demand, among many others, made by a collection of media personnel. In the bicycle tour of Beijing, students were joined by a group of leading writers and poets. All were braving official criticism and a possible backlash later on, part of the familiar pattern in the treatment of intellectuals in communist China. They could easily be labelled as 'bourgeois', suffering from westernisation and in need of a dose of Marxist-Leninist-Maoist thought, the ideological medicine they are usually forced to take. But they persisted in their calls for artistic and academic freedom.

The day after the 'bike demo' there was another demonstration in Beijing, not directly related to the students' pro-democracy movement but possibly inspired by it. About 4,000 Muslims marched from the predominantly Muslim sector of the city near the universities to Tiananmen Square to protest over a book labelled as China's *Satanic Verses* (a reference to the Rushdie affair). A socio-anthropological study on sexual customs of ethnic minorities in China was seen as insulting and degrading to those of the Islamic faith. The protesters wished to see it banned immediately. The sight of students coming out *en masse* over the previous weeks had possibly inspired them publicly to draw attention to their own grievances. The students' calls for democracy and free speech were taken on board with ironic consequences here because the book was eventually banned.

It is interesting to consider this example of minority protest and how it related to the majority Han Chinese students' aims. Respecting the rights of the minority groups would be in line with calls for human rights and democracy but go against the spirit of patriotism expressed by the students, who were proud of their vast motherland extending from Tibet to Taiwan, and from Hong Kong to Outer Mongolia. Some of the minority groups felt that they could only gain true freedom and human rights through independence from China, Tibet being a case in point here.[1] Devolution of power in the Chinese state was probably antagonistic to the ideas of the 'patriotic democrats', but this is a problem to which they simply did not give serious thought. The soon-to-arrive Gorbachev was having difficulties himself with the issue of nationalities and minorities and probably could not have offered any advice if it was called for. The students at the time were more concerned with general political concepts centred around the notion of democracy, and as the day for the visit drew closer another opportunity to state their case presented itself.

The streets of Beijing and other cities had been relatively quiet since 4 May but the campuses were still alive with pro-democracy discussion and activity. It was not clear whether another large-scale demonstration would greet the Russian delegation or a smaller event. What transpired was probably more effective than anything else carried out by the students.

THE STUDENT HUNGER STRIKERS WELCOME THE RUSSIAN PRESIDENT

It was decided that a group of several hundred students would go on hunger strike. They would refuse food until the leaders agreed to a genuine dialogue according to the preconditions laid down two weeks before. The stakes in this struggle for political change were suddenly and dramatically raised.

Up to this point, no lives had been lost and the numbers of injuries sustained were very few, especially when considering the large numbers of participants in the mainly peaceful protests. The possibility of just one dead student, an instant martyr for the struggle, made this move a very serious one indeed. The government would be deemed responsible for any deaths resulting from the hunger strike and the consequences of this would be unpredictable. They would have 'blood on their hands', ultimate proof of their lack of concern about the nation's youth. The hunger strike was, therefore, a dangerous but clever move by the student leaders, most of whom would be refusing to take food themselves. But initially there were few volunteers for this action. Organisers at Beida and Beishida, two of the most active campuses, managed to find several hundred willing participants after emotive appeals especially by Chai Ling, the 23-year-old female student who was already seen as one of the most influential leaders of the movement.

On Saturday 13 May the young volunteers ate their 'last meal', a special, lovingly prepared dinner made by teachers and fellow students. It was essentially a ritual. Chinese meals are often full of symbolic significance and meanings, and their ritual aspects have been studied by western social anthropologists. This last meal before the hunger strike was particularly significant in every way. Some of the students could not eat the food before them, according to Chai Ling who later tearfully recounted the event. Many were scared that the authorities might crack down before they could get the hunger strike under way. They could die at the hands of soldiers rather than from starvation. Their youth - some were only twenty years old - added further pathos to this occasion as the struggle for democracy entered a new emotive and dangerous phase.

After the meal, they put on the white headbands symbolising self-sacrifice, complete with the Chinese characters for 'hunger strike' (*jue shi*) and marched to Tiananmen, accompanied by many thousands of supporters. In the square, they set up a makeshift encampment and prepared to wait, without food, for as long as it would take to move the government from its uncompromising position.

News of the hunger strike brought crowds into Beijing, many of them sympathetic to the students and deeply touched by their gesture of self-sacrifice. Their standing in the community rose still further as the 'heartless' politicians ignored the pleas of the young people made on behalf of the nation. 'They are only children', said some of the on-lookers, many in tears. Cast into the role of dependents, no longer students so much as children of the motherland, demanding democracy for everybody, they were viewed in a sympathetic and protective light. The citizens of Beijing were more than willing to offer assistance to the young people and in taking their side, came to despise the corrupt government led by Li Peng even more. This protective attitude persisted after the hunger strike had ended and in part contributed to the pledge of the citizens to prevent the students from being hurt by the army. Feelings were aroused and deep sentiments touched by the student hunger strike. Political argument gave way more to emotive appeals, some commentators would say emotional 'blackmail', in the effort to influence the government's position with regard to political reform and the corruption issue. 'They should listen to the young people before someone dies', was a common view. But would they?

It appeared not. Throughout the first night of the hunger strike more people converged on the square offering help and solidarity. More students joined in, refusing to eat until top officials came out and addressed their demands. Factories sent delegations of workers with money and words of encouragement. Residents sent representatives from their blocks with drinks and messages of encouragement. Tiananmen once again became the centre of attention as an occupation got under way which would last until the troops moved in on 3 June. By the following evening, an estimated 100,000 people were packed into the area with flags and banners across the length and breadth of the square. 'Give me democracy or give me death', read one banner, in English as well as Chinese for the benefit of the many foreigners around the world who were watching the developments. Reporters sent to Beijing to cover the Sino-Soviet summit found themselves in the midst of another historic event, with China's youth taking on the old men in power. Student speakers at the base of the monument, which became the headquarters of the encampment, appealed for massive support to legitimise their campaign. They were still asking for Li Peng to come out and address them. He remained inside.

The Chinese leadership were busy making their own appeals. The square should be cleared. 'Good citizens' of Beijing should do their 'patriotic duty' by returning home quietly. The forthcoming international summit had to take place in an atmosphere of order and calm, not the turmoil being created by the hunger-striking students, The pleas fell on deaf ears. Sympathy was with the young people.

There were some attempts to defuse the tense situation, but talks between student representatives and government officials were no more successful than on previous occasions. No real gestures of conciliation or compromise came from the authorities and the students were not willing to dilute their preconditions for dialogue. Consequently, with the Russian leader already on his way, Tiananmen remained in a state of occupation. Beijing was described as being in a 'ferment', an adjective which would be used repeatedly over the next few weeks.

Armed police were moved into the streets near the square and the Great Hall of the People to seal off the area. This tactic had the effect of keeping people in as well as preventing others from joining the crowds already gathered there. The leadership of the most populous country in the world appeared to be in a state of siege. By Monday 15 May, the third day of the hunger strike, there had been no forceful attempts to move the students. The organisers arranged for some of the encampment to be shifted in order to make way for the visiting statesman, but the official reception planned to take place in the square, along with an inspection of the military guard of honour, was rearranged for the airport. This was the first of a number of embarrassing itinerary alterations caused by the student occupation and hunger strike.

Thousands of people waited eagerly for Gorbachev's arrival, some carrying his picture or placards bearing a greeting. The city centre was choked by the crowds: few were at work. The students took charge of traffic and crowds, with their own stewards keeping some sort of order. Members of the traffic police had capitulated to the rule of the young and joined the spectators instead, some openly supporting the hunger strike. The students were determined not to give the authorities any reason for describing the situation they had caused as 'da luan', chaos, although there had already been references to 'turmoil' in the official media. They recognised the need to keep the demonstration peaceful and orderly at all times. Their own stewards managed to maintain a semblance of order on the Beijing streets despite the massive numbers of people on the move, mainly heading in the direction of the square.

The official entourage had to manoeuvre around the occupied area and the honoured guests entered the Great Hall through a back door, hardly a fitting welcome for the first Russian premier on Chinese soil for nearly three decades. The students seemed to feel apologetic about this unsuitable welcome. The leaders felt angry and embarrassed. The crowds cheered Gorbachev, but gave a cool reception to their own leaders. The gulf between them was growing, but the Chinese authorities could do nothing to take their revenge for this major loss of face before Gorbachev. The first day of his visit was certainly historic in more ways than one, with Beijing in a state of 'orderly chaos'.

Some of the hunger strikers were already suffering the strain of being at the centre of all this activity as well as feeling the effects of lack of food and the heat. The constitution of the average student in China is not strong because of his poor diet and living conditions. Even a few days without food could lead to medical problems, especially under aggravated conditions such as in Tiananmen at that time. Consequently, some students, exhausted and weak, gave up their fast on medical advice, but there was no shortage of volunteers to take their place. Other hunger strikers agreed to receive treatment before resuming the fast. The sound of wailing ambulance sirens became a new addition to the existing cacophony of sounds around the square as sick students were ferried to nearby hospitals. A few weeks later this eerie sound would be heard again, in the early hours of 4 June as wounded students and people were rushed to the crowded hospitals, victims not of the hunger strike but of the army. In May, it was hoped that there would be no martyrs and a concerted effort was made to prevent any young people from dying.

On Tuesday 16 May, the crowds swelled as spontaneous acts of support for the hunger strike broke out all over China. Gorbachev's visit was being eclipsed. The planned wreath-laying ceremony at the People's Monument was cancelled because the students were in the way and the Forbidden City was also impossible to tour. The Gorbachevs missed the opportunity to see the former home of China's imperial rulers. Widely broadcast pictures showed Deng Xiaoping losing his grip at a state banquet, dropping food from his chopsticks. Zhao Ziyang cleared himself of any responsibility for the crisis by telling Gorbachev that Deng was still the supreme leader who had political power therefore, by implication, he was to blame for the scenes on the streets which obviously upset the visiting Russian leader. The students were slightly disappointed that he did not speak out in their favour. Gorbachev attempted to be diplomatic in an extremely difficult situation and the only reference he made to the crisis was a warning against being too 'hotheaded'.

Chinese intellectuals were less circumspect and came out in favour of the students. On 16 May, a group of around 3,000 leading figures issued a declaration describing the student demands as 'legitimate'. Numerous teachers also demonstrated their support for the young people even though they were very worried about the eventual outcome. The major universities sent their school buses to the square with supplies and supporters, but there were attempts by the authorities to persuade the hunger strikers to give up their dangerous action. Scenes of tearful teachers with young students looking sick and weak were televised worldwide.

Several thousands of young people were now refusing food and some even water. Many were hospitalised. Gorbachev had walked right into a divided Chinese Communist Party and a popular protest movement. Party officials attempted to ease the situation by visiting the hospitalised hunger strikers. They shook hands and offered their sympathy, but the sick students still had the same messages for the leaders: something must be done to control corruption and political reforms were essential. They would not be dissuaded from their course of action. Several student leaders, looking dishevelled and exhausted, were invited into the Great Hall of the People to talk with Premier Li Peng. This was an unusual act on behalf of the government, but many students were suspicious of their real intentions, claiming it was just another 'media trick'. It was an unusual meeting with the unkempt student leaders, Wu'Er Kaixi for example, still in his pyjamas and toting round a saline drip, sitting in the stately reception room of the Great Hall where Gorbachev had been received. But once again there was no real dialogue. Li Peng adopted a somewhat haughty attitude, telling the students they should give up and return to the campuses. They walked out in disgust with Wu'Er addressing Li Peng in less than respectful tones, telling him they came on their own accord, not at his behest and anyway, he was 'too late'. Wu's strident individualistic manner may not have been supported by all the students, but he was a popular represent- ative. His behaviour in the Great Hall probably sealed his fate: he was to become an 'enemy of the people'.

The hunger strike was set to continue with antagonism and mistrust mounting on both sides. Beijing was in the grip of the 'hunger strike fever'. Hardly anyone was at work and hundreds of thousands were on the streets. The student stewards were doing their best to control the crowds and traffic, making way for the continual stream of ambulances ferrying the critically sick to the hospitals. The cries for dialogue, democracy and freedom were growing louder. Ordinary citizens and workers, once wary of becoming involved with anything not organised by the party, were active in demonstrations, rallies, slogan shouting and poster writing. The media came out in favour of the students who, after all, spoke on their behalf as well. Although journalists and other person- nel were restricted in what they could say about the hunger strike and general situation in Beijing, for several days there was relative freedom in reportage. The demonstrations could not be ignored and scenes from Tiananmen were broadcast in the news bulletins along with reports in the newspapers. This was also unprecedented in communist China.

Interviews with tearful mothers were shown on the CCTV news, a clear expression of where the television reporters' sympathy lay. 'The length of the broadcasts was extended to an hour or more and footage from the square made it clear that, partly as cause and partly as consequence of the coverage, support for the strike was mushrooming' (*Article Nineteen*, 1989: 54). The Party appeared to be losing its control over the important media organs and their own power could only be weakened as a result. The political crisis deepened as the top leaders such as Deng and Li, Yuan Mu, Hu Qili and Qiao Shi as well as Zhao Ziyang, attempted to undertake 'damage control' at the Sino-Soviet summit. But all over China, there were protests and hunger strikes.

It was doubtful that these grassroots campaigns for more freedom and democracy could continue once Gorbachev had left China. The hardliners in the government were angry, obviously waiting for their guest to leave before acting to restore order. The Russians left a capital in 'turmoil' for Shanghai, where they were also greeted by demonstrations and a sit-in. There was rampant speculation about what would happen when they finally left on the Thursday. It was rumoured that Deng was going to step down and the reformers in the party take over. Others pointed to the build-up of troops near the capital and Deng's reminder that power came from the barrel of a gun.

The Gorbachevs were probably as pleased to leave China as their hosts were relieved to have them out of the way so that the political crisis could be dealt with. China was at a turning point of reform or repression; it was difficult to imagine any middle road. The students in Tiananmen were euphoric about their success in capturing a worldwide audience for their demands, but also fearful of the immediate consequences. The hunger strike continued, indeed it could have gone on indefinitely as long as participants agreed to receive medical help, but the government was unlikely to allow the sacred ground of Tiananmen to be furthered 'abused' by the students and determined not to lose any more face internationally. The situation in Beijing was reaching an unpredictable climax.

THE DECLARATION OF MARTIAL LAW

Friday 19 May arrived with unkempt and exhausted students sleeping rough in the square. At dawn, Premier Li Peng and Party Secretary Zhao Ziyang went down to address the students. At last, Li went among the students on their 'own' ground. It was another gesture rather than an act of commitment or compromise. Li was curt and non-committal, telling the students that they should go home now. He appeared unmoved, almost embarrassed by the scenes in the square and did not stay long. Zhao, on the other hand, appeared genuinely sorry, apologising for not coming earlier. His famous words, 'I've come too late', were proven correct. This was his last appearance in public. His tears were probably due in part to the realisation that the hardliners would soon be in control and he along with the students had little chance of winning the argument for political reform.

After the visit, about one million people again took to the streets of Beijing calling for Li and Deng to resign and expressing support for the hunger strike. 'Save the children! Save the nation!', people chanted. From road sweepers to policemen, the feeling seemed to be in favour of the students, who were still trying to keep order in the city. It was another day of protest. The student leaders held a vote on whether to continue the hunger-strike tactic. By a narrow margin, it was decided to call it off for the time being because of the deteriorating situation. This was not an entirely popular decision and there were some differences in opinion about the next move. The occupation of the square, however, continued.

In the early hours of Saturday morning, at a specially convened party congress, a grim-faced Li Peng declared martial law in parts of the capital. He talked of the 'turmoil' and 'chaos' created by the students and the threats to the party and the nation. A dangerous 'handful of conspirators' had stirred up trouble which most citizens, he claimed, wished to see ended. The situation posed a threat to national security. He was backed by senior party member and Long March veteran Yang Shangkun, who headed the army. Other elderly officials from the Long March era, deemed to have retired years before, were brought out, some in wheelchairs, to applaud the declaration. The hardliners had clearly won the power struggle with the Deng-Li-Yang 'faction' in control. Zhao Ziyang was conspicuous by his absence.

On hearing Li's speech broadcast across Tiananmen through the government loudspeakers, the students booed and jeered. They were still calling for the resignation of a leader they had come to despise. Fear, however, quickly descended during the night since most people believed the troops would be sent in to clear the square by force. Groups of students and onlookers drifted away, scared for their lives, but thousands stayed. Some of them began writing 'yishu', the Chinese equivalent to a last will and testament, believing this to be their final few hours alive. The authoritative voices over the loudspeakers advised them to go home for safety's sake. Instead the student 'hardliners' sang the 'Internationale' and China's national anthem repeatedly. They appeared prepared to sacrifice themselves in this struggle for democratic reform and human rights and all the other demands made over the preceding month of protest. Onlookers feared a 'bloodbath' and attempted to persuade the young people to leave. 'It's our duty. We have to stay, even if it means death', was often the reply. Whatever happened, they would remain non-violent, maintaining a peaceful campaign. But the workers and citizens of Beijing had pledged to protect them, if necessary. It soon became obvious that the students needed help.

As the PLA troops moved in from the outlying districts of Beijing, residents rushed out to set up roadblocks using buses, trucks and dustbins. They then assaulted the soldiers with arguments in favour of the students and against the use of force. 'Don't hurt the students!', was the general message and some of the perplexed young soldiers, who had little idea of what had been going on in the capital, were won over. Tearful old ladies pleaded with them to go back and young children were sent forward with food and drink. The guns held by the confused soldiers, many of them no older than the students they were supposed to move, seemed irrelevant as the pro-democracy movement took yet another extraordinary turning. 'People power' had been set loose on the streets. Only a few scuffles were reported throughout the city where at most major intersections, large army convoys were stopped literally in their tracks. It was a sight any follower of Gandhi would have been proud of. The Chinese people also felt relieved as they prevented the army from getting anywhere near the students and the night passed into a jubilant, if uncertain day. The dawn deadline, to clear the square by 5 a.m., passed but the occupation continued. Li Peng's attempt to enforce 'his' martial law had been foiled by the citizens he claimed were so eager to see a return to normality.

Over the weekend, a strange stalemate ensued as the people continued to block the army. Not one shot was fired. Some troops even drifted back to their barracks with their commander's blessing. The army itself seemed to be divided and some were listening to the students' arguments rather than the government's.

There seemed to be a unity among the people that had been absent for decades. 'We all had the same mind, the same idea', an elderly Beijinger later told me when looking back over the first few days of martial law. 'No one told us what to do. We just went out onto the streets to stop the army. The party no longer controlled us', she said. 'I was on the barricade we put up near here all night', she said proudly. 'When the alarm was raised by banging dustbin lids and shouting "the army is coming", we all went out to protect the students'. Asked why she and the other residents all took this risk, breaking martial law and putting themselves in the line of fire, if there were any shooting, this old woman declared, 'Because the students are great! They surely are the hope of China. We love them'. She, along with thousands of other Beijing citizens, had been touched by the actions of the young people and in fact they agreed with many of their demands. Their patriotism had put the 'corrupt Li Peng government to shame'. This old lady had seen many things in her long life, but this was something 'special', I was told, as she continued with tears in her eyes. 'We all love the students'.

Outside of Beijing, there was also opposition to the attempt to impose martial law. Demonstrations and sit-ins took place in Shanghai, Nanjing and Wuhan, where martial law was also declared briefly after students blockaded the important Changjian River bridge. Troops were stopped in Shanghai. Even relatively conservative Guangzhou, the economic trendsetter in China, saw thousands of young people out on the streets demanding democracy. The whole country appeared to be the scene of a popular, peaceful revolution, but it was not clear who could replace the leadership of Deng and Li, if they should fall from power.

Wan Li, the NPC chairman, widely seen as a 'liberal', cut short his visit to the States to return home, amid speculation that he would form a new government. He was declared 'ill' on arrival in Shanghai, however, and taken out of circulation. Zhao Ziyang had still not reappeared, in spite of calls by the demonstrators to bring him back and dismiss Li Peng. 'People power' might be ruling the streets, but not the corridors of political power. The doors were still firmly closed and the hardliners had the upper hand in the party.

A whole week of martial law passed by with military impotence and a lack of clear direction from the besieged leadership. For several days, up to a million people marched, cycled or rode on commandeered buses and trucks along the Beijing streets, usually converging on the square. All shouted the now familiar slogans of the campaign or made up their own. A general feeling of support for what the students had started was expressed boisterously and cheerfully, accompanied by song and dance. The citizens had seen off the martial-law troops using words not weapons and the government had been verbally attacked time and time again in ever stronger terms. Li Peng's attempt to bring the situation under his control had seemingly failed, therefore it was believed he had to listen to the demonstrators and talk with the student leaders. Messages of support came from Chinese people the world over as well as from compatriots in nearby Hong Kong and Taiwan.

After a week of this, when probably half of Beijing was hoarse with shouting and discussing politics well into the night, Deng Xiaoping and his chosen deputies had still given no indication that they were prepared to alter their course and put China back onto the road of modernisation and democratisation. Deng had actually been keeping a low profile during this week, an ominous sign of what might take place in the near future.

China was still on the 'brink' and no one could say for sure what was about to happen next. This was still a matter of speculation. I decided to leave for Beijing to see for myself what would transpire during the final stage of the patriotic democratic movement.

DEMORALISATION OR CONSOLIDATION AMONG THE STUDENTS?

From reading the newspapers aboard a Beijing-bound flight on Saturday 27 May, I learned that the student movement was in its final throes and would soon be over. There would be nothing much for me to see according to the foreign correspondents' reports and like the unfortunate Zhao Ziyang, I would arrive in Tiananmen 'too late'. I planned, therefore, to gather first-hand accounts of what had happened, how students and ordinary people had acted and felt during the period of the biggest popular upheaval in communist China. That would be gratifying enough in itself even if there were no student encampment left to see. I could assess the situation for myself in the immediate aftermath of the hunger strike and martial law declaration.

Looking at the newspaper photographs, it seemed that this particular day had arrived like a huge, collective hangover in Beijing. The street party was over but the communist party was still intact. The student expressions captured on film seemed to be asking, 'What has it all been for? What has been achieved by all the excitement and infectious behaviour?' The pictures of dishevelled students sleeping on mounds of tatty bedding and clothes amidst piles of rubbish in the square gave a sense of sobering up after a 'good time'. Everyone had let their hair down, had lots of fun and no-one gave a damn about tomorrow. But it had arrived and, outwardly, nothing had changed in China. The hard-liners in the government refused to budge from their position. The *People's Daily* editorial of 26 April attacking the students still stood, as did Deng's statement that a little bloodletting was not a serious matter in the restoration of law and order. The dialogue that the students campaigned for had never taken place.

The reports told of the students being 'demoralised' because of their failure to bring about any substantial change and the prospect of their movement fading into oblivion. Throughout the history of the spring campaign, the foreign media had portrayed the students in a number of ways according to the predominant image of the day: now as heroes, spoilt, privileged children, brave warriors, neglected waifs, would-be martyrs, well-disciplined and responsible young adults, naive and idealistic dreamers and now as demoralised youth who expected too much, too soon. Some accounts spoke of them 'idolising' the west, especially the USA, and having no clear thoughts on the most suitable version of democracy for China. They were 'confused', it was claimed. Like many media images, however, an element of truth mingles with the over- simplifications necessary to put across a clear message to the public and to make a 'good story'. By drawing upon my recent contact and experience with this particular social group, I had been attempting to judge all the way through the movement what was really in the minds of the students, what their aims and moods were. My reflections sometimes led me to reject aspects of the media reportage.

It is true that they may have been naive to dare to think they could take on the overwhelming power of the state, backed as it is by the military. Idealism tinged with a little romanticism for past heroic struggles was also omnipresent, but such is the stuff revolutionary movements are made of. As a driving force it worked well. There had been nothing concrete achieved in political terms, but the mass campaign, beginning as it did from a chance occurrence, had inspired and mobilised the Chinese people in a manner unseen before under communism. Mao Zedong had millions of youths out on the streets and trekking across the country at the height of the Cultural Revolution, but that was a top–down movement, led by a highly charismatic and powerful leader. The students in 1989 had instigated a grassroots movement outside party control and influence. Officials could only look on in despair or join in, as some had done, breaking all precedents and rules. This surely was a major victory in itself.

Their autonomous union, classified as illegal by the authorities, had organised and co-ordinated more collective action in a few weeks than its official counterparts had done in years. It had also set an example for other groups struggling to find an independent voice. For several days in May, the media had been relatively free, with journalists and television presenters refusing to censor the news. An Autonomous Workers' Federation had also been set up with different groups of workers eager to join and put forward their views on Chinese political and economic problems. There was the possibility of this organisation spreading to other cities and establishing links with trade unions overseas. All these developments were of significance even if short-lived. A precedent had been set which would be hard for the government to erase from people's minds no matter how much 'ideological work' they carried out.

I suspected, therefore, that the description of 'demoralisation' was another media exaggeration. The students were probably by this time tired, weary and not too healthy, but I expected them to keep a sense of achievement about their movement rather than return to their former 'it's useless, nothing can be done' attitude. If the movement really was over, the students would have to swallow their pride and retreat from the square in a dignified manner, even though none of their demands had been considered. I wondered how they could do this, if indeed they would cease their occupation, as I drew closer to China.

9   One week in Beijing

OVERVIEW

Once in Beijing, I was immediately caught up in the pro-democracy 'fever'. The young taxi driver and his friend who touted for fares outside the airport could hardly stop talking about the students and demonstrations as we drove into Beijing. Both were very animated, explaining how they had joined in, giving up several days' work (and money) to support the students because the movement was something 'special'. We even took a special detour via Tiananmen so I could see for myself what was left of the student occupation. 'You should have come before. It was really big', they told me. I was to hear this statement many times during the course of the final week of the 'patriotic democratic movement', which will be described in this chapter. I hope to portray some of the sights, sounds and emotions of those last days, from the unveiling of the students' 'Goddess of Democracy', right up to the days after the brutal military crackdown which resulted in such a tragic loss of life in Beijing and of hope throughout China.

JOURNEY TO SEE A GODDESS

The historic and somewhat incredible events of Beijing's spring were soon described by many Chinese people keen to tell me what I had missed. I listened for hours to stories of 'people power' and demonstrations, gaining valuable insight into the movement. The strength of emotion had obviously been quite overwhelming for the Beijing citizens, who had supported the students and their demands. Beijing was not the same as it was when I had left earlier in the year and people's attitudes had changed. During one conversation a CCTV news bulletin came on. 'Li Peng's news. We don't listen to it anymore', I was told. The official reports of what was happening in China were dismissed as propaganda.

The dark figure of Li dominated the news broadcast, wearing what I called his grey martial-law outfit. Since the declaration of martial law, he had not been seen wearing his usual western-style suit. 'Mao suits' were back in fashion. When I commented that clothes were matching the political regression, people laughed but I could see my companions were exhausted after the events of the past few weeks.

Before leaving, I had been told the students were building a statue for Tiananmen Square which ought to be seen. 'Something will happen because of it', they said. I was also warned to be careful. 'Things are not so safe now. It is a critical time'. I departed with these words in mind.

Early next morning, Tuesday 30 May, I cycled in the direction of Tiananmen. Remnants of posters could be seen on walls outside colleges and work units with small groups of people gathered on street corners holding impromptu discussions. The scenes looked very different from the massive demonstrations of the previous week and there was an air of normality in the city. Many people were back at work and the student-led movement seemed to be over, for the time being at least. The building of the statue I had been advised to see was possibly the final public action of the democracy campaigners.

On Fuxingmen, one of Beijing's main roads which leads into Changan Avenue and eventually Tiananmen Square, there were more posters and people. Pinned or pasted to trees, lampposts and walls, the posters were an obvious channel of communication between students and the public, an alternative to 'Li Peng's news'. Cyclists on their way to work dismounted to read any bulletins posted up, while those with more time on their hands, such as the old men, quietly discussed the major issues. Now that the large crowds had dissipated, people were feeling more vulnerable. Consequently there were furtive glances over shoulders and a wariness in case plain-clothes police were around, taking note of who was reading the posters and their strong criticisms of the government. Some of the *dazibao* I briefly read were simplistic rallying cries, others offered more detailed and sophisticated arguments in favour of the pro-democracy movement (see Appendix for translations). They were all strongly opposed to Li Peng and his 'faction'.

The journey to the square took me past Zhongnanhai, where a large crowd of student supporters and general sightseers were sprawled across the road. Spectators were taking photographs of this pocket of resistance and I went to take a look for myself. A large white banner with bold characters reading, 'It is not the government who decides for the people but the people who decide for the government', was strung across the entrance to the leaders' special enclave, where six weeks before Hu Yaobang had died and now Zhao Ziyang was possibly under house arrest. A group of about twenty students were camped out by the entrance, their disorder and unkempt appearance contrasting sharply with that of the soldiers sitting by the famous doorway, uniformly crosslegged. Sleeping-bags, clothes and food were scattered across the small cordoned-off compound. Like the sight of Tiananmen Square the day before, this was indeed a strange scene for me to witness, accustomed as I was to the normal orderliness of this hallowed place. The occupation, now in its second month, was a daring one. The most powerful leaders in China lived and worked within the walls of Zhongnanhai, yet the students had the audacity to sleep on their doorstep, demanding that they come out to address them face to face.

The crowds of onlookers strained at the ropes, but were held back by young stewards; the students were taking the responsibility for their own movement. 'Are you a reporter?', they asked when I passed over some drinks and food and I was beckoned over the rope to talk to the students. I declined at first, aware of the video camera pointed in our direction, recording all the proceedings. I felt in a slight dilemma, but quickly resolved this and accepted the invitation to talk with people who had been an important part of this student movement. Stepping over the rope gave rise to a burst of applause from the crowd. They were slightly disappointed that I was not a journalist. They were eager to talk to foreign correspondents because they thought it would help their cause if the whole world knew about their campaign. Under the glare of the crowds, I tried to discover the reasons for their occupation and how long they were prepared to stay. Some of them had been there since the beginning and would not leave until the leaders had emerged to speak to them. They wanted to talk freely about corruption among the party officials and the future of China's development. 'This government is too corrupt. . . .'We love our country', they said. They were prepared to give up their own future for the good of the nation, they explained, and had come here to make their views known. I commented on the miserable conditions they had placed themselves in, but I was told they were quite comfortable with enough to eat and drink. Their greatest need was 'democracy' for China. They appeared to be accustomed to the wearying experience of being on constant public display.

When I asked if the movement was coming to an end with a planned withdrawal of students from the square, they shrugged their shoulders as if unaware of such a move. They had no clear plans to leave, just to stay and continue their struggle. I was informed they would still be there the next day and I was 'warmly welcomed' to come again. 'Don't you want to go home?', I asked, but they laughed and mumbled, with no clear answer given. In retrospect, they probably had little choice about leaving

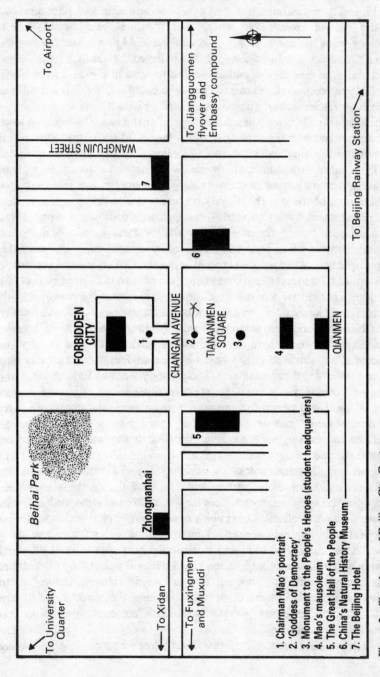

Figure 2 Sketchmap of Beijing City Centre

1. Chairman Mao's portrait
2. 'Goddess of Democracy'
3. Monument to the People's Heroes (student headquarters)
4. Mao's mausoleum
5. The Great Hall of the People
6. China's Natural History Museum
7. The Beijing Hotel

or staying. These were activists, militants even, by virtue of their sit-in, with easily recognisable faces after all the attention and photography. They had not attempted to conceal their identities, being proud of their act of 'remonstrating' with the government. Although the authorities had promised 'no retributions', no one believed them. Li Peng had, after all, declared martial law and attempted to send in armed troops. They could not trust such a man and therefore could not possibly leave their posts at Zhongnanhai. There was no turning back.

'Zaijian!', 'Bye! See you again!', they called out as I stepped back over the rope and into the smiling crowd. I never did see them again as the events of that final week overtook my plans. The next time I attempted to visit there, armed martial law troops had arrived before me with tear gas, preventing any more social calls. We did not know at that time that this would be the way the illegal occupation was to end.

I continued along Changan Avenue, where a distinct atmosphere was building up among the swelling crowds. Posters pasted up along the roadside were being read and discussed by onlookers. I soon heard the loudspeakers of the square screeching out their messages and eventually arrived in Tiananmen, parking my bicycle near to the Great Hall of the People. The square was quite a different sight now to the many previous occasions I had visited there. Tents, banners, groups of students, piles of rubbish and food were scattered across the square mile or so of Tiananmen 'guangchang'. There were some areas relatively clear of any signs of occupation, although in the weeks before, students had crammed into every inch of this famous place. Some were preparing to leave even as I walked around, but many were intent on remaining. I estimated around 2,000 were still occupying the square from my initial reconnaissance. These were the 'hangers on', few in comparison to the more heady days of the movement but their determination to stay put was significant none the less.

Municipal hygiene trucks were driving around disinfecting the paving slabs. It did not smell particularly bad, considering the numbers of people who had congregated here for weeks on end. Some students were sweeping up small piles of rubbish over to larger piles which would be collected by council workers. Thinking about the rubbish and mess which can usually be seen and smelt in the corridors of most crowded student dormitories, the situation here I decided was not too off-putting. It reminded me of a normal day at Beijing railway station, where thousands have to camp out while waiting for tickets in far less satisfactory conditions. At least the fresh air could prevail in this outdoor encampment.

The young occupants of the square were housed in a variety of dwellings, from brightly coloured 'igloo' tents donated by the Hong Kong students, to makeshift structures which looked precarious indeed. Larger, green canvas tents were also on the square, again donated by outside supporters. It took some time for me to adjust to this campsite in the middle of one of China's most hallowed places, normally full of tourists and photo-stands. There were still tourists, but that was only because the encampment had become the new attraction on the Beijing itinerary and other more established tourist 'traps' were closed due to the 'crisis'. The nearby Forbidden City had been out of bounds since before the imposition of martial law.

Looking around at the banners, I could see that many of the major Beijing colleges were represented as well as contingents from provincial institutions: Jinan, Shanghai, Qingdao and Tianjin. I spoke to one group who had recently arrived from Shanghai and were planning on staying at least till 20 June, when the next NPC was scheduled. 'That meeting is important', one young man said. 'They should talk about the problems facing China.' But that was still three weeks away and anything could happen before then. 'We will wait and see', I was told.

On this hot morning, some students seemed tired of waiting, looking listless, restless and apprehensive. Others were busy preparing food or writing their diaries. A few continued to sleep under the gaze of a curious public, but many had gone over to the northern part of the square, where the latest addition to Tiananmen was receiving its finishing touches. A large crowd had gathered around the spot where this thirty-foot tall, white 'goddess' figure had been erected. It was still partially covered by plastic sheeting with scaffolding around the base. Several students from the Central Art Institute were wearing tee-shirts bearing the 'goddess' emblem. They were slowly sawing through the tubular steel and preparing the statue for an unveiling ceremony. It had been brought into the square the night before, I was told, and was going to be officially 'christened' that morning. Situated near the main road (Changan Avenue) more or less opposite Chairman Mao's portrait, it would be highly visible and provocative. The students had already angered the authorities with their continued presence in Tiananmen: the statue took their action one step further. The unveiling ceremony was sure to be a good publicity stunt.

I saw that the clearing around its base had been reserved for journalists and other foreign media personnel as well as their Chinese counterparts. Martial law forbidding the reporting of the pro-democracy activities was being flaunted with the students' full encouragement and assistance. An out-of-date Gorbachev visit press pass assured me a place among the reporters and camera crews, many of them set up to shoot since dawn. We were put in this privileged viewing position in order to transmit full reports back to our respective countries, thus ridiculing the government's attempts at a news blackout.[1] The student leaders knew full well the power of the mass media. 'Take some good pictures!', young people were shouting over to the cameramen. Throughout the movement they had used the media to their best advantage, not only to publicise their struggle worldwide, but also as an indirect form of protection.

They presumed that the western democracies would support their attempts to bring about political reform in China, or at least give moral support as they had to the nascent 'Solidarity' movement in Poland. The more information that could be sent out, the greater would be the level of international sympathy. This would then bring pressure to bear on the Chinese leadership, who had stressed their commitment to the 'open door' policy. For this reason they might exercise a degree of self-restraint not conceivable otherwise and refrain from attacking the students. If the eyes of the world remained on Tiananmen Square, maybe Li Peng would not try again to send in the troops. The British Foreign Office echoed such a hope when they stated, after the declaration of martial law, 'We are watching them. The whole world is watching them' (BBC Radio Four 21. 5. 1989). At that time there were great fears of a possible bloodbath. It did not happen that night.

Judging by the large presence of foreign media representatives, the world was still watching, although the Chinese authorities had told them after Gorbachev had left that there was nothing to see and legally proscribed reporting. Now that Tiananmen had become part of the 'global village', the Chinese government could not brutalise its own people behind closed doors. Everyone would see it. The students sincerely hoped this would offer another line of defence to supplement the one offered by the Beijing residents and workers. They also hoped it would revive interest in a story which was considered to be almost 'over'. The unveiling ceremony of the 'Goddess of Democracy' was intended to recapture interest and support, with the organisers of this event intent on maximising publicity. But it was not clear whether they would leave the square or stay put once their highly provocative symbol had been officially brought into the world.

The unveiling ceremony was not, however, merely a publicity 'stunt'. It was infused with patriotic feeling and sentiment. The 'Goddess' was the students' own creation, a physical image of the ideals that were driving them into an ever-closer and serious confrontation with the hardliners in the CPC. Much has been said about the symbolism of the statue, so closely resembling the famous one standing at the entrance to

New York harbour. I heard one American cameraman complain about the students incorrectly 'copying' the original and others asking why they could not think of something original for themselves. I do not accept that this was merely a 'copy', just as the young people in the movement were not campaigning to bring about the American (or British) form of democracy in China. They wanted to learn from the West but to have the most suitable way of running China along democratic principles brought into action. They wanted debate and discussion, such as their 'May Fourth' predecessors had instituted, rather than the centralised form of dictatorship now running the country. The pure, white figure of 'democracy' in Tiananmen was an easily recognised symbol for people to understand, but it was the students' own version, with definite Chinese characteristics.

The use of a female figure has been common in many political struggles throughout history. In this sense, the creators of the 'Goddess' were following a time-honoured tradition.[2] It was also reflected, I noted, in the language being used throughout the ceremony with students calling each other 'tongbao', compatriot, which literally means in Chinese, 'from the same womb'. This form of address seemed to have replaced the more usual one in communist China of 'tongzhi' (comrade), which had lost some of its meaning in the previous years of economic reforms.

The statue also served the function of 'totem',[3] a symbol around which like-minds could gather to share opinions and emotions. Here the common cause was 'democracy' with all its varied meanings and connotations. The 'Goddess' could be a new rallying point, even if the student occupation finished. The movement looked set to enter a new highly critical phase as the 'Goddess of Democracy' vividly expressed the great gulf between the leaders and their young subjects who refused to obey their orders.

Slowly the scaffolding was taken away. 'Sit down, sit down!', stewards kept calling out to people around the statue who were blocking the view of those behind. 'Please be patient, we will begin the ceremony soon', a female student pleaded to the restless crowds over the PA system. The sun was already hot and in the square there is no shade. 'Can the cameramen stop moving around, please!', the girl shouted. People were becoming irritable in this drawn-out wait for the goddess to make her formal entry into the world. At times, the crowds pushed forward, straining to get nearer and gain a better view. These sudden surges threatened to become minor stampedes over the 'foreign friends' of the media. They were not aggressive, but natural bouts of enthusiasm and impatience. The stewards, all official with their arm and head bands, had developed effective crowd-control techniques and were able to keep the proceedings orderly without outside help. There were no police here, except of course those in plain clothes, who had come for reasons other than everyday law enforcement.

Most but not all of the ever-growing crowd of onlookers were young people, as impatient as the foreign reporters for the proceedings to start, giving the impression of wanting to physically embrace the statue, to fall at its feet and dedicate themselves to the struggle for democracy. Emotions were running high as the temperature climbed and we were all eager for the wraps to come off the statue. It already seemed a strong source of inspiration for the followers of the pro-democracy movement. The noise was also increasing with the government loudspeakers around the square continuously blasting out their propaganda with speeches calling for the Chinese people to adhere to the socialist road and obey martial law. These were interspersed with strains of the national anthem, as were the students' own announcements over their own *ad hoc* PA system. Both sides were claiming to be the true patriots and representatives of the Chinese peoples' best interests. Both sides appropriated sentiments of national pride. The verbal battle of the airwaves continued unabated. Handel's 'Hail the Conquering Hero' from Judas Maccabaeus was also played over and over in the build up to the unveiling of the statue. Whether the choice of this piece was deliberate or through convenience remains to be seen. The students may have viewed the statue as a 'conquering hero'. The ceremony eventually took place at midday.

The 'Statue of Liberty' had been used before in student movements; there were references to it in the winter demonstrations of 1986–7, and during the spring of 1989 students in Shanghai had carried a small model of it through the city streets during one of the numerous protests. Now, however, there was a large Chinese-style version right at the heart of the Chinese capital, gleaming white and facing Chairman Mao's portrait, which had been defaced the week before and had to be cleaned up.[4] The ideals of freedom, human rights, democracy and free speech were all encapsulated in this polystyrene statue, which was dedicated to the hunger strikers. The speeches made during the ceremony were all addressed to 'compatriots' and made many references to democracy and freedom, as well as criticisms of the Li Peng government. The style of the addresses was rousing, somewhat reminiscent of the Cultural Revolution, as several Chinese intellectuals pointed out. There was very little real substance or argument, but plenty of rhetoric about struggle. The female speaker who gave the major address often resorted to shouting slogans rather than offering reasoned arguments why anyone should support the pro-democracy movement. It appeared that the main aim of this ceremony, apart from the dedication of the statue, was to revive enthusiasm and spirits which had been declining since the days of the mass demonstrations. Just as with the party itself, the 'hardliners' in the student movement had won the day: the occupation of the square would continue, the struggle would go on.

The similarity of the style of language now used by the students to the government's own propaganda was also interesting to note. Either the young people were trying to 'beat them at their own game' or they had failed to develop their own style of language in political argument and debate. They were using the same music as the authorities, with the national anthem and the 'Internationale' being very popular, but the unveiling ceremony had an odd mixture of other tunes. Dvořák's 'New World Symphony' was added to a medley of old Communist Party songs which a small choir sang loudly. The speaker declared that a 'new age' had begun in the square that day and a 'democratic republic' established in the heart of the Chinese capital would set an example for the rest of China. The patriotic nature of this pro-democracy campaign was pre-dominant throughout the ceremony and at times the speeches verged on xenophobia. The students were trying to avoid being seen as traitors or unpatriotic as they had been labelled in the official media. They only wanted to serve the nation and save it from itself, as did their predecessors of the 'May Fourth' movement.

Amidst loud applause and cheering, the goddess was noisily intro-duced into the world. 'Long live democracy!', 'Long live the people!', 'Long live the republic!', were the final cries of the ceremony, slogans now familiar to the movement's participants. The content would not have been out of place seventy years before and the style would have been suitable for twenty years before. The goddess certainly had an interesting heritage, a symbol of all the different ideologies which the students wanted to embrace and synthesise into a suitable form for modern China. Their reference to the 'republic' was somewhat ambigu-ous, not stating clearly if it was the 'People's Republic' already in existence they had in mind or something different.

But ambiguities were left aside as the crowds surged forward. The abrupt ending of the ceremony had left the enthusiastic young sup-porters feeling agitated and excited, but they had no way to expend their energy apart from pushing to get nearer the statue. The rallying cries and speeches had set the adrenalin flowing and infused the onlookers with the desire for action, but there was no real outlet for their 'revolutionary zeal' at that time. There was something a little fearful about the noisy, agitated crowd. I quickly left this scene and headed back towards the centre of the square. Given enough provocation, this pent-up frustration could spill out into violence. So far the movement had remained peaceful and most people hoped it would stay that way, but the Cultural Revolution style talk of 'struggle' appeared slightly out of place in this otherwise very contemporary movement for democracy.

I reached the nerve centre of the Tiananmen occupation located around the base of the People's Heroes Monument. The whole area was roped off to the general public and a press pass or some other identification was needed to gain access. This exclusively appeared as a contradiction to the democratic principles espoused by the students and their commitment to equality. The necessity of official 'pieces of paper' also indicated a degree of bureaucracy had entered the movement, something else the students were opposed to. Why were the student leaders practising what they wished to see reformed in the Chinese political system? As I stepped over the rope, I decided that there were obvious practical reasons for keeping this area out of bounds to everyone. The student leaders needed some form of protection from government agents come to 'spy' on them and also the inquisitive general public. The strain of constant public attention was quite evident on the faces of some of the students around the monument. I recognised the symptoms of 'over exposure' from other long-term political campaigners I had seen elsewhere. They were in need of some degree of peace and quiet, rare commodities in the middle of Tiananmen Square. The pragmatism of the exclusion rule was acceptable even if at odds with their stated demands, a feature picked up by other foreign commentators.[5]

The foreign media were welcome here because of their valuable role. An assortment of camera crews and reporters littered the steps leading up to the monument, all waiting for something to happen. Many appeared bored, the unveiling of the goddess having failed to enthuse them as much as the young Chinese. Some had been in the capital since the Gorbachev visit and had wearied of the student movement.

The information or 'propaganda' department[6] of the movement was located here under a canvas awning, complete with desk and a flower in a vase. Student press 'officials' were busy putting together leaflets using an old but functioning banda duplicating machine and piles of donated paper. These would be distributed throughout the city in an effort to keep the movement alive. As it was noon-time, some of the students were eating lunch. 'Our food is given to us', I was told. Food supplies were brought in by sympathisers, mostly consisting of bread and noodles as far as I could see. These basic items could probably not supply a balanced diet, but this is often an unattainable goal for students even in normal circumstances, with their low incomes and poor-quality campus meals. Some looked drawn and weary, lying around under the shade of makeshift structures.

I approached a few occupants of the 'residential area' who were not taking the usual post-lunch nap. 'Come in and sit down!', they said. I took up the offer and asked them about their living conditions and their plans. They assured me that they were quite comfortable and intended to stay for as long as it took to make the government change its mind. They were proud of their 'goddess', but knew the leaders would be angry, 'very angry' with this gesture. 'Soldiers will try to knock it down but not yet. We must protect the statue', they informed me. 'Take some good pictures!', they urged, 'in case it does not remain there for long'. I was invited to visit again soon; perhaps they too sensed they would not be there much longer in spite of their stated intention to stay. Every statement seemed to be hedged with a certain doubt about the future.

By the following day, some of the encampment had shifted to the foot of the statue with the igloo tents forming a circle inside the crowd barrier. The new symbolic head of the movement was being surrounded by the students, who were also consolidating their own position; they had 'dug in' for the duration. Talk about ending the occupation was now dismissed as the hardcore remained. Many Beijing people went to see Ms Democracy and take photographs of the new attraction.

A summer squall early on Wednesday evening brought down most of the remaining makeshift structures. Some students packed up and left, but many moved into the larger military-style tents also donated by supporters. These could house around twenty people and were more sturdy. Someone remarked that it looked like the army had already gone in, but so far the statue had only elicited the expected verbal response from the government. It was, to them, a piece of sheer effrontery to the sacred nature of Tiananmen and the Communist Party. Also it spoiled the 'beauty' of the square and should be removed immediately. It would also prevent the children of the city from holding their annual Children's Day parade on 1 June. 'Big brothers and sisters, please leave the square so we can celebrate our special day', ran a piece in the *China Daily* on 30 May. Children from many middle schools had actually visited the students in Tiananmen to express their support of what they were trying to do, but the official media did not run these stories. More appeals were made, intermingled with serious threats, but the situation remained virtually the same. The square was occupied and the students now had their own symbol which was relayed all over the world.

FROM FALSE ALARMS TO ALARM

By Wednesday night, rumours were rife that troops were poised to go in to demolish the offending statue and clear the square. Whilst cycling in the northwestern suburbs about 11 p.m., I saw half a dozen motorcycle combinations speeding towards the city centre. 'This is not normal', I was told and there suddenly seemed to be substance to the rumours. Perhaps this was the night martial law would be strictly enforced, so I turned around and cycled towards Tiananmen.

The streets were quiet at first with few people out. If the troops did come, the citizens might not be prepared to erect the barricades again in time to halt a military advance. Once on the main road, I felt less anxious because there were crowds of people, awake and alert. The closer I drew to Tiananmen, the greater the numbers of people, more than in the daytime. Although it was past midnight, whole families were in the vicinity of the square, enjoying the cool night air and the sight of the student occupation. It was like a festival and everyone appeared to be enjoying themselves. Normally there is little to do for entertainment at night in Beijing and the citizens were making the most of this unusual spectacle.

Numerous food stalls had been set up around the perimeter of the square, selling everything from Xinjiang kebabs to Sichuan noodles. The pedlars were seizing the opportunity to make some money and the high prices charged by some of them highlighted the negative aspects of economic reforms. These 'get rich quick' *getihu* (small businesses) would justify their profiteering by pointing out the risks they take and problems faced in setting up small businesses. They were a symbol of Deng's reform programme, a partial and incomplete success story. The students around the monument, in contrast, epitomised the failures of the decade.

The noise was quite unbearable with the government propaganda blasting out in competition with the students' versions. Delegations from autonomous workers' unions were giving speeches which initiated a great deal of discussion among the spectators. The leadership was under verbal assault, Li Peng coming under particularly heavy criticism. The sounds of laughter, singing and music merged into the general cacophony which was Tiananmen at night during the student occupation. I walked over to the nerve centre and joined some students there, settling down for a night of conversation and waiting for the soldiers to come. I was pleased they did not appear that night and interrupt the conversation I had with those young intellectuals, the 'hope of China'. I was relieved the motorcycles had turned out to be a false alarm, and we sat on the steps of the monument sharing thoughts about freedom, democracy and life in general. I was fortunate to have known these young representatives of the student movement before it all ended so tragically, along with, perhaps, their own lives.

'Are you a journalist? Where are you from?', they enquired. I told them about the military movements I had seen earlier that night. They asked about the details of the motor-cycles and their passengers. 'They could be armed police, not soldiers', they concluded. They were not too concerned about this particular sighting because others had been recorded that night. 'The situation is growing more dangerous', I was informed. 'What will you do?', I enquired. 'The workers and citizens will protect us. We will not fight. We are prepared to die', were the sort of replies I received. They would not desert their 'posts' at the Tiananmen headquarters.

These students were probably fairly typical of those who occupied the square at that time: mostly from out of town, about twenty years old and very committed to what they were doing. I was told about the 20 June congress, where they hoped their demands would be discussed seriously and Li Peng would be forced to step down. They needed to stay in the square till then and would not return to the provinces until after that meeting.

'Maybe we'll stay after 20 June if the result of the meeting is not satisfactory.' They were a little uncertain about the future and worried about the dangers that could force them out of the square. Their families were also scared on their behalf. 'I saw my mother today', said one young man, a particularly gentle and frail character. 'She wants me to go home but I can't now. Maybe later. The government is bad and the people of China have to know.' His voice was weak and his health poor, he admitted, since he could not sleep much here and the food was not nutritious. But he was going to stay and he wanted to talk, refusing my encouragement to find a place to sleep.

'What do you think is the biggest problem facing China?', another young man asked me. After some discussion we agreed that the huge population was a pressing problem which any regime would have to deal with. The underdeveloped education system was another serious and related difficulty, they said. 'In the countryside the peasants receive little education and they have too many babies. It's backward.' 'How can there be democracy when many people can't even read and write?', they asked. The government, they suggested, should spend more money on education and raise the status of those involved with the transmission of knowledge. This would secure them a better future because of their intellectual status. 'Now things are too bad for us. We're too poor.' I nodded in agreement, recalling the many similar conversations I had shared with young teachers and students over the previous year.

They wanted to know about the political and education systems in England and how British democracy differed to the American version. They were as eager to learn from me as I was from them. This type of open discussion and free exchange of ideas they felt was lacking in China but was badly needed in order to probe into what was wrong with the 'sick man of Asia'. Without real debate there could be no real development in their opinion. 'We need freedom of speech and the media', they insisted, to further the exchange of ideas and promote intellectual activity. 'Otherwise China will remain backward.' They all saw a clear relationship between the major problems facing China, but they were not agreed on what should be tackled first or, indeed, how. There was a consensus, however, that the existing regime was corrupt and should not be steering China into the twenty-first century. Coming back to the question of the leaders, the students were depressed and pessimistic. A form of democracy was necessary to rid China of such dictators but the exact form it would take was unclear. They suggested a multi-party system so that the Communist Party had some competition.

The conversation continued, fluctuating between bouts of deep pessimism and moments of great hope. We also laughed a lot, sharing jokes about Chinese and English politicians. Eventually I was left with the one frail but enthusiastic student who refused to sleep. We sat on the steps of the monument, enjoying the peacefulness which had finally descended over the square. Most of the sightseers had gone home and the loudspeakers were silent at last. The assorted banners and flags of the encampment fluttered in the breeze and inside the tents the young people slept. 'Isn't it beautiful here?', he said. I agreed, having never seen such a sight in China before. There were shades of unreality about this usually cold, empty square at the heart of the Chinese capital. Tiananmen had been transformed in a way previously beyond imagination. Would the students succeed in transforming Chinese society in a similar way?

A scream suddenly interrupted our quiet reflections. People were soon rushing around. Foreign camera crews sprang into action as the girl continued to yell. 'Are the troops coming? What should we do?' I asked in a panic. There was no need for concern, the matter was soon resolved. The young woman had woken up in pain and had trouble in breathing. She was taken to the medical tent. There were no soldiers. 'I don't think they'll come now', my student friend assured me but I still felt very vulnerable there on the monument. Peace returned to the square as the false alarm died down. We went back to our conversation and waited for dawn to come. 'I'd like a photograph taken here, perhaps you can do that for me next time you are here. I can give it to my mother', the student asked. He had found some food for us and other people still awake in the small hours and I wanted to return the favour. I promised to do that for him, a promise I would be unable to keep.

When it was light, we said 'zaijian' ('bye, see you again'). My student friend was facing another day of bustle in the square after a sleepless night. My admiration was mixed with pity. How much longer could they carry on? 'Try to sleep. Get something good to eat', I advised him. I felt reluctant to leave but wanted to get back while the roads were still quiet.

Cycling down Changan Avenue, so calm and clean, I considered myself fortunate to have spent a whole night talking to those students. The early morning road sweepers smiled as I went by and I reflected on how beautiful the city appeared in the early morning light, before the rush hour got under way. But this uneasy calm was only for a few days longer: the dream would soon be shattered and this street was to be renamed 'blood road'. The next time I went to the square at night, on Friday evening, 2 June, I could not find the students I had spoken to during the week. The situation had changed around the steps of the monument due to a new hunger strike and the atmosphere had also raised the tension. A weekend of chaos and death was about to begin as this struggle for democracy ended.

As I cycled along Fuxingmen on Friday evening, by now a familiar route, at around 10 p.m. I came across a large crowd blocking the road. People were pouring out of blocks of flats flanking the roadside, some still in their nightclothes, to see what all the commotion was about. Police were also on the scene. After asking around I found out there had just been an accident and three, maybe four cyclists were dead as a result. I could see the twisted cycles on the roadside, the offending police vehicle and bloodstains. I did not wish to see the bodies which were still lying there. An ambulance had just arrived on the scene to take the victims away. I enquired into the cause of the accident and found out that the police van had been driving at high speed and hit the cyclists. 'It was going too fast', several people said. 'Four people are dead now who should be alive.'

The anger of the local residents was clear. 'The police are murderers', someone whispered. The atmosphere was tense. Police were telling people to go back to their homes. There was nothing to see but few were leaving the scene. Everyone was talking; some voices were raised in anger and Li Peng was mentioned in critical terms. He was not driving the offending vehicle, but he might as well have been: it was his fault in the eyes of those Beijing citizens. These deaths were attributed to the attempts by the authorities to suppress the student movement. The police van had been speeding towards the square maybe as an advance vehicle, heralding an assault on Tiananmen, people were suggesting, rightly or wrongly. It had been two weeks since the abortive efforts to enforce military rule and clear the square. Now blood had been spilt, the first lives lost in this otherwise peaceful movement. There was the feeling that something would happen because the student movement had four 'martyrs', even though they were not killed in the square and may have had nothing at all to do with the pro-democracy campaign.

After pushing my way through the agitated crowd I continued on my way more warily. There were large numbers of people out on the streets as news of the accident was relayed down the road. At every intersection, small groups of citizens engaged in animated discussion and some shouted angrily at passing police vehicles. The mood had rapidly changed as the approach to Tiananmen became more hectic. Thousands of people were either milling around or walking purposively towards the student encampment.

It was even more lively and noisy than on previous evenings. The foodsellers around the square were doing a brisk trade while the competing PA systems were pitched to a frenzy. Family groups were still very evident, even though the situation was probably more dangerous now because of the accident. I wanted to tell the student officials about this, but it seemed they already knew. There was nothing to be done about the deaths, which were being linked to Li Peng and the martial law directive and were obviously going to be used as another way of attacking the government.

Listening to speeches being made in the square that evening, the attacks were growing more vituperative. One speaker referred to the ploy earlier in the week by the authorities to pay people to join in a pro-party, martial-law 'demonstration'. In return for a few yuan, sun visors and popsicles, some people in a local township had marched, carrying banners in favour of Li Peng and his regime. The whole affair was somewhat farcical and made the situation look worse for the beleaguered officials. 'How much do we have to pay for people to join our demonstrations? Not even one yuan!', the speaker shouted out, seizing the opportunity to score moral points over the government. The loud applause indicated they were succeeding. Some workers were also making a case for the recently arrested 'getihu', the small businessmen who had acted as messengers during the height of the crisis after martial law was declared. The police had rounded up some of them and they faced prison sentences. It was even suggested that the police stations themselves should be 'stormed' to free these people. This was perhaps a little beyond what the students had planned.

They had begun, that very afternoon, a new hunger strike, only this time not with mass participation. Four celebrities were the volunteers including Hou Dejian, a famous popstar in China who had originally come across from Taiwan. I went over to the monument, where the four young men were preparing to starve for democracy. The white tent with its slogans and declaration was clearly visible in spite of the large crowds which had gathered there. The stewards shouted through megaphones that the hunger strikers would come out and address the public shortly. They emerged to rapturous applause just after midnight. The quartet clasped hands and smiled, looking victorious already. They were the new heroes in the eyes of the students. They walked down the steps as if descending a conquered Everest and stood right in front of their thrilled supporters. They said a few words then retreated to their tent, accompanied by more applause, shouts of encouragement and clicking of cameras.

'Did you see them? Are you all right?', a young man standing nearby asked, concerned because I was being pushed by the crowd behind. 'You should go over, take some good photographs', he said, urging me over the rope. One of the stewards tried to stop me climbing over. On this evening, they were enforcing tightly the exclusion policy because of the changed situation, but at last I was able to go over and walk up the steps to where the hunger strikers' tent was positioned. This latest action had made the monument a hive of activity. Medical attendants were on hand by the tent, one of them I noticed eating several large buns which seemed an odd juxtaposition as those inside began to slowly starve themselves.

On my arrival in Beijing less than one week before, many people had told me that it was all 'over', but it seemed that they were mistaken. I spoke briefly with some students in the headquarters and they seemed to be expecting something to happen as a result of the accident earlier on that evening. It was clear I would be unable to find any of my student acquaintances and few others were willing to talk much. I did meet one student who wanted me to talk with him and his classmates and had come up from out of town. We left the hectic nerve centre and went down to 'tent city' where his friends were staying. But they were all asleep. 'Come back later. Don't forget where we are', he urged, explaining the exact location of their tent again. I moved on to see what else was happening in the early hours of Saturday 3 June.

At around 2 a.m. I was alerted to a commotion by the Great Hall of the People. A crowd of about 1,000 were marching outside there shouting, 'Li Peng, Deng Xiaoping resign!' They did not look like students. 'They are Beijing citizens', I was soon informed. 'They've come to protest about the killing tonight of four people on Fuxingmen.' I was not surprised that the local residents had left the scene of the accident and come to Tiananmen to protest. Men still wearing their singlets and young children in nightclothes were in the procession, adding their voices to the growing dissent in Tiananmen.

I decided to contact some friends and cycled quickly to Changan Avenue, on the east side of the square. I saw groups of workers pulling construction equipment out from a nearby building site onto the road, to form a barricade. Suddenly there were more people running around in different directions and shouting something about the army coming. I did not know what to do and in my indecision was swept along with the crowd heading down a side road by the Beijing Hotel. We were met head-on by a column of soldiers. What followed next was a good deal of confusion, shouting and scuffles. The soldiers halted and were quickly surrounded by the crowds. People surged in front of me, so I could no longer see clearly in the dark. 'Get out of the way!', some shouted at me while others encouraged me to take a good look. A few soldiers were getting beaten up, but the physical attacks soon subsided into a verbal onslaught once it was clear the soldiers had no guns.

There were cries of 'more soldiers' from the opposite direction back down Changan Avenue. I rushed around the corner with hundreds of other onlookers and we saw another column of soldiers. Similar scuffles and confusion occurred. Kitbags were snatched away from the soldiers in the front row and the contents held up for all to see and ridiculed. Food, drink and other supplies were pulled out and thrown to the ground. The anger which had spilled over into violence was now rapidly subsiding into pity. 'Don't hurt them!', women were calling. Others said, 'Don't take their things. Leave them alone'. This seemed to be a curious reversal of Mao's old dictum to the PLA during the days of the civil war. They were not to take anything from the villages they passed through not even 'a nail or thread', from the people. This had earned the army an excellent reputation and many Chinese people viewed it as truly the 'people's army'. Over the previous few weeks the relationship had become strained with the attempts to enforce martial law. This latest attempt to take the square had caused more conflict. The crowds were trying to restrain the rage they felt about this move as they stopped the soldiers in their tracks so close to Tiananmen.

Once the confusion had died down and the scuffles ended, it was possible to walk along the column of troops and observe their condition. They were exhausted, having jogged along the main road from some distance out of town. They were in civilian clothes rather than full uniform. Even without uniform, 5,000 or so soldiers could hardly be missed. The most striking point about them was their age: they all appeared very young. 'Look, they're sending children to kill children', people were saying. 'This is how bad the government is.' I was told to note the scene carefully by numerous Beijing residents who had come out onto the streets. At first there was a sense of anger with the leadership, but this soon evolved into a feeling of national shame and humiliation that Chinese people could treat each other in such a way. Some citizens did not want this image relayed across the world and some foreign correspondents attempting to capture the scenes of frightened young soldiers squatting in the bushes had their cameras knocked out of their hands. This column of the PLA was hardly a sight to be proud of with the cowering young men, shaken and tired, obviously wishing they were somewhere else. Many of them seemed to be new recruits, just up from the countryside.

No one could ascertain just who was in command of this ragtag column of soldiers. At one point, a 'commander' was found and he was quickly encircled. Wearing civilian rather than military attire, he refused to address the crowds. Sympathy was extended to the young men all along the column which stretched to the east of the city. They were offered food, drink and cigarettes but were unsure whether to accept or not. Mostly they squatted along the roadside as if waiting for orders and some put on their army jackets and caps. They stayed until daybreak, huddled into the bushes along Changan Avenue. Then, like snowmen, they melted as the sun came up.

It appeared that half of the city attempted to resume normal life that morning, cycling along the main thoroughfares, skirting barricades and broken glass. Just off Changan, down the side-streets, old people were practising their Tai'Ji[7] as usual, as if nothing untoward had happened. Some of the roadblocks were removed, but many were left in case they should be needed again. Squads of students and workers with white headbands were rushing around, rallying the people and preparing for more army moves. I could hardly rush after a night on the streets, but there was too much happening around Tiananmen for me to return to my base in the suburbs. It was clear that events were building up to the final climax and I decided to stay to witness the outcome of this extraordinary movement. The 'toy soldiers' of the night before had been easily stopped. People were feeling both confident and apprehensive about what would occur next. Various isolated but related incidents happened throughout Saturday 3 June which I saw for myself or heard about through reliable witnesses as well as rumour. The main events that followed are detailed below.

EYEWITNESS TO A MASSACRE

Crowds of students from the Beijing campuses were coming into the city centre throughout the day to reinforce the numbers already in the square. I was watching a small procession along Changan Avenue in the afternoon when people urged me to go down the road by the side of the Great Hall of the People. 'Quick, have a look!', they said. There, inside a compound, were armed troops preparing to come out. Large crowds were shouting at them, both threatening and pleading with them not to try and enter the square. Men were climbing up the railings, trying to get in and physically confront the soldiers. It was about 3 p.m. when the unit came marching down the road towards Changan. It was a terrifying sight, very different from the raw recruits of the previous night. They were fully clad in riot-gear and armed. I thought they would open fire if their intended passage was blocked. But groups of people ran in front of them, screaming and shouting. The soldiers quickly came to a halt. Sticks, stones, eggs and tomatoes were flying through the air along with verbal abuse. A public bus was soon commandeered for use as a barricade to hold back the wall of green.

Once it was certain the soldiers had stopped, the pleading and arguing began in earnest, as before, with citizens and students united in a verbal confrontation against the military. The troops were ordered to sit down and there they stayed in the blazing sun. Another 'fiasco' appeared to be under way, but this was not the only scene of action. Over towards Zhongnanhai there was another commotion where troops had also advanced. I cycled through the crowds, noticing a few spent canisters of tear-gas on the ground and an acrid smell in the air. The situation was chaotic, with groups of people heading in all directions but no one getting very far. It was impossible to reach the Zhongnanhai compound, where a few days before I had chatted quietly with the student protesters.

By chance I saw a former Chinese colleague who was surprised to meet me there at this time. He warned me to take care and not attempt to go towards the western suburbs. 'There are thousands of soldiers there. They have guns and are coming this way. They will be here soon.' The situation seemed to be deteriorating rapidly. I promised my friend to be careful, but was uncertain how to follow this advice. Returning to the Great Hall, the troops were still trapped by the Beijing citizens. The top of the bus-barricade was covered by many people, trying to talk to the soldiers down below or just get a better view. Some were arming themselves with sticks and stones slung around their waists.

'Yes, we will win', one of the students in the square told me. 'Victory is in the hands of the people.' The atmosphere throughout the Tiananmen encampment was growing tense as people prepared themselves for some sort of military advance. Many students wanted to sit quietly and were reluctant to talk any more with the crowds of excited foreign journalists. Others were rushing around in a state of high agitation, attracting attention with their banners and slogans. There was a clear division between those who would fight back if attacked and those who would remain non-violent.

There were reports of violence, however, in the western suburbs. 'The soldiers are whipping people with their belts. They are firing bullets with nails in them into the crowds', several people told me. One man showed me marks on his face he claimed were from the soldiers. 'There are big fights out there.' Facts mingled with rumours to add to the growing confusion and anxiety in the square. The sight of armed soldiers outside the Great Hall had been alarming and although they eventually withdrew it was clear they could come out again at any time. No one could estimate just how many troops the government had positioned all over the city. Groups of people surrounded the Great Hall shouting for Li Peng to come out, but not knowing if he was even in there. Students were singing the national anthem and the 'Internationale'; some were writing their 'yishu' – last wills. This was the scene as dusk fell over the square.

I stayed in and around Tiananmen for most of the evening. Around 9 p.m. I was cycling along Changan, near the museum, when a single line of soldiers suddenly came running down the street. They were young, unarmed and scared. The watchful citizens soon stopped their progress and fighting broke out. Some of them were beaten, but as on the previous evening, the violence was soon stopped. 'Don't hurt them! Stop fighting!' A few were helped away by women to receive attention for their wounds and probably a lecture about the students being right and the government being wrong. The authorities seemed to be playing cruel games with their own people, teasing and provoking them by sending in such vulnerable groups of soldiers, raising tension and anger all around.

'One, two, three, pull!', was now the communal chant as men and women pulled the neat bicycle-lane barriers across the road. These could only be minor hurdles for heavy military vehicles, but offered a token of the people's resistance to the army advance. To west and east, masses of troops had been sighted. A government broadcast that evening had warned people to stay off the streets and not to go to Tiananmen because their safety could not be guaranteed. Yet thousands, if not millions were out all over the city, many of them in the central area. Family groups were still strolling around enjoying the spectacle, unperturbed by the threats. Many wanted to help protect the students and possibly believed that the soldiers would not attack if there were women and children on the streets. This assumption was soon to be proven tragically wrong, but in the meantime, the barricades were going up all over Beijing.

I cycled back to the centre of Tiananmen, near to the headquarters on the monument, which had been virtually sealed off by the stewards. The competing loudspeakers continued to throw out different versions of the 'truth' about the situation. Students and workers were giving speeches and there was the usual singing of the national anthem and the 'Internationale'. The noise was wearying. Yet through all of this, some slept in the tents. I was advised to go home and be safe, but it was too late for that now. I left the centre of the square for the final time at around 11 p.m. because I could no longer stand the suspense of waiting for the troops to arrive and I was scared of what was going to take place.

I cycled eastwards towards the Jiangguomen flyover, where, it was reported, a large convoy of soldiers had been stopped by the citizens. The main road was by now difficult to negotiate due to the barricades and crowds. Arriving at Jiangguomen I saw the flyover completely packed with men, women and children surrounding military trucks. I counted over twenty vehicles, all full of young armed soldiers. People were appealing to their better nature, students with megaphones were giving political lectures, but the young men in green remained mostly impassive, not wanting to get involved with the Beijing people or ideological discussions. They refused cigarettes and other items offered to them. The crowd appeared to have this unit 'captured', but down below on the main road was an armoured personnel carrier driving at top speed. I moved off to take a closer look. There was little to get in the way of the armoured personnel carrier as it covered this stretch of road several times, clearing the way perhaps for more trucks and, I was told by a taxi driver, tanks which were waiting in the suburbs. I could hardly believe that the authorities were intending to bring in tanks, but they had been seen. It was a terrifying sight in itself to watch this armoured car in the middle of the city. I cycled back to the flyover after the armoured car had turned off in the distance. The situation there appeared to be stalemate.

From the direction of Tiananmen came the sounds of what seemed like shots and shelling. Flares were going up into the night sky. What everyone had dreaded for weeks was obviously happening. It was well after midnight by this time. I raced back towards the square, having to take the 'hutongs' (alleys) since the main roads were both impassable and dangerous. I followed a tricycle rickshaw carrying a foreign journalist back to the scene of the action. Once we had reached the Beijing Hotel, I was advised to go inside and keep myself out of danger, but I could not leave the streets. Instead I went with the crowd back towards the eastern corner of the square thinking there would be safety in numbers. We got as far as the museum and just ahead was the armoured car I had seen earlier, now in flames. I was told that three or four people were dead inside.

It was impossible to see beyond into the centre of the square because of the crowds and the darkness, but we could hear the official propaganda bellowing out its threats, and everyone said there were cordons of soldiers just in front of us. They had arrived in Tiananmen a short time after I had left for Jiangguomen. There was a great deal of noise and confusion, no one could say for sure what was happening. 'Is that shooting?' I asked at one point. 'No, it's nothing. Don't be frightened', I was told. It was about 2 a.m. when suddenly there was reason to be frightened as real bullets started flying in our direction. Many still thought they were blanks or that the soldiers were firing in the air to scare us away. But people started screaming as they were hit or others nearby were bloodied. I was already running. Screams, shouts and gunshots were the awful sounds that rang down Changan Avenue for the next few hours.

After the first volley, it appeared safe to go back and stay with the crowd. We went forward again. More shots. I dived onto the ground, then over into the bushes, shaking with fear and disbelief. It was incomprehensible that this was happening, that the army were shooting unarmed citizens indiscriminately and that people were dying around me. I quickly realised that the small bushes along the walls of the Forbidden City were not much protection against bullets which at times seemed to be coming from two directions: from the square and from the side-streets alongside the Forbidden City. I was concerned for the students in the square, now surrounded by armed troops and beyond the protection of the people, some of whom were paying with their own lives for their gestures of support.

Gradually I managed to scramble away from the killing zone. A succession of shots cut people down as they fled and I particularly remember hearing mothers screaming for their children. Later, as I stood outside the Beijing Hotel, I saw bodies on the road and learned of the large numbers of casualties. A crowd had gathered there, mostly people fleeing from the area around the square and they were sharing their grief and disgust. I stayed with them rather than go inside the hotel, apparently now under 'fascist' command. By staying outside, I missed getting a beating from the hotel 'staff' (probably plain-clothes security forces) who were trying to snatch films and recordings of the events from foreign media personnel.

People tried to tell me calmly but tearfully what they had seen and how they felt. 'The fascists are killing our children', I was told. 'We hate the Party. The Party is now dead for us', others said, commenting that it had never committed such atrocities against the people before. Men told me of what they would like to do with the 'dogs', Li Peng, Deng Xiaoping and Yang Shankun. They really hated the leaders. 'It's all over for them.' All this time, the dead and wounded were being ferried out of the square and its surroundings on the backs of rickshaws, handcarts or anything the volunteers could use. There was clearly not enough transport to get them out to the hospitals. People raged with great anger and emotion at the fleet of locked taxis outside the Beijing Hotel, all neat and clean, which could have been used to transport the wounded. I saw two small ambulances plying the hazardous journey between the square and a nearby hospital. Along with the Chinese people, I cried at this pitiable lack of resources to deal with the terrible situation unfolding before our eyes. Like them, I was sickened by the sight of young people covered in blood piled up on the backs of carts. Some must have been dead already as other students raced down Changan, hoping to save their lives. All the time there was shooting along the road. 'Another two! Another four!', we could hear as more people fell victim to the soldiers' guns. Some students had commandeered buses and drove them wildly towards the square to the loud cheers of the watching crowds.

I felt useless. All I could think of was to stop an ambulance and volunteer my services and my blood at a local hospital and I even wandered out into the road with this intention at one point, half-dazed, but was quickly pulled back. I went back to the crowd outside the hotel. A young man arrived, looking particularly distraught and crying bitterly. I took him to one side and put my arms around him. He told me of his escape from the square, but somehow he had got separated from his girlfriend and classmates. He assumed they were all dead. On his way down Changan Avenue, he had seen two young girls, three and eight their mother said, both very beautiful. They were dead. 'They were so pretty, how could they do that to children?', he said crying. 'China, China! The young people are all dead. They had no chance, no future, no opportunities to live their lives. They were all so young!', 'hen nianqing', so very young. This 21-year-old student continued to pour out his grief, not knowing how he could carry on with his life after this night. 'There is no hope for China now. I should die too', he said.

There was absolutely nothing I could do for him or his fellow students. His feelings of despair probably summed up the general attitude during those early hours of 4 June, when the Chinese leaders so cruelly threw away the progress and hope of the decade. I could not dissuade this young man from returning to the square. He thanked me sincerely and said I was very kind then walked away. It was nearly dawn and the troops were clearing Tiananmen of all traces of the students' pro-democracy movement. I doubt he could have survived.

After he had gone, I went inside the hotel. All the phone lines had been cut by the 'staff', but they were no longer beating people up. I stayed there till daybreak, listening to the shooting and screaming in the streets. 'Ba gong!', people were shouting, 'Go on strike!'

THE AFTERMATH

The hours of darkness eventually gave way to light on Sunday morning 4 June, but the nightmare of reality continued uninterrupted until daybreak. There was still some shooting on the streets and around 8 a.m. I half-heartedly ventured onto a balcony of the Beijing Hotel to see what was happening. I did not want to see any more of the horror I had experienced throughout the night, but I also had some slight hope that perhaps things were not as bad as they had appeared.

Everything was gone. It was all over. Tiananmen was now full of army green, having become a military encampment packed with tanks and soldiers. There were even helicopters swooping down to deliver supplies or top personnel to the Great Hall of the People. Everything to do with the student-led movement had been cleared away. It had all been obliterated, as if it had never happened. I tried to come to terms with this new, frightening reality and all its implications for the Chinese people.

Soldiers on Changan Avenue were lined up in battle formation. There were two rows lying down, their guns pointing straight ahead, another two or three rows behind, crouching, guns also aimed at the crowds still on the street, and behind them three or four rows of soldiers standing, poised to shoot. Some people were still trying to get close enough to say, 'The People's Army loves the people. Stop shooting and start a dialogue!' But the days of dialogue were over. Shots rang out if anyone got too near. Some were hit.

I looked over at Tiananmen and wondered how it could have been cleared so quickly. There were a few things burning in the square; the soldiers had made bonfires of the students' tents and belongings. Thick black smoke rose from the spot where the 'goddess' had stood. I could only assume that the statue was on fire. Beyond the square in all directions were clouds of smoke and the sound of shooting. It seemed as though the whole city were being destroyed. The weak sunshine was being blotted out by clouds of smoke.

Nearer to the hotel, just on the intersection between Changan and Wangfujin, was a wrecked bus, used on the previous night as a barricade. It had just been set ablaze and was slowly catching light. The main road stretching eastwards to the Jianguomen flyover was littered with broken glass, the twisted remains of bicycle lane barriers and various other items used in the attempt to stop the troops and tanks. It was all evidence of the resistance put up by the Beijing citizens who had kept their promise to protect the students but had been overwhelmed by the heavy military onslaught. Both sides had been provoked into brutality by the government's actions.

Some were still resisting. There were hundreds of people on Changan even then, cycling around the wrecked buses or walking along the streets in small groups. Later that day, after I had left the hotel, the by now world famous student Wang Weilin stepped out in front of a column of tanks and made history. For a few minutes the tanks stopped and even tried to manoeuvre around this solitary man. He wanted to talk to the soldiers, to reason with them and drive them back with words, but he was hustled away by friends before the tank drivers could respond. His eventual fate is uncertain, but there are unconfirmed reports of his arrest.

I had to leave the hotel but was unsure about returning to the university quarter and too unnerved to go very far. Nowhere seemed safe, but I had been out on the streets for two nights and could no longer drift around the capital on my bicycle. As I went to take a look at the burning bus on the intersection, a volley of shots came from down the avenue. People scattered for cover and I left the area; fifteen minutes later a dozen people were killed outside the hotel.

I spent the rest of the day in another hotel nearby hearing more about the events of the night before and its aftermath. Unofficial estimates of 2,600 dead were put forward and the hospitals were overflowing with the wounded. Soldiers were reported to have shot into people's homes at Muxidi. There was a rumour that Li Peng had been shot by a soldier sympathetic to the students and that civil war was about to break out between warring army factions. It was also reported that soldiers were being lynched all along Fuxingmen, but it turned out that just one army member had been captured, burnt and then lynched for his crimes against the people. In any case, the situation was volatile and dangerous and the prospect of cycling alone over fifteen kilometres through the side-streets of Beijing did not seem a sensible act at that time. Embassies were telling foreign nationals to stay in a safe place and leave as soon as possible. The campuses were preparing to be stormed by the troops, even the diplomatic quarter was coming under some fire from soldiers riding around in tanks. There was no possibility of my leaving the relative safety of the hotel that day.

In the days that followed, the picture became a little clearer and the streets safer, although there was still danger as sporadic bursts of shooting continued. I went out, travelling around the capital with British media personnel, during that week and saw the scars of battles all over the city. To begin with, the people were still keen to talk, to tell us what had happened and how they had tried to see off the 'fascist troops'. They hated the leaders who had destroyed the student-led movement they had all supported. Fighting had occurred not just on Saturday night and Sunday morning but over successive days. To the west and east of the city centre street battles had raged, 'very fierce', people told me openly. All of them had been witnesses to deaths and wounding and had a story to tell. But they had to stop talking by the end of the week under threats from the martial-law authorities, whose public notices were being slapped up on every wall and door. The rounding-up of activists, sympathisers and 'rumour-mongers' had begun in earnest and history was being rewritten by the Deng-Li-Yang 'clique'.

The citizens of the capital were reluctantly drifting back to work under some duress and the strike collapsed. It was difficult to stay away from work with threats of reprisals and lack of money to buy food, which was becoming scarce. People had little choice but to go to work. The hourly news bulletins showed pictures of the 'counter-revolutionary rebellion' as it had been labelled by the government and crimes committed by the 'hooligans' who took part. No one died in the square, people were informed. Three hundred or so were killed elsewhere, mostly soldiers who only opened fire after being threatened and attacked by 'thugs'. The soldiers were 'heroes', highly praised by the officials. The PLA had saved the nation and therefore was to be honoured, while the students were to be despised as traitors. Shots of those already arrested, looking bruised and humiliated as they were paraded, were broadcast to remind people of the seriousness of the June events and the strength of those now in control. They were intended to cow the public into passivity. Those arrested, from young students to old men, the so-called 'counter-revolutionaries' looked less than human on screen. The first executions were planned for Shanghai. Terror tightened its grip all over China, but particularly in Beijing, which had witnessed the massacre. Other cities had their own smaller 'counter-revolutions'.

But what of the students, especially those who had been active throughout April and May? We visited several campuses three days after the massacre to try and find out. The troops had not 'stormed' in as threatened or rumoured beforehand, but there was still fear that such an act was possible. Plain-clothes agents were out in force, however, mingling with the crowds who visited the major universities. The main gate of Beida, in many ways the home of the patriotic democratic movement, was covered with the characters for deep mourning and white paper flowers, traditional symbols of mourning.It was a cool grey day, unusual weather for the season, but appropriate to the sombre mood on campus.

The remaining students were going about their daily activities, washing clothes, fetching food, as usual, but the numbers were depleted and they looked downcast. Few of them dared to talk to us and they were in mourning for lost classmates. The fate of those 'missing' was not clear: they could have been killed as feared, wounded and taken to hospital or arrested. They may also have gone into hiding or just gone to stay in some other place, too scared to go back to campus. Most of the student leaders had fled already and some had been arrested. No one could put a number to the casualties or describe for certain what had occurred in the centre of Tiananmen during the last few hours of the pro-democracy struggle. It was not known how many young lives had been lost and those still around were understandably reluctant to talk about it. The term had been brought to a sudden and violent end.

Torn and ragged *dazibao* remained on the crowded noticeboards and walls of Beida, where one year before I had read posters mourning the death of the student Chai Qing Feng and calling on the government to act in favour of young intellectuals struggling to make ends meet in worsening economic circumstances. The contents of the 1988 *dazibao* campaign had all the elements which would spill out into the massive patriotic democratic movement of 1989. But apart from the unfortunate student whose murder had triggered off the campaign, no one had lost their lives that year. June 1989 was very different.

To the old posters from the previous weeks were added new ones, and some were painted over with the characters for mourning. Revenge was hinted at for the deaths. 'Blood has been spilt, more will be lost in the struggle for democracy.' The peaceful movement had been given an unknown number of martyrs. I reflected on the many previous times I had visited Beida. I was not even sure if all of the students I knew there were safe.

At Renda, the atmosphere was the same with 'deep mourning' posted everywhere and white paper flowers in memory of the dead. On another campus, the foreign teachers were packing up to leave, having been effectively evicted after electricity and water supplies had been cut off.

Some wanted to leave because of the fear and uncertainty, but others did not wish to abandon their Chinese colleagues and students. Foreign interference was already being cited by the authorities as partly responsible for the uprising, and this was a predictable response from the government. 'Bourgeois liberalism' was an unwelcome facet of the open-door policy, which had not been kept under control. Although the door would stay open, westerners, and particularly intellectuals, were not especially welcome in those days after the massacre. Their Chinese colleagues feared that once they had all left the country the troops would then come on campus and their lives would be in danger. 'We are preparing to die', several middle-aged teachers said. They had signed a petition in May supporting the students and criticising the government policies. Many had also been to the square, taking food and drink and offering encouragement to their students to participate in the pro-democracy movement. 'If they don't kill us, we will be arrested. The Cultural Revolution has come back.'

I had to say some sad farewells. Some of the students were still angry and prepared to resist if the soldiers came. Girls were crying in the dormitories, not over broken romances or poor assignments, as they had done in previous years, but over their lost classmates and in despair of China's future. The campuses were depressing places to be, but the whole of Beijing had that same air of despondency and loss. The troops never stormed in as rumoured. Students deserted their colleges and those on the government wanted list were arrested as they attempted to leave Beijing. A number of intellectuals were also arrested as the net widened, and the crimes of 'counter-revolutionaries' were detailed over the following days. It became apparent that there would be no sudden assault on the universities, rather a slower, more painstaking victimisation.

The repercussions continued across the country, even in small towns. The news spread of what had happened in Beijing, running counter to the government's own version of events. But what of the rest of the Chinese students scattered all over the world? Their response needs to be considered in the final chapter. My attention turned to them after I left China. My departure day was grimly marked by the first executions of 'counter-revolutionaries' in Shanghai.[8]

10 The movement in exile and prospects for the future

OVERVIEW

News of the events in Beijing quickly reached Chinese students all over the world and brought thousands of them onto the streets of the major capitals to demonstrate against their government's actions. But after the initial shock and outrage caused by the June events what could be done to help bring about political change in China? This was the urgent question asked during the summer months of 1989 as Chinese intellectuals already out of the country organised themselves to take action along with those who managed to escape the Chinese authorities and reach safety. This chapter will cover some of their activities post-Tiananmen. The problems facing Chinese students, many of whom have become political exiles in one form or another, will also be addressed in an attempt to ascertain whether the patriotic democratic movement has been transferred abroad. The situation on Chinese campuses will also be briefly analysed using the limited material available after the military crackdown.

OUTRAGE, ORGANISATION AND AGITATION

From Los Angeles to London, Sydney to Hong Kong, students from the People's Republic demonstrated against the Deng-Li government for the military assault on the pro-democracy movement. Even normally politically apathetic members of distant Chinese communities joined in to voice their outrage and sorrow at the Beijing killings and the strict imposition of martial law with its associated human rights violations. Chinese from all walks of life, even those who had never set foot on Chinese soil, expressed their deep-seated patriotism. 'We are all Chinese', was the message as thousands marched on Chinese embassies the world over in a massive display of disapproval. The embassy officials for their part remained behind closed doors, unable to address the demonstrators.[1]

After these protests, however, it was not clear exactly what could be done by overseas students to show solidarity with those inside China, let alone help bring about some form of political change. The June events left many in a dilemma. Becoming active in anti-government campaigns while abroad could jeopardise their own prospects on returning to China. Doing nothing, on the other hand, could be read as tacit approval of the regime's actions. The existing dilemma for thousands of overseas students of whether to return or stay away for as long as possible was also sharpened. More would now choose to find a way of remaining outside China to protect their own personal interests and safety. But should they decide to return later on, their extended absence could still cause problems.

One strategy was to keep a low profile by not becoming involved in any pro-democracy rallies, giving interviews to the press or associating too much with more radical students. Yet many quickly resolved to become active even if it meant taking risks. No doubt a large proportion of this group had already decided to stay out of China as a result of poor opportunities and lack of freedom. What happened in June further strengthened their resolve. 'I can never go back while the party is still in power', one Chinese student in the USA told me. Others were less radical, stating that the demise of Deng and Li and the rise of more reform-minded members of the party would be sufficient. Most agreed that as long as the 'hardliners' were in control, they would press for change from the outside, almost like a pro-democracy movement in exile, because inside China there could be no pressure groups, no 'alternative'.

The developing overseas student organisations were motivated initially by outrage at the military assault on Beijing, but many realised that this anger alone could not sustain a new movement. Questions of how to keep up the pressure were addressed by the newly founded associations across the world, but the test of time will judge their ability to maintain the struggle for democracy in exile.

The Federation of the Independent Chinese Student Unions in the USA[2] is probably the largest such group. There are around 40,000 Chinese studying in America and many were represented at the Federation's first congress held near Chicago at the end of July 1989. Some 183 colleges sent delegates and the total attendance was in the region of 600 people.[3] The main aims were the representation of the interests of Chinese students and the furtherance of the democracy movement in the USA,[4] but the Federation also approved a thirty-nine point constitution as well as debating during the three-day meeting the next steps to take. (See Appendix for the Federation's manifesto.)

The delegates were addressed by two leading personalities of the Beijing Spring, student activist Wu'Er Kaixi and the influential political scientist Yan Jiaqi, who used to hold office at the Chinese Academy of Social Sciences (CASS). Wu'Er, although exhausted by his escape from China through Hong Kong and the subsequent journey to Paris, managed to rouse the audience with his words and urged them to continue the struggle. 'The hope is just beginning', he said, 'I believe the Chinese can be united and will erect a Goddess of Democracy in Tiananmen one day' (AP Chicago 29. 7. 1989). He stressed his commitment to carrying on with the cause, but his fighting words did not impress all of the congress members, some of whom had been out of China for a number of years and were more concerned with the practical realities of the situation than with rhetoric. It was implied that Wu's charisma, which had been so valuable in Tiananmen Square, would have to adapt to the different social and economic environment of the USA.

When I saw him myself at a similar meeting a few weeks later in Los Angeles,[5] the student leader appeared tired, depressed and unsure of himself. His address was unprepared and disappointed many of the audience of Chinese students who were eager to see for themselves this highly acclaimed young man, one of the few to escape the regime. Wu admitted he was confused by the changed circumstances he found himself in. 'I'm only twenty-one, yet I'm a political exile. What should be the best time of my life may turn out to be the worst.' He was despondent about those (such as Wang Dan) whom he had left behind in the hands of the authorities. He would obviously have to clarify his own personal situation before being able to contribute as effectively as before to the pro-democracy movement.

The other members of the panel, such as Yan Jiaqi and Wan Runnan all spoke about the problems and the potential of the movement in exile. 'Fighting talk' was not suitable in the United States, where Chinese students had to maintain public support and sympathy as well as trying to extend visas and achieve other practical goals so that that they could stay away longer. They had to balance all the factors in the social equation. The more mature members of the panel realised this. Yan Jiaqi, for example, gave a thoughtful address stating that the shortcomings and difficulties of the economic reforms were the basis for the democracy movement but the struggle, he believed, went back further. 'Ever since 1911, blood has been shed for democracy and probably more will be shed', he said. The Chinese people were living under an Imperial State. He was loudly applauded for demanding that it should be the people who decide their rulers and that there was only one true form of democracy, one true form of free speech.

The Front for Democratic China which he and the others were attempting to establish in Paris was going to unite all those people and political groups outside of the Communist Party to 'overthrow the imperialist state through rational and non-violent means'.[6] He realised that this placed him firmly in the category of 'counter-revolutionary' also that, along with the others who spoke, he could not return to China until radical change had been brought about. A young student on the panel who had escaped from China, Shen Tong, sounded very depressed at this prospect. He was clearly shattered by his experiences and by homesickness.

Wan Runnan, former head of 'Stone Company', China's largest computing company, whose success was often acclaimed by the reformist party members as the model business for the future, also addressed this meeting. Wan, an intellectual turned businessman, believed that economic reforms could not be completely realised without political reforms and he had put himself on the wrong side of the government for saying so. He said that Deng was sacrificing the success of reforms for outmoded political principles. He claimed that their exile was the end of one period and the start of another in Chinese history. 'Our dreams of reform from within were shattered by the massacre. It has opened our eyes and awakened our consciousness that democracy is the only future for China.'

The five speakers all addressed audiences and answered questions as they would do at other universities in a brief tour to raise support and money for the Front. It was clear that the exiles were as diverse as the audiences to whom they spoke. The main unifying factor was the desire for democracy in China, but the exact form was still unclear. A multi-party system with universal suffrage appeared as the major model, but there was also discussion of 'democratising' the Party.

The different backgrounds and beliefs of the Chinese students and intellectuals would have to be carefully orchestrated in order to maintain a united front against the hardline regime in Beijing. Some were wary of the idea of bringing together all concerned groups outside of the party. Associating with Taiwan organisations, for example, was seen as problematic not just because of the historical conflicts between the communist mainland and the nationalist republic. The government would be quick to label such action as 'collaboration with the nationalists' and discredit the exiles back home. (Wu'Er Kaixi had already upset some Chinese inside the States for meeting unofficially with representatives from the Taiwan government in Washington DC.)

Although the Taiwanese were viewed as compatriots, 'from the same womb', any co-operation with them had to be cautious. This issue and many others were discussed with Chinese students in groups in the USA as well as other countries. There was naturally disagreement, but at least, as one student pointed out to me, the discussion is free, not like in China'.

At the end of August, Wu'Er Kaixi visited London to address students and their supporters at a number of meetings. During the Institute for Contemporary Arts 'Hands up for China' Day, (28 August 1989), his message was less radical than his stance in the States, claiming that the aim of the Democratic Front was neither to form a political party nor to overthrow the Communist Party but to clarify what happened in Tiananmen in June. Their 'higher purpose' was to set up the conditions for political change by sharing power rather than by overthrowing the government. This seemed to be more in line with Yan Jiaqi's idea of preparing the intellectual groundwork soundly before acting rashly as scholars had done before in China. Moving away from a confrontational approach may have been a more pragmatic and acceptable stance to the older students living and studying outside China. It may also have avoided their being immediately discredited back in China.

The Federation for a Democratic China[7] was officially established in Paris by people such as Wu'Er, Yan Jiaqi and other exiles, at a large conference on 22 September 1989. There were major speeches, discussions and declarations about the aims of the newly formed Federation, the main one being to work towards bringing about political liberalisation in China from the outside. The means of doing this were not clear, but maintaining the pressure, retaining foreign support and sympathy and preparing the groundwork intellectually and politically for an alternative form of government were top priorities. There were historical precedents for this throughout the world and in the case of China, Dr Sun Yatsen's organisation had operated largely outside of the country before returning to lead the overthrow of the last dynastic regime.

The Beijing authorities quickly labelled the Federation as 'treacherous' and dismissed their efforts as futile. They were nothing more than a group of 'troublemakers', who could not persuade the Chinese people from the true road of socialism. Outwardly the government did not accept the Federation as a threat, but inwardly there must have been anxiety that such a diverse group of exiles could come together and establish a movement dedicated to political change. The hardliners probably hoped that it would all just die down and come to nothing. The suppressed reformers in the Chinese leadership may have taken some hope from this movement in exile. At the time of writing, it is too early to make sound judgements.

The fortieth anniversary of the PRC on 1 October 1989 was marked worldwide not by celebrations but by protests. The June massacre had irretrievably discredited the image of the Communist Party. Meanwhile China support groups continue to help those students fearful of returning when their visas expire and any others who have escaped the regime. Various activities were organised to raise money and support for the pro-democracy campaign and the casualties of the June events, as well as to keep the movement alive. The initial shock and outrage have inevitably subsided, but the desire to redress the balance of power in China and help bring about some form of peaceful change remains strong outside the country. But what about the students and intellectuals inside the People's Republic as the grip of repression tightened in the months following the events in Tiananmen Square?

Wu'Er Kaixi was fortunate to escape but others were caught by the authorities. Wang Dan, another of the major leaders in the pro-democracy movement, was arrested and put into prison. His eventual fate is unknown. There have been conflicting reports about Chai Ling (see Postscript): some claim she too was arrested (THES 15. 9. 1989: 11), while others state she is still in hiding in China. Thousands of other activists and participants were arrested and imprisoned from among the student population across the country. The true extent of the purge is unclear.[8]

Those who remain free have had their study programmes and lives brought back under the party's strict control. Particularly in Beijing, where the movement started, the authorities began the new academic year by dictating a new agenda to returning and new students. The whole freshman class at Beida were sent for military training at a camp in the countryside, to instil discipline and obedience and deter them from 'bourgeois liberalism.' Whether the 'short, sharp, shock' tactic will succeed in winning them over to the side of the government, or instead cause still further alienation, remains to be seen.

Enrolments for the new academic year were lower than normal, with some departments, notably social sciences, history and politics virtually starved of freshmen. These disciplines had produced a disproportionately large number of pro-democracy activists; consequently the authorities wished to avoid any recurrence in the future by limiting admissions in these departments. Other departments were also affected by lower recruitment and tighter controls generally on what they could do. Teachers in these departments, especially those who had been active during the movement, were told not to turn up for classes. The new term was delayed at most major higher education institutions in Beijing to enable staff and students alike to participate in compulsory political courses which included learning Deng Xiaoping's speech about the June events. The 'truth' of what happened was to be inculcated and intellectuals had to offer self-criticisms along with accounts of what they did during the period of the uprising. People were encouraged to inform on each other. The older teachers were not unfamiliar with such procedures. 'We just keep our heads down and go along with the motions', was a typical comment on these political study sessions.

Dissatisfaction with this state of affairs has deepened the desire of many educated youth to go abroad. But the opportunities have grown more scarce and the regulations tighter in the aftermath of June. Graduates will not be permitted to leave China until they have worked for at least five years and they will have to pass certain political criteria rather than academic or linguistic ones. 'Redness' rather than 'expertise' looks set to be more important in the immediate future under the changed political circumstances. There will be fewer places holding the all-important TOEFL tests and those who intend to finance themselves will not be allowed to leave before the age of thirty-five. These new measures, if fully implemented, will effectively stop the exodus of young graduates from the country and limit the spread of 'bourgeois liberalism' from returnees. Meanwhile, students continue to go abroad if everything was arranged before the crackdown, but later on there will be a noticeable drop in the numbers of Chinese students overseas.

As before, these tighter regulations will probably have an adverse effect. Those already outside China and unsure about returning will have their minds made up for them. Thousands will stay away because they may never have another chance to 'get out'. Those left behind can only feel deep despondency and pessimism about the future of their nation and their own circumstances. The underlying negative trends discussed earlier can only be exacerbated with the renewed and strict repression of China's brightest youth. The question 'why study?' will once more be on the lips of many young people.

The campuses are, therefore, quiet. The movement has been repressed, but has it been completely stamped out? This is hard to say with accuracy, but my feeling is probably not. This round of anti-bourgeois backlash is certainly more harsh than any seen for many years and looks set to continue, but the underlying causes of the 'patriotic democratic movement' remain. The desire for democracy will not go away. 'Democracy' as an idea and an ideal as well as a form of political organisation is quite alien to Chinese culture and society. I have traced its origins there back to the 'May Fourth' movement, but I have attempted to show that it never had much chance to blossom. Yet in spite of oppression it has never disappeared. Since the 'open door' policy and economic reforms, the demand for democracy has grown stronger, eventually spilling out in spring 1989 into a fully-fledged pro-democracy movement. Students in China may now find it impossible to freely air their views and ideas, but they will not suddenly stop wanting to do so. For a brief period of time, it looked as though they might succeed in bringing about some form of political liberalisation, but that was not to be. The desire still exists. The fact that an unknown number of their colleagues were killed and imprisoned for this desire will only serve to strengthen the students' aspiration for democracy.

The silence of the campuses in the months following the June crackdown is understandable and predictable, but by no means assures 'victory' for the hardliners. The armed suppression of the pro-democracy movement was a desperate act of an unstable leadership which had little legitimacy among the educated elite, both young and old. Keeping quiet is a strategy the Chinese know only too well from past experience. They could just be biding their time until they have the chance again to speak out. That may be when Deng Xiaoping eventually dies. Although he stepped down from his official post as chairman of the Central Military Commission early in October 1989, he is still the symbolic head of the regime and retains some power. He is known as the leader who killed students and children on the streets of Beijing. His death, therefore, will possibly unleash some of the pent-up feelings of the campuses and trigger off another power struggle. Although he has appointed and designated new officials and 'heirs' such as Jiang Zemin, they are there largely because of his blessing. The party is not a united body. Deng's death could bring divisions into the open with un-predictable consequences. The students would probably take advantage of any instability to show their anger and grievances.

Meanwhile, the students have not been totally acquiescent or submissive and there have been several small but significant displays of dissent. In late July 1989 there was a small protest at Beida. Dozens of graduates marched around the campus to protest against being rejected by their prospective work units because they were viewed as 'trouble-makers'. About 300 people eventually took part, joining hands and chanting slogans (*Newsweek* 7. 8. 1989: 37). There were also reports in September of students commemorating, in spite of being warned not to do so, the end of a 'hundred days' of mourning – a traditional custom in China. White paper flowers appeared in several places to remind the government that the deaths had not been forgotten. On the other hand, the official fortieth anniversary celebrations were largely ignored, in another 'protest' against the crackdown. The authorities had planned a number of significant events such as specially chosen students dancing in the square on 1 October, near to a polystyrene 'statue' of a peasant, worker, soldier and intellectual erected by the government more or less on the sport where the 'goddess' had stood. There was little enthusiasm, however, apart from among the diminishing numbers of party faithful. Many students chose to stay in their dormitories all day to register their contempt for the government. The sight and sound of fireworks in the evening of 1 October must have been sadly reminiscent of the gunshots and fires of that night in June when the patriotic democratic movement was brought to an end.

The desire remains for democracy, for freedom, for a better life and for an end to the perennial purges of intellectuals. Pessimists say that the pro-democracy movement is dead and finished in China. Optimists say that it is merely taking an enforced break and continues in the hands of the overseas students who will one day return home. In the meantime, they may clarify what form of democracy they wish to institute in China and make the difficult decisions now facing newly-liberated former communist states such as Czechoslovakia and Romania. I hope that on the basis of the information offered here, readers will be able to make their own decisions about China's students and their longstanding struggle for democracy.

CONCLUDING COMMENTS

I have discussed the Chinese students' struggle for democracy with only brief attempts to define the concept of 'democracy'. I wanted the students' own ideas to speak out instead, with all their complexities and contradictions rather than impose a definition based on western intellectual tradition. Some commentators have criticised the students' lack of clarity and the absence of any definite programme of action: I hope to have shown that such judgements were misguided. The students wanted to explore the various political ideologies in the true spirit of their 'May Fourth' predecessors who were themselves cut short in their discussions by a national crisis. The students in 1989, as in 1919, were concerned about the Chinese political system, the state of society and, indeed, their own lives, and they wished to seek ways of improving all of them. They desired the freedom to decide for themselves what democracy could mean.

The events in Eastern Europe at the end of 1989 and in Russia in early 1990 must eventually have some effect on China, which, it could be said, had set the trend for 'people power' by seeing off the troops in May 1989 – at least initially, although in the end people died in this struggle, daring to speak out and demanding the right to speak out. The struggle, I believe, is not over yet.

Postscript

Since completing this work on China's students, the first anniversary of the 'Beijing Massacre' has come and gone without any major disturbances or renewed displays of dissent. The Chinese authorities showed signs of nervousness throughout the spring of 1990 with its series of anniversaries, beginning with 15 April (the death of Hu Yaobang and the outbreak of the student movement) and ending with 4 June. During this period Tiananmen Square was frequently cordoned off and declared out of bounds for the general public, with various official activities organised there to keep it acceptably occupied. Tight security was maintained in the capital throughout the spring, although martial law had been lifted earlier in the year.

Approximately 2,000 postgraduate students gathered on the Beijing University campus to hold a candlelit vigil during the early hours of 4 June and commemorated the anniversary. They sang the 'anthems' of the student movement from one year before and although there was some shouting and smashing of bottles, the protest was peaceful. The contingent of armed police surrounding the university did not intervene. There were several other small acts of protest to mark the occasion, but basically people remained subdued and remembered the events of one year before in silence.

Other developments include the emergence in the west of student leader Chai Ling whose whereabouts since her disappearance after 4 June had been unknown. She escaped after nearly one year with the assistance of various people in China sympathetic to the pro-democracy movement and angered by the actions taken by the government to suppress it. Her successful escape indicates that some form of 'underground' movement exists in spite of the crackdown.

One of the other student leaders who escaped immediately after

4 June, Wu'Er Kaixi, continued to receive a 'bad press' throughout 1990, with accusations of misappropriation of funds and unacceptable egoistic behaviour. The student movement in exile will probably discreetly disown him because of the negative effects on their cause to promote democracy in China.

Plans to broadcast news, information and music to China from the dissident ship, the 'Goddess of Democracy', were finally abandoned at the end of May 1990, when the Taiwanese authorities refused to offer the necessary assistance or secure safe passage in the South China Sea. The nationalist government had been making conciliatory gestures to the Beijing authorities, seeming eager to establish closer links, especially in the field of trade. Helping the dissident ship would not further their own objectives, consequently the 'Goddess' could not begin its broad- casts, an outcome which pleased the Beijing leaders.

The Taiwanese authorities found they were host to another guest of uncertain status in June: the popstar Hou Dejian who had been prominent during the student movement and was one of the four personalities on hunger strike at the time of the military onslaught on Tiananmen. Originally from Taiwan, Hou had defected to the mainland in 1983 with the communists claiming a moral victory over his choice of homeland. He soon became an embarrassment, however, because of his outspoken criticism of the regime and 'liberal' tendencies. Just before the tense anniversary period, Hou along with several other leading dissidents, was 'removed' from Beijing, eventually emerging in Taiwan. The others were released in Beijing.

Several hundreds of people, including students and journalists, arrested after 4 June 1989 were released in the spring of 1990, but it is unclear how many others are still being held by the authorities. These releases were declared a gesture of goodwill and proof of the Chinese government's intention to improve their record on human rights. Both western and Chinese observers, however, point to China's need to resume trade and other economic links with the outside world, especially the USA, and see the slight relaxation of repression as a cynical move to tempt back foreign business. The official verdict on the student movement is still that it was overtaken by a 'handful' of 'counter-revolutionary plotters' who intended to overthrow the Communist Party and the state. The main objective for every dutiful Chinese person, as emphasised by the *People's Daily* editorial of 4 June 1990, is to help maintain social 'stability' at all costs and be on the guard against these negative forces. 'Bourgeois' ideals of democracy and freedom continue to be viewed as inappropriate in the Chinese setting and the Communist Party remains the supreme political organisation in China. As communist states crumble all over Europe, the old Chinese leaders steadfastly cling to traditional Marxist-Leninist dogma.

Although the immediate impression is indeed one of 'stability' at the time of writing, there is a general feeling of tension and fear of further political 'turmoil'. It appears that the political situation in China is not resolved and the present leadership sit uncomfortably in Zhongnanhai. Outside, people are waiting for the old men to die and the fate of their chosen protégés, such as Premier Li Peng, will then be uncertain. Another death could trigger further student protests or perhaps something even more bloody and large scale. But there we are in the realms of uncertainty and guesswork. If we can learn anything from the history of China, it is that unpredictability appears as the only predictable characteristic of Chinese society.

Like the Chinese, we have to wait and see.

Appendix 1

Extracts from an interview with Su Xiaokang, one of the 'Heshang' ('River Elegy') authors, taken from *Zhongguo Qingnian Bao*, 16 August 1988

R–Reporter; SXK–Su Xiaokang

R: Last month in Hainan, you received a telegram from Beijing which urged you to return. What was it that was so urgent?

SXK: After 'Heshang' was shown, there were different reactions. At that time there was a meeting going on. University presidents were worried, afraid that 'Heshang' would arouse radical reactions among college students. But many people thought that 'Heshang' was basically positive. As for that telegram, there was nothing really urgent, but it was natural because whenever something new emerges in the cultural/ideological area, those who are concerned or enthusiastic about the future of China are unconsciously nervous. This is a logical result of our previous experiences.

R: Will there be any revision in the programme when it is reshown? If there is any, what is the principle for doing so?

SXK: At the end of July, the leaders of the Central TV station (CCTV) informed us that 'Heshang' could be reshown but with some revisions. Before this, some people had offered different ideas. Our conclusion is, we won't revise those concerned with academic opinions which can be discussed in society. But those sentences and paragraphs which are likely to arouse some misunderstanding are likely to be revised.

R: I remember at first, you and Xia Jun and Lu Xiang (the co-writers) named the TV series, 'The Main Artery' but you then changed it into 'Heshang'. What does it mean?

SXK: At first, we wanted to reflect the fate of the Yellow River culture through the subject of the Yellow River by writing about the river as a main artery in China, symbolically, with no subjective flavour. When we were writing, we read a lot of material, visited experts, scholars and gradually formed such a way of thinking. The Yellow River culture was a rational civilisation based on agriculture. When industrial civilisation developed in the West, agricultural civilisation immediately became weak and vulnerable. Owing to all sorts of reasons, such an overspecialised civilisation lacks the inner ability to adapt to changing circumstances. Hence its failure to alter into a new civilisation over time. That is, what should have died still exists. Therefore we changed the name.

R: Some people think the 'River Elegy' is destructive rather than constructive in its implication. From your original emphasis, what do you stress?

SXK: The Yellow River civilisation was not bad at its birth and our treatment of this civilisation was not one of destructive criticism. Those who think otherwise have not really understood 'Heshang'. In our narration, the seventeenth century is a very important part. Somebody raised the question whether it is good to compare industrial civilisation with the Yellow River civilisation. I think every society has to go through agricultural, industrial and post-industrial stages with the last form the highest form of civilisation. Although industrial civilisation also has problems and sufferings, it is a kind of suffering on a higher level. We refuse to reject it because of its problems. The only other option is agricultural, utopian socialism. Our age-old civilisation has become a burden on our advancement, therefore we must look back together and there will be criticism. Of course, criticising an old culture must be directed towards the construction of a new one. That's why we compare it to industrial civilisation. Part Five talks about the general chaos today in China's society. The ruinous effects of such chaos on society and production, which are both thrown into disarray by disorganised forces. Our worries about the possibility of future disorders reflect our expectations that the reform programme will build a new civilisation which will not let things run their 'natural' course. This is a constructive opinion.

R: I think our television lacks independence, but it has achieved something equally valuable, i.e. scholars and writers seldom have anything to do with it, but 'Heshang' seems to have realised a kind of integration between the thought of the intellectual elite and the mass media. Do you think this will finally emerge as an inevitable trend?

SXK: When we were writing 'Heshang', we wanted to introduce new ideas into television to improve its quality and so that the ideas would be more widely disseminated. Social science workers have done much valuable theoretical work, but the effects still remain among the intellectual elite because the only means to spread these theories is by books. We should let the masses think together with the theoretical workers. After 'Heshang' was shown, there was strong reaction in the different levels of audience which proved that we had too low an estimation of the intelligence of our audience. The strong reaction resulting from 'Heshang' was due to the power of the new thoughts expressed by means of television. Of course as a new attempt there are still many shortcomings in this style; for example, in the TV series, ideology occupied too much airspace. We should have given more space to music and images.

R: Regarding 'Heshang', we hear both praise and criticism. Some of the criticism is very sharp. What do you think about that?

SXK: 'Heshang' mainly aims at raising questions. When offering answers sometimes we cannot avoid hasty replies. Some opinions have aroused different reactions, this is normal. If the audience could receive 'Heshang' with tolerance, why can't 'Heshang' face all sorts of criticism with tolerance? After all, one of the goals 'Heshang' is to advocate criticism, assessment and discussion.

Appendix 2

Extracts from student leaflets of the Pro-democracy Movement, May 1989

NEWS BULLETIN 22 MAY, EDITORIAL

Protect the square! Protect the capital! Protect the People's Republic!
Tiananmen Square is in danger!
The capital of Beijing is in danger!
The People's Republic of China is in danger!

Since April, the great patriotic democratic movement of the university students in Beijing has opened the most magnificent page in China's history. The rationality, self-restraint and orderly manner of the students have not only evoked admiration towards the Chinese people from the world over, but have also greatly increased the self-confidence of the Chinese nation! It has proved that the Chinese people are a promising people!

However, from the very beginning, the Li Peng government has adopted an extremely irrational and bad attitude towards this great patriotic democratic movement. It has made one mistake after another. On 20 May, it outrageously ordered the army to march into Beijing and Tiananmen Square, imposing martial law on the orderly, thriving capital of Beijing! This shows that the Li Peng government is no longer the people's government! The Li Peng regime has stood completely on the opposite side to the Chinese people! He has labelled the great patriotic democracy movement supported by the whole nation as 'turmoil'. He declared that Beijing is in a state of anarchism, ignoring the fact that Beijing during the movement is in good order, without any traffic accidents or crime. He said that transportation in Beijing was paralysed because of the 'turmoil' in spite of the fact that it is the municipal government which ordered the bus company to stop transport. He has confused truth and falsehood, mixed up black and white. Even Goebbels and Yao Wenyan[1] would feel embarrassed.

The evil action of the Li Peng government flies in the face of the will of the people and it has been reasonably met with strong protest from the people! Up to today, the great patriotic democracy movement of the Beijing students has developed into a national patriotic democracy movement and into a Chinese constitutional movement in which people are fighting to defend the constitution. Every student, worker, Beijing resident, lower official and intellectual has taken part in this struggle for democracy. More and more officials and soldiers in the PLA who were deceived have come to know the truth and stood by the side of the people against the martial law! There is not a single person who does not know that those who produce chaos are neither students, nor workers, nor Beijing residents, nor cadres, nor intellectuals, nor the police, but a small clique in the Li Peng government!

Nevertheless, Tiananmen Square is still in danger! The capital of Beijing is still in danger! The People's Republic of China is still in danger! The disaster-ridden Chinese people are at a critical juncture! The Li Peng regime is continuing to press the army to carry out martial law. It is still making a show of strength. They have brazenly repudiated the appeal of the generals who think that the army should not occupy Beijing. They have brazenly refused the request of the members of the Central Party Committee that an emergency meeting should be held. They have brazenly refused the request that an emergency meeting of the People's Congress should be held. They have brazenly refused the request for the minority parties to hold an emergency meeting. On the whole, they have brazenly refused to discuss and solve the problems on the basis of democracy and law. They want to draw the Chinese people into the abyss of history through martial law and military control.

The hunger strike of the students has turned the square into the symbol of China's freedom and democracy. The great support from Beijing residents has turned Beijing into the new model of freedom and democracy in the contemporary world! The support from all over the country, from Hong Kong, Macao as well as overseas Chinese is a sign that the Chinese will be the most promising people in the twenty-first century! The Chinese people will never allow the small number of Li Pengs to turn back the whole of history. We must defend Tiananmen Square with our lives! Defend and protect the capital! Defend the People's Republic! We will build up a new Great Wall with our blood and flesh!

Abolish martial law! Call an emergency meeting of the People's Congress! Defend the constitution! Down with turmoil! Down with Li Peng! Long live the people! Long live freedom!

STUDENT LEAFLET, 27 MAY 1989

The student movement and the democracy movement have been a spontaneous mass movement. It is more significant than any other movement since the 'April 4th' movement because it has been and will be a people's movement, independent of the political struggle within the ruling party. No one has been able to control this movement. Instead the movement demands that individuals or any interest groups conform to the people's will embodied in the movement.

The starting point of the movement is to promote political reform and speed up the growth of democracy in contemporary China. Only through this can we effectively eliminate the corruption which exists in the government and the party. Because of this, the movement has been supported widely by people all over the country and in the world.

Therefore, the attitude towards the movement had become the measure of the ideological and political attitudes of every Chinese and of the Chinese leaders. In other words, to conform to the movement is to conform to the process of democratisation in China. To act against the movement is to be against the process of democratising. Every party and leader has to pass a severe test before the movement and to be judged by the people.

The reason why Premier Li Peng and some other leaders have lost the support of the people is that they denied the movement from the very beginning and even tried to suppress it. This is clearly shown by the 26 April editorial and their refusal of a dialogue. Thus we have good reason to believe that such leaders cannot promote the democratisation of China nor can they lead China to modernisation. The martial law imposed by Li Peng on 20 May is a further step towards undermining democracy and establishing fascism. It has made the people realise that as long as Li Peng and his fellow officials are in power, people who have supported the movement are in danger. It is because of this that the people demanded, after martial law was declared, the resignation of Li Peng, He Dongchang and others.

Secretary Zhao Ziyang is undoubtedly responsible for the corruption in the party and the government. However, after he came back from North Korea he called for solutions to problems on the basis of democracy and law and has a correct attitude towards the movement. That is why people have a good feeling towards Zhao and hope the conflict can be solved according to Zhao's words.

From the above words, one can see that this movement does not aim at supporting or overthrowing certain leaders of the country. People's attitudes towards the leaders are decided by how these leaders look at the movement. Those who stand by the side of the people are supported by the people and those who oppose the movement are opposed by the people.

Unfortunately some leaders today still have a traditional mentality. They always regard the people's democracy movement as the reflection and instrument of the political struggle within the party. They always assume that the people's movement is backed up by some high-ranking officials in the government and the party. Therefore they think that once they have controlled the struggle within the party, they have solved all the problems. This way of thinking is not only out of date but also undervalues the political intelligence of the students and the people. We want to point out that this way of thinking will fail to come to terms with the situation today.

The end of political struggle within the party will not lead to the end of the democracy movement because it is not this struggle which decides the fate of the movement but vice versa. As we have seen, the movement is broadly supported by party members too. In this case, no matter who is in power, he has to be on the side of the movement to get support from the party members.

The movement will go its own way forever. Our short-term goals are as follows: (i) to abolish martial law and withdraw the troops; (ii) to discredit the 26 April editorial and Li Peng's 20 May speech so that the great patriotic democratic movement and the autonomous student union are officially recognised, along with other autonomous organisations, as legal; (iii) to hold a meeting of the People's Congress as soon as possible to discuss the people's demands and the dismissal of Li Peng.

Undoubtedly this will be a long struggle. We declare to the people of China and the world that the peaceful movement on the square will hold on till 20 June, when the National People's Congress starts, on the condition that an emergency meeting of the congress is not held before.

The significance of this movement also lies in the fact that it has been a rational, self-restrained, orderly and peaceful movement. We want to tell the Chinese leaders that oppression and threats will not work. To use military measures to solve the problem is playing with fire. One who uses military force to suppress the people's movement is to put the government and the army to an end. Because a military crackdown of the people's movement will change the nature of the government and the army. The consequences of a military crackdown are beyond imagination.

The peaceful demonstration of 27 April is a glorious page in modern Chinese history. Today, after one month of demonstrations, we make this declaration to mark this great date. We urge the Chinese people to name 27 April the 'Festival of Freedom for China'.

Long live the students' movement and democracy!
Victory belongs to the people!

Appendix 3

The manifesto of the first congress of Chinese students in the US, 30 July 1989, Chicago

We, the delegates of the Chinese students and scholars from all over the United States, with our belief in democracy, with deep love of our motherland, and with our historical responsibility of promoting the democracy movement in China, solemnly declare the establishment of the Federation of the Independent Chinese Student Unions.

We hereby proclaim our persistent pursuit for democracy, which includes our claims for such basic human rights as life, freedom, property and pursuit of happiness; our belief that people have the right to choose the form of government, to participate in political processes, and to decide the fate of their nation. Our cause, for which numerous Chinese with lofty ideals have devoted their lives since the May 4th movement, is based upon the intuitive and common knowledge in the whole civilized world. It represents a historical trend of human society progressing from barbarism to civilization, from backwardness to advancement. This trend cannot be defied by any force.

We hereby extend our admiration of the 1989 Democracy Movement in China. This great movement signifies the new awakening of the Chinese people. It challenges the federalist dictatorship that has dominated China for over 2,000 years and any other hideous things that oppose democratic principles. It ignites the hope for vitalizing Chinese nationality.

We hereby condemn strongly the crimes committed by the Deng, Li, Yang regime. The suppression of the democracy movement and the persecution of democracy advocates only helped reveal its viciousness, barbarity, and weakness. The hope for democracy is still alive, and the flames of democracy are not extinguished. The day when people bring Deng, Li, Yang to trial cannot be remote.

We hereby demonstrate our unity and power. We overseas Chinese students unite not for any special group interests. We shall, in this favourable condition in the U.S., work hard, accumulate our power, and cultivate the basis for new waves of the democracy movement in China.

The support that we have received surmounts the boundaries of nations, nationalities and political differences. All the Chinese people and democratic forcés all over the world are with us. This is the source of our power.

History is calling upon us. We are determined to defeat the tyranny and dictatorship through a long and difficult struggle by resorting to peaceful, rational, and nonviolent means. May our ideals of democracy, freedom, equality, and rule of law come true in China.

Notes and references

INTRODUCTION

1 A spokesman for the Chinese government, Yuan Mu, claimed in a CCTV broadcast, 6 June just after the massacre, that 300 people, mostly soldiers, had been killed and up to 5,000 wounded. Later official figures slightly increased the number of dead and raised the proportion of civilian to soldier casualties. *China Daily*, speaking for the government, denied the unofficial Red Cross figure of 2,600 dead had ever been given, indicating that it was a 'foreign lie' (17 June 1989). The authorities also denied that any students had been killed in Tiananmen Square, see the Amnesty International Report, *Death in Beijing*, October 1989.

2 The 'reform decade' is the term used to describe the ten years of rule by Deng Xiaoping starting from December 1978, when he instigated a programme of economic reforms with Zhao Ziyang and Hu Yaobang as his main advisers.

3 The students preferred to describe their campaign as the 'aiguo minzhu yundong', which translates literally as the 'patriotic democratic movement'. It was particularly stressed in all speeches and pamphlets emanating from the square during the last week, when the government propaganda increasingly attacked the students for their 'unpatriotic' behaviour. (See also the appendices for examples of student literature.

4 See Nathan (1986) for a full explanation of this tradition, which is also discussed in Chapter 1.

5 The Nationalist Party, previously written as the Kuomintang.

6 Test of English as a Foreign Language, a US-administered English examination which is a required test for prospective overseas students. A certain score is required before students can be considered for scholarships and assistance to go abroad to study. (See Chapter 5)

7 These were all government slogans related to various political campaigns of the 1980s.

8 This is a famous, often-quoted part of a speech Mao gave to Chinese students in Russia in 1957. See, among others, Hooper (1985), p. 3.

9 Wu'Er Kaixi was one of the most prominent student leaders to emerge during the spring movement of 1989. Coming from the Uighur ethnic minority group, his real name is Uerkesh Daolet, but the Han Chinese transliteration was usually used in the media. He became known as Mr Wu to many foreign journalists, but Uighurs I spoke with preferred to call him Uerkesh.

CHAPTER 1 TRACING THE HERITAGE OF THE 'PATRIOTIC DEMOCRATIC MOVEMENT'

1 In an interview with Dr David Wong in early July, Li Peng said, 'They were students until they committed crimes. After they committed crimes, they were backed by other groups and became counter-revolutionaries' (*The Independent* 7. 7. 1989).

2 See Tsao Hsueh-Chin and Kao Ngo, *A Dream of Red Mansions*, translated by Yang Hsien-yi and Gladys Yang, Hong Kong: Hong Kong Commercial Press, 1986.

3 I am grateful to a Chinese student for translating and explaining the importance of these to me.

4 Tsao and Kao, *op. cit.*, p. 202.

5 The notion of 'bourgeois liberalism' has often been used by the Chinese leadership as an umbrella term to refer to any unhealthy tendencies in society which have their origins in the western capitalist nations.

6 Several other commentators have noted the fact that there were few Marxist writings entering China at that time, therefore the intellectuals had very little exposure to this political philosophy and doctrine. They were more likely to be familiar with Hobbes, Spencer, and Rousseau for example, rather than Marx and Engels.

7 The Treaty of Shimonoseki, 1895, granted Japan large indemnities, the right to open new ports and to establish factories along with businesses in China. It also gave them control over Formosa (Taiwan). See Nathan (1986), p. 138.

8 Ten previous attempts to overthrow the Manchu Imperial dynasty were made by the revolutionary movement in exile, Tung Meng Hui, led by Dr Sun Yatsen. The eleventh and successful attempt took some members by surprise, as if they were not ready to establish the republic. See J.C.F. Wang (1985).

9 *Xin Qingnian* (*New Youth*) was a publication of this period as well as a general concept often used to refer to the contemporary generation of educated young people.

10 'The Society for the Study of Marxism' was founded at Beijing University in the spring of 1918 at the suggestion of Li Dazhao, who 'realised that we could not accept the messianic message of the Russian Revolution and yet completely ignore the doctrinal presuppositions on which it was presumably based' (Schwartz 1966: 16). Many of its members, like Mao Zedong, later became important Communist Party personnel.

11 Tsingtao or Qingdao, is an important city on the Shandong coast formerly controlled by the Germans.

12 Wang Zhangqi, speaking on BBC television's *Panorama* in a documentary entitled 'The Rape of Liberty', 12 June 1989.

13 Although held in 'secrecy' in Shanghai's French concession, the police disturbed the proceedings. No official accounts of this first 'congress' were preserved, as the delegates had to flee for their own safety.

14 For a detailed and comprehensive account of this period, see Israel (1966).

15 The essay by Lu Xun, 'In Memory of Miss Liu Hezhen', can be found in *Nahan* (*Outcry*), August 1989, pp. 108–9.

16 The far-ranging influence of 'May Fourth', intellectually, politically and socially, has been discussed thoroughly in most of the works cited in the text.

17 Chiang Kaishek was captured on 12 December 1936 near Xian while visiting

the region. There had been student demonstrations with thousands calling for an end to the civil war and immediate resistance to Japan. The communists who captured him were not agreed on releasing him, though they did so after he agreed to co-operate with them to help overcome the Japanese.

18 The Long March started from the Jiangxi communist base in October 1935 with around 150,000 people. After the hazardous 6,000 mile trek to Yenan in Shaanxi Province, there were only about 20,000 survivors.

19 The preparations, the anxieties, the clashes with the authorities and so on, were all reminiscent of the spring 1989 demonstrations. The students were both fearful and daring about their action, prepared to pay the price for speaking out against the leadership but knowing that a price would have to be paid. A full account of 'December Ninth' can be found in Israel (1966).

CHAPTER 2   SHAPING THE REVOLUTIONARY SUCCESSORS: STUDENTS UNDER MAO

1 Being both 'red and expert' meant to be a good communist, full of revolutionary zeal, able to serve the country through the application of some expertise and training. But being too red often went against expertise, i.e. over-emphasising class struggle or some other form of political activity rather than pursuing higher education. Many articles were dedicated to the discussion of this problem during the 1950s and the stress on one or the other varied according to the predominant party line.

2 See J.R. Townsend, *The Revolutionisation of Chinese Youth: A Study of Chung-kuo Ch'ing-nien*, Berkeley: University of California Press, 1967, p. 14.

3 Young people between the ages of fifteen and twenty five were eligible to join in the early days of the League's re-establishment. According to the new constitution adopted by the Eleventh Congress in 1982, any Chinese youth between the ages of fourteen and twenty-eight could apply for membership (FBIS China Report, no. 390, 10. 2. 1983, p. 23).

4 Several researchers have commented on this tension between wanting to be a good young communist and gaining the rewards which success in the League and Communist Party can bring. See, for example, Chan (1985).

5 During the late 1980s, the official media often claimed that because the young people only had memories of 'new China', their lives had been relatively easy. They wrongly compared China with the developed, western nations rather than 'old China' and thus came up with mistaken conclusions. They had not 'tasted the bitterness' of the old society and did not know any better.

6 In the first years of the People's Republic, the government tended to adopt the USSR's line on education which recognised the important role of the intellectuals. Their conditions, therefore, improved at the outset of 'New China'.

7 This idea of a 'conspiracy' has been tendered but cannot be proven. I am grateful to participants at the School of Oriental and African Studies' 'London–China Seminar' for ideas on this (November 2nd 1989).

8 The removal of negative labels was part of the process of rehabilitation, but for thousands of 'rightists' the wait was a long one, with some not officially cleared until the 1980s.

9 'Xiafang', referring to the 'down to the countryside movement', continued

throughout the 1960s and 1970s. It was seen as a possible solution to the urban unemployment problems of the late 1970s, but was not carried out on such a large scale as previously because of changing economic and political circumstances.

10 The party is often wrongly viewed as a united body, without recognition of different 'factions' such as the 'modernisers' or 'developmentalists' as they were sometimes called during the 1950s. Deng Xiaoping was usually viewed as a 'moderniser' and later as a 'reformer', in contrast to the 'conservatives'.

11 See Bibliography for writers in this field.

12 *Ten Years of Turmoil (Shi Nian Dong Luan)*, in Chinese, by Hei Yan Nan, Xian: International Cultural Press Company, 1988.

13 See, for example, SCMP 4002, 16. 8. 1967, p. 10, for a typical Red Guard chant: 'Long live the victory of the great proletarian cultural revolution! Thoroughly smash the Liu Shaoqi renegade clique! Down with Liu Shaoqi, China's Krushchev! Long live the invincible thought of Mao Zedong! Long live Chairman Mao, the reddest sun in our hearts! A long, long life to him!'

14 Many of the major universities in the Chinese capital have an attached middle school for the children of the staff, and often have a relatively high academic reputation.

15 See Chan (1985) pp. 204–25.

16 The 'Great Link Up' or 'Liaison' to exchange revolutionary experiences, with Red Guards travelling all over the country, learning from each other and from the 'masses'.

17 Chan (1985). See book-jacket, where this quote is used.

18 'Shengwulian' is the shortened form of the title of the Hunan Provincial Proletarian Revolutionary Great Alliance Committee, made up of more than twenty organisations, not all of them students. Their October 1967 essay, 'Whither China?' has been referred to by a number of commentators on contemporary Chinese politics, and can be found in SCMP 4190 (May 1968).

19 'Whither China?', *op. cit.*

CHAPTER 3 NEW BEGINNINGS: STUDENTS IN THE ERA OF REFORM

1 See J. Gardner in Benewick and Wingrove (1988) p. 11.

2 Several scholars have remarked that Deng Xiaoping was accused of inciting the Tiananmen Incident to further his own ends. See, for example, J. Gittings (1989) p. 103.

3 The concept of 'seeking truth from facts' has a long history in the Communist Party and has been used at various times over the decades. It was a phrase liked by Mao, but it has recently come to be associated with Deng Xiaoping in the reform decade.

4 'Democracy Wall Movement', also known as the 'Beijing Spring', began in late 1978. For a full account of this, see for example, K.E. Brodsgaard (1981).

5 The 'Li Yi Zhe' document, see Brodsgaard (1981), p. 752.

6 See A.J. Nathan (1986) for an account of these problems, especially p. 15.

7 Not only during this time immediately after the Cultural Revolution but also right up to the present, petitioners descend on Beijing in an effort to redress injustices against family and friends. They remain outside the relevant

government office hoping to catch the attention of officials who may help them. See, for example, J. Becker in The *Guardian* 25. 7. 1989, 'Justice goes begging in suburbs of Beijing'.

8 There were many underground journals being printed during this time. See FBIS China Report, 27. 7. 1979, for translations of a selection.

9 See Gittings (1989), p. 161–2 for a fuller account of the contents of the 'Li Yi Zhe' document.

10 See also Gittings (1989) pp. 166–7 for more on Wei Jing Sheng.

11 The idea of a 'scarred generation' comes from the 'lost youth' of the Cultural Revolution decade. In the late 1970s, a 'New Realist' type of literature, often referred to as 'scar' literature emerged which addressed the personal damage done over this period. See, for example, H.F. Siu and Z. Stern, *Mao's Harvest* New York: Oxford University Press, 1983.

12 The 'Gengshen Reforms' are discussed by Nathan in his work on *Chinese Democracy* pp. 80–3.

13 See Nathan (1986) for a full account of the events.

14 Under the withdrawal of the 'four great freedoms', legitimate protests were deemed illegal along with other activities formerly protected by the Constitution.

15 Student activist Liang Heng left Hunan Teachers' College with his American wife in July 1981 and has since written about his experiences.

CHAPTER 4 DEEPENING THE DIVIDE: STUDENT DISSATISFACTION AND DEMONSTRATIONS

1 Tournebise and Macdonald (1987), p. 46.

2 *Far Eastern Economic Review*, 16 June 1988, p. 31. According to Ethridge (1988), p. 192, the number of institutions is 1,063.

3 Susan Shirk (1982).

4 The 'banzhuren' is the teacher-cum-guardian of each class and has the responsibility for the students' health and welfare, generally keeping an eye on their behaviour.

5 *Beijing Review* 28 (22. 4. 1985), p. 27.

6 According to the 1982 census, there were 243 million people between the ages of fourteen and twenty-five, roughly one-quarter of the population. See Hooper (1985), p. 2.

7 FBIS *China Report* 112 (4. 11. 1985), p. 41.

8 The 'football riot' was short-lived but still quite shocking for the Chinese authorities as well as foreigners in Beijing at that time. It was reported in the foreign media and eventually in the Chinese press.

9 Gittings (1989), p. 172.

10 See Gittings (1989) for a fuller account of these scholars and D. Kelly, 'The Chinese Student Movement of December 1986 and its Intellectual Antecedents', *The Australian Journal of Chinese Affairs* 17 (January 1987).

11 Tournebise and Macdonald (1987), p. 65.

12 For a discussion of this, see R. Munro in Benewick and Wingrove (1988).

13 *China Now* 120 (Winter 1986/87), p. 5.

14 Tournebise and Macdonald (1987), p. 79.

15 Professor Fei Xiaotong was China's foremost sociologist in the era before the

People's Republic and carried out much work of great interest and importance on rural China. After the communists came to power, his discipline was considered largely as a 'bourgeois' one, virtually banned from the universities until after Deng's rise to power. Prof. Fei suffered during this time along with other sociologists, but was rehabilitated and given many honours after 1979.

CHAPTER 5 DILEMMAS AND DIVERSIONS: STUDENT STRATEGIES AT THE END OF THE REFORM DECADE

1 Figures for students going overseas in the early twentieth century are taken from T.C. Wang (1928).

2 There were a number of articles discussing the 'clash of values' within the younger generations caused by the rapid changeover from the 'old to the new' society. For example, see in the CASS's own journal, *Wei Ding Gao*, Nos. 8 and 9 (1988)

3 The TOEFL examinations, previously discussed, as a prerequisite for overseas study.

4 A number of small, pro-democracy groups were established during the late 1980s, usually by Chinese students in the USA and Australia. For example, a group of students at the Australian National University organised themselves in 1988 as 'Democratic China' and wrote to Li Peng complaining about their treatment. Fang Lizhi, who visited ANU in August 1988 was greeted enthusiastically by the Chinese students, but he was apparently concerned about their actions. (Thanks to David Kelly at ANU for this information.)

5 I was told that the government would only be sending 2,000 students overseas in 1988 and would allow fewer self-financing students than in previous years. The rules were being made more stringent.

6 'Socialist commodity economy', translated from the Chinese 'shehuishangpin jingji', was discussed frequently in the media throughout 1988, being cited as the natural state of the economy during the 'primary stage of socialism'. It made clear allowances for elements of capitalism to be introduced within the Chinese economy, but the official line denied that China was 'turning capitalist' though free-market forces were in operation.

7 *Di Sidai Ren (The Fourth Generation)* by Zhang Yong Jie, Beijing, Dongfang Xueshu Congshu (Eastern Academic Series), 1988. See also an interview with the author in ZGQN 1. 10. 1988.

8 For an explanation of 'banzhuren', see Notes for Chapter 4, note 4.

9 The 'women's movement' in China was a new phenomenon coming to the fore in the late 1980s. Comprised largely of female intellectuals and academics, they were observing and analysing the negative effects of the reform programme on women workers. The first 'Women's Studies' conference was held in 1986 with much pioneering work done by Li Xiaojiang, a lecturer at Zhengzhou University.

10 A number of articles expressed concern about the rising numbers of teenage pregnancies and the renewed outbreak of venereal diseases which had been largely eradicated after the accession of the communists. Social scientists were urged to study these 'unhealthy trends' and find solutions. The government often blamed the open-door policy. Sexual behaviour was to be strongly

discouraged among young people.
11 The idea of a 'moral panic' in society comes from Stan Cohen's *Folk Devils and Moral Panics* London: Macgibbon & Kee, 1972.
12 GMRB, 21. 6. 1988 p. 13; 23. 6. 1988, p. 3; 1. 7. 1988, p. 13.
13 *Wen Hui Bao* 28. 6. 1988, p. 3. See also RMRB, 12. 6. 1988.
14 *Heshang*, Beijing: Modern Publishing House (Xiandaihua Chubanshe), 1988.
15 For a fuller account of the interview with Su Xiaokang, see Appendix 1.

CHAPTER 6   1988: THE WRITING ON THE WALL

1 There are small factions within the NPC mainly consisting of intellectuals but they have no real power and cannot present themselves as a political 'alternative' to the all-powerful Communist Party.
2 See R. Cherrington, 'The Protest Posters that Spell Trouble for the State', in *The Times Educational Supplement*, 22 April 1988.
3 At the beginning of May 1988, the major basic food items went up considerably in price, but the authorities made much of the fact that subsidies in the city could be claimed by many people such as students, which would 'protect' them from the price rises. But the feeling on the ground was generally that most urban residents were a lot worse off than before.
4 *Hong Gaoliang (Red Sorghum)*, represented a breakthrough in Chinese cinema, part of the 'new wave' genre and won considerable acclaim in China and abroad. It was also controversial, with its realism and attitude towards sexual matters. It became something of a 'cult' in 1988.
5 'Xuechao Fenxi' (Analysis of the Student Movement) was a detailed survey carried out by social science students at Beida in June 1989.
6 Far *Eastern Economic Review*, 16 June 1989, p. 22.
7 Student poster, Beijing University, June 1988.
8 Student poster, Beijing University, June 1988.
9 *China Daily*, 28 December 1988.
10 Many people commented on the help and economic aid which China had given to underdeveloped African nations over the years, such as in building railways, agricultural aid and so on.

CHAPTER 7   THE OUTBREAK OF THE 'PATRIOTIC DEMOCRATIC MOVEMENT', SPRING 1989

1 There were many articles in the media at this time about attempts to cut back on official expenditure, but many Chinese felt that these were just 'empty words', and that the corrupt cadres would still be holding massive banquets and giving 'gifts' for services rendered over the years.
2 According to Chinese astrology, 1988 was the Year of the Dragon, not a particularly good sign. In the last dragon year, twelve years before, the Tangshan earthquake occurred, killing many thousands, and Chairman Mao had died. As it turned out, 1988 did not bring anything quite so drastic, but it was not considered a good year. The snake, 'little dragon', could also be calamitous.
3 Foreign Exchange Certificates (FEC) is the currency usually given to foreigners when they change money in China, rather than the renminbi, which

is the 'people's money'. FEC has a higher value because it can be used to purchase goods not available to the majority of people and this system lends itself to black marketeering and corruption.

4 This phrase was one frequently used to describe what happened during the 'ten black years' of the Cultural Revolution.

CHAPTER 8 THE BEIJING SPRING

1 Tibet (Xizang) has long been a thorn in the side of the Beijing administration. It was fully incorporated into the PRC in 1959 as an 'autonomous region', but not without a struggle. Martial law was declared in Lhasa, the capital of Tibet, in March 1989, after violent clashes between the Chinese security forces and monks. It seems that the Tibetan people want to be free from Chinese rule and this is an unresolved, ongoing problem.

CHAPTER 9 ONE WEEK IN BEIJING

1 Just after martial law had been declared on 20 May, the Chinese authorities 'pulled the plug' on live satellite broadcasts, thus causing difficulties for the foreign media who were trying to get the news out of China.

2 The French often depicted 'la liberté' as a female, for example.

3 The concept of 'totem' relates to the social functions which religion can play in maintaining social solidarity, it being a physical representation of shared beliefs and so on.

4 There was some confusion here about the motives of those who managed to splatter paint over the Chairman's portrait. Some viewed it as an attempt to discredit the students, who denied that it was any of their supporters but suggested that it may have been 'agents provocateurs'. Two people were later arrested and imprisoned, apparently not students.

5 See, for example, Jane Macartney's article in G. Hicks (ed.) *The Broken Mirror: China after Tiananmen*, Canberra: Australian National University Press, 1990. She is highly critical of the students' tendency to mimic the government and indeed offers scathing criticisms of their general behaviour.

6 'Xuan chuan', the word used here, translates as 'to publicise or propagate'; 'xuan bu' is often translated as 'publicity or propaganda department'.

7 Tai 'Ji Quan is an old form of martial arts as well as exercise and is popular in China, particularly among older people, who usually practice in the streets and parks early in the morning.

8 Three people were sentenced to death on 15 June 1989, for their part in the 'counter-revolutionary rebellion' in Shanghai. The three 'workers' were accused of killing people and riotous behaviour at Shanghai station, where a sit-in had taken place on 6 June in protest against the military crackdown in Beijing.

CHAPTER 10   THE MOVEMENT IN EXILE AND PROSPECTS FOR THE FUTURE

1 I saw a video of a protest demonstration in Washington where an unknown member of the Chinese embassy staff had pulled the curtains across the windows into a 'V' shape, the students' victory sign.

2 The Federation of Independent Chinese Student Unions in the USA was set up at its first congress at the University of Illinois, at the end of July 1989. See *The Chronicle of Higher Education*, 9 August 1989, USA.

3 See *The Chronicle of Higher Education, op. cit.*

4 Details of the congress were given to me in a personal interview with one of the leading delegates and founding members.

5 'Forum On Democratisation in China', a meeting held at University of Southern California on 12 August 1989, organised by overseas Chinese students at West Coast universities and members of the large Los Angeles Chinese community.

6 Notes from Yan Jiaqi's address to the forum.

7 For an account of this conference and the establishment of the Federation, see *Nahan*, (Outcry) 2 (Winter 1989), Manchester.

8 For an account of the government backlash and estimates of arrests and executions see Amnesty International, 'Death in Beijing', London, 1989.

APPENDIX 2

1 Yao Wenyan was a well-known propaganda writer during the Cultural Revolution.

Bibliography

Article Nineteen Censorship Report No. 1. August 1989 *The Year of the Lie: Censorship and Disinformation in the People's Republic of China.*

Benewick, R. and Wingrove, P. (eds) (1988) *Reforming the Revolution*, London: Macmillan.

Brodsgaard, K. (1981) 'The Democracy Movement in China', *Asian Survey* 21: 747–73.

Chan, A. (1985) *Children of Mao*, London: Macmillan.

Chan, A. (1989) 'The Challenge to the Social Fabric', in Goodman and Segal (1989).

Cleverley, J. (1985) *The Schooling of China*, Sydney: George Allen and Unwin.

Ethridge, J.M. (1988) *Changing China*, Beijing: New World Press.

Gasper, B. (1989) 'Keypoint Secondary Schools in China: the Persistence of Tradition?' *Compare* 19: p. 5–20.

Gittings, J. (1989) *China Changes Face*, Oxford: Oxford University Press.

Goldman, M., Cheek, T., and Hamrin, C.L. (eds) (1987) *China's Intellectuals and the State: In Search of a New Relationship*, Harvard Contemporary China Series, Cambridge, MA: Harvard University Press.

Goodman, D. and Segal, G. (1989) *China at Forty: Mid-Life Crisis?* Oxford, Clarendon Press.

Hooper, B. (1985) *Youth in China*, Harmondsworth: Penguin.

Israel, J. (1966) *Student Nationalism in China 1927–1937*, Palo Alto, CA: Stanford University Press.

Kelly, D.A. (1987, 'The Chinese Student Movement of December 1986 and its Intellectual Antecedents', *Australian Journal of Chinese Affairs* 17: 127–42. (1990) 'Chinese Intellectuals in the 1989 Democracy Movement', in G. Hicks (ed.), *The Broken Mirror: China after Tiananmen*, Canberra: Australian National University Press.

Levy, M.J. (1968) *The Family Revolution in Modern China*, New York: Athenaeum.

Liu, A.P. (1976) *Political Culture and Group Conflict in Communist China*, Clio Books, Santa Barbara, California: Clio Books.

Mclellan, D. (1977) *Karl Marx, Selected Writings*, Oxford: Oxford University Press.

Nathan, A.J. (1986) *Chinese Democracy: The Individual and the State in Twentieth-Century China*, London: Tauris.

Saich, T. (1985) *China: Politics and Government,* London: Macmillan. (1988) 'Reforming the Political Structure', in Benewick, R. and Wingrove, P. (eds) *Reforming the Revolution,* London: Macmillan.

Scalapino, R. (ed.) (1972) *Elites in the People's Republic of China*, Seattle: University of Washington Press.

Schwartz, B.T. (1966) *Chinese Communism and the Rise of Mao*, Cambridge, MA: Harvard University Press.

Shirk, S.L. (1982) *Competitive Comrades*, Berkeley: University of California Press.

Tournebise, J.C., and Macdonald, L. (1987) *Le Dragon et la Souris*, Paris: Christian Bourgois Editeur.

Townsend, J.R. (1980) *Politics in China*, Toronto: Little & Brown.

Wang, J.C.F. (1985) *Contemporary Chinese Politics: An Introduction*, Englewood Cliffs, NJ: Prentice Hall.

Wang, T.C. (1928) *The Youth Movement in China*, New York: New Republic.

Watson, J.L. (ed.) (1984) *Classes and Social Stratification in Post-Revolution China*, Cambridge: Cambridge University Press.

White, G. (1981) *Party and Professionals: The Political Role of Teachers in Contemporary China*, New York: M.E., Sharpe.

Wu, N.K. (1986) 'From Half-Step Bridge to Cambridge', *The Cambridge Review* (June 1986), pp. 101–8.

Newspapers and Periodicals

The following is a list of Chinese and foreign newspapers and periodicals utilised in this work. Wherever possible, an English translation of the Chinese title is given.

Beijing Wanbao (Beijing Evening News)
China Daily
China Now
China Reconstructs
The Economist magazine
Far Eastern Economic Review
Guangming Ribao (Enlightenment Daily)
The *Guardian* newspaper
The Independent newspaper
Jiefang Ribao (Liberation Daily)
Newsweek magazine
The *Observer* newspaper
Renmin Ribao (People's Daily)
The Sunday Times newspaper
The Times Educational Supplement
The Times Higher Educational Supplement
Time magazine
Weiding Gao (draft journal of CASS)
Zhongguo Funu (Women of China) magazine
Zhongguo Qingnian (Chinese Youth) magazine
Zhongguo Qingnian Bao (Chinese Youth) newspaper

Index